By the Evidence

Other books by L. S. B. Leakey

The Stone Age Cultures of Kenya Colony   1931

Adam's Ancestors: The Evolution of Man and His Culture   1934

The Stone Age Races of Kenya   1935

Kenya: Contrasts and Problems   1936

Stone Age Africa   1936

White African   1937

Olduvai Gorge   1951

Animals in Africa (*Photographs by Ylla*)   1953

Defeating Mau Mau   1954

Mau Mau and the Kikuyu   1955

The Progress and Evolution of Man in Africa   1961

Olduvai Gorge, Vol. I   1967

Animals of East Africa   1969

Unveiling Man's Origins (*with Vanne M. Goodall*)   1969

L. S. B. Leakey

By the Evidence

Memoirs, 1932–1951

Harcourt Brace Jovanovich

New York and London

Printed in the United States of America

Library of Congress Cataloging in Publication Data

Leakey, Louis Seymour Bazett, 1903–1972.
  By the evidence: memoirs, 1932–1951.

    1.   Leakey, Louis Seymour Bazett, 1903–1972.
I.   Title.
GN21.L37A32   569'.9'0924 [B]   74-7376
ISBN 0-15-149454-1

First edition

B C D E

Illustrations

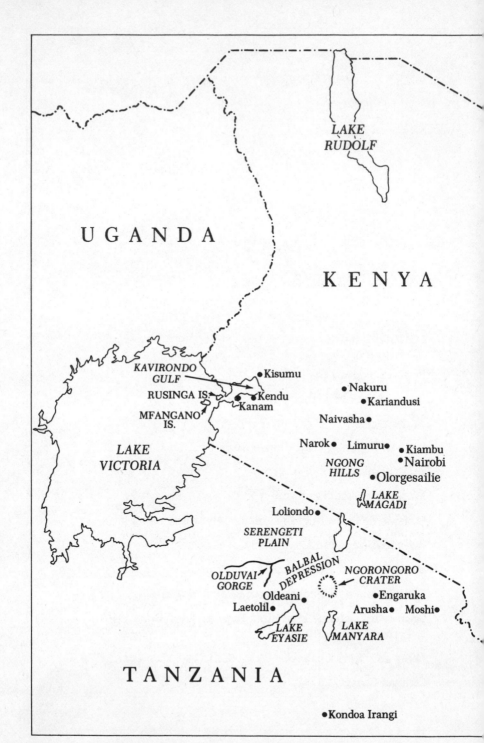

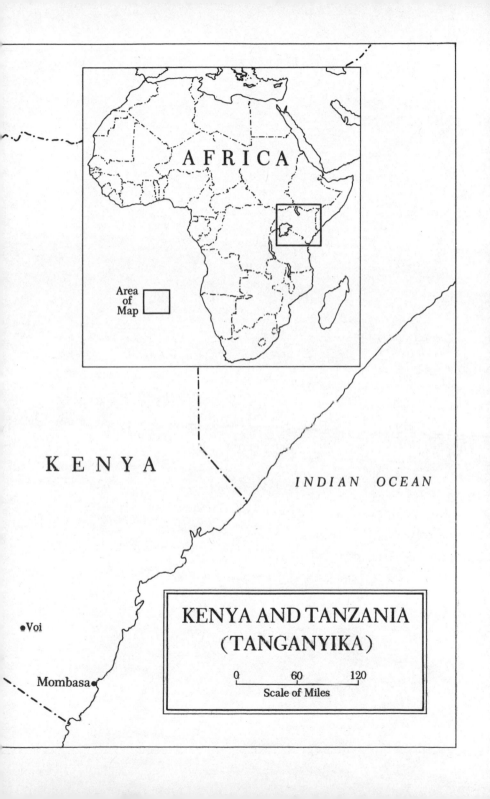

AFRICA

Area
of
Map

KENYA

INDIAN   OCEAN

•Voi

Mombasa•

KENYA AND TANZANIA
(TANGANYIKA)

0   60   120
Scale of Miles

By the Evidence

Publisher's Prologue

Louis Seymour Bazett Leakey (1903–1972) was a man of infinite variety. He is best known, of course, for his discoveries of fossils and artifacts related to human evolution. When Leakey was born, man was thought to have arisen in the Far East little more than 100,000 years ago. By the time he died, Africa, as Darwin had predicted, was established as by far the most probable cradle of humanity, and the time of genesis had been pushed back several million years. Much of the evidence leading to these conclusions was produced by Louis Leakey himself during a lifetime spent hunting for fossils under a blazing tropical sun.

But, as readers of this book will soon discover, his interests were not confined to palaeontology. Growing up among the Kikuyu of Kenya, to whom his parents were missionaries, he early became intimate with their beliefs and customs, and when he was thirteen he was initiated into the tribe. Throughout his life he strove to interpret African culture to the white man and warned against the wrongs and misunderstandings that breed race hatred. As a social anthropologist, he worked to preserve a knowledge of the old ways; his works in this area range from a

3

monograph on the string figures of Angola to a monumental *Study of the Kikuyu People* (written before World War II, but just now being prepared for publication).

He was a fine naturalist, taking as much delight in the live creatures of the wilds as in the bones of their long-extinct ancestors. As a boy he had a passion for hunting, which was later transmuted into deep concern for the survival of African wildlife. Forty years ago, long before the conscience of the world was aroused by the slaughter of the great herds, Louis Leakey was working for the establishment of game preserves; subsequently, he became a founding trustee of Kenya's National Park System. On their many expeditions, he and his remarkable wife, Mary—an anthropologist whose accomplishments match his own—worked surrounded by field pets that included wildebeest calves and a monkey. At home, near Nairobi, they bred tropical fish and pedigreed Dalmatians, and kept antelopes and hyraxes as pets.

Stalking wild animals with his bare hands was a favorite pastime in Leakey's younger years. He brought the same sporting instincts—and the scientific curiosity of his professional pursuits—to the solving of crime. Leakey fancied himself as an amateur detective. Introduced to the world of Inspector Lestrade as an intelligence officer during World War II, he retained a fascination for the trade, as the anecdotes he tells here show. His most dramatic involvement occurred during the Mau Mau uprising and cast him in the role of interpreter at the political trial of Jomo Kenyatta—past acquaintance, future president of an independent Kenya.

Handwriting expert, gourmet cook, benevolent Svengali to a whole generation of young anthropologists and animal behaviorists, Louis Leakey is a hard man to pin down. But it is his determined, unceasing, and, ultimately, phenomenally successful search for evidence of man's evolution that qualifies him as one of the great men of this or any century, and makes this second installment of his memoirs (an account of his early years, entitled *White African*, was first published in 1937) a record of extraordinary importance.

Since that record is an engagingly personal account, it may well attract readers who are not fully aware of the background

4

of Leakey's work. For them a brief sketch of the highlights may be in order.

The science of palaeoanthropology, for all its recent accomplishments, is little more than a hundred years old. In the present book, it is fascinating to read of a 1929 conversation about the young Louis Leakey's recent discovery of skeletons that were some 25,000 years old. Even in the second quarter of our own century, some people refused to accept that date, on the grounds that at so early a period heaven and earth, to say nothing of man, had not yet been created.

In the seventeenth century, the date of creation had been calculated by Archbishop Ussher of Armagh as precisely 4004 B.C., and for over 200 years his finding went unquestioned. It was only when the inexorable testimony of the rocks—many of them products of a sedimentation process that took millions of years to accomplish—was accepted by mid-nineteenth-century geologists that the idea of an earlier origin for life could be entertained.

Even then, man himself was assumed to have entered upon the scene at a remarkably recent date. Discoveries like those of Mary Leakey's great-great-great-grandfather John Frere of stone tools together with the bones of extinct animals, or of what we now know to be the remains of prehistoric men, were long explained away The famous Neanderthal skull found in Germany in 1856 was not acknowledged for what it was—an extinct type of man—for thirty years, although the more modern-looking Cro-Magnon man, first unearthed in 1868, was accepted with less reluctance.

Slowly but surely, however, literal interpretation of the Bible gave way to the awful truth of evolution. Paragon of animals though he may be, man is a member of the order of primates, to which apes also belong; the two families share a common ancestor in an unimaginably remote past. In 1894 Eugene Dubois, a Dutch army doctor in Java, proclaimed that he had found the "missing link," fossilized bones that provided proof of man's humble origins. He called his find *Pithecanthropus* (*pithecos*, "ape," plus *anthropos*, "man") *erectus*—"the ape-man who walked upright." Today, *Pithecanthropus* is known to be fully human. Popularly labeled "Java man," his scientific name has been upgraded to *Homo erectus*.

The discovery of Java man—and some thirty years later, near Peking, of a related species—seemed to confirm the Far East as the birthplace of mankind. When, in 1924, Raymond Dart, of the University of Witwatersrand in South Africa, announced the discovery of a still earlier human ancestor, the reaction was the familiar one of disbelief. The geographical improbability was compounded by the dissimilarity between Dart's find, which he called *Australopithecus africanus* ("South African ape"), and the celebrated Piltdown man, discovered in England in 1912. Although now known to be a hoax, the latter, with its high, domed braincase and apelike jaw, long deceived many scientists into believing that, in the words of Sir Arthur Keith, an early authority, "the essential mark of man lies neither in his teeth nor in his postural adaptations, but in his brain."

Disconcertingly, Dart's *Australopithecus,* though its teeth were quite manlike, had a small but domed braincase scarcely larger than a chimpanzee's. The discovery of similar species by Dr. Robert Broom during the thirties did little to change the experts' opinion; it was not until 1947 that the australopithecines, as they were collectively called, were admitted to be hominids—members of the family to which man, his immediate ancestors, and related forms belong. Today, they are known as "near-men"; some anthropologists place them in the direct line of human descent, while others (including Louis Leakey) believe they have only a collateral relationship.

It is evident from even this brief sketch that most of the famous names in palaeoanthropology are associated with their major discoveries: Eugene Dubois with Java man; Davidson Black with Peking man; Louis Lartet with Cro-Magnon man; Raymond Dart with *Australopithecus.* But how does one define Louis Leakey? On his very first expedition in an Africa where, up to that time, only a handful of human fossils had been found, he unearthed a whole series of remains, dating from late Palaeolithic through Neolithic times. He was at Olduvai Gorge in Tanganyika (now Tanzania) as early as 1931, and though that famed treasure house was not to yield any significant fossils related to man for many years, the stone tools that for decades Louis and Mary Leakey painstakingly collected revolutionized previous ideas about early human development.

In 1932 came his disputed finds of primitive *Homo sapiens*

remains—the Kanam jaw and Kanjera skulls, which he claimed dated back, respectively, to over half a million and 100,000 years ago. In 1948, working with Louis on Rusinga Island in Lake Victoria, Mary Leakey found the first almost complete skull of *Proconsul,* a 25-million-year-old primate once believed to represent the very point on the evolutionary tree where the human stem emerged from the branch common to both apes and men. (It was later decided, by Louis Leakey himself, that this was not true and that *Proconsul* had already proceeded beyond the point of no return.)

Then, in 1959, began the drumfire of discoveries that were to make Leakey the most famous—and most controversial—name in anthropology. First there was "Nutcracker man," a grotesque-looking skull with huge jaws and heavy eyebrow ridges, which Leakey formally named *Zinjanthropus,* or East African man (it is now known as *Australopithecus boisei*), and which proved to be 1,750,000 years old. In quick succession came *Homo habilis* ("man with ability," a name suggested by Raymond Dart to emphasize this specimen's superiority to *Zinjanthropus*); an African version of *Homo erectus* (the species, formerly called *Pithecanthropus erectus,* to which Java and Peking man belong); a creature the Leakeys nicknamed "George," which initially appeared to be a primitive form of *erectus,* but is probably another *habilis;* and an earlier and a later species of *Kenyapithecus,* an ape Leakey believed was the most likely candidate to replace *Proconsul* as man's immediate ancestor.

Any one of these finds would have made its discoverer famous. But all of them together represent only the high points in the vast and minutely detailed knowledge of human evolution that Louis Leakey compiled in forty years of "crawling," as he himself described it, "up and down the slopes of [Olduvai Gorge and other African sites], with eyes barely inches from the ground." It is no wonder that everyone knows his name. What may surprise those who are not themselves anthropologists is the assessment of Leakey's achievement by many of his colleagues. For although the outstanding importance of his fossil discoveries is universally acclaimed, Leakey's own interpretation of them is not. It is to his credit that this fact never embittered him. And it is one of the better dispensations of providence that he lived long enough to see some of his theories strengthened by the amazing fossil finds his son Richard is now making in the Lake Rudolf area of northern Kenya.

The disagreement among anthropologists is not, of course, confined to Louis Leakey's model of human evolution; there are, in fact, almost as many models as there are anthropologists. The reason lies in the fragmentary nature of the evidence. Oblivion blindly scattereth her poppy, and in the millions of years that separate us from our ape progenitors very little of significance has escaped. But whereas the human family trees drawn by most anthropologists coincide at some points though they may differ at others, Louis Leakey's model is almost uniquely his own.

"The study of human evolution is a game," according to the University of California's Sherwood Washburn. Sometimes it resembles the famous croquet game in Wonderland, where the arches are constantly getting up and walking away. Fossils cannot walk away, but they do seem mysteriously to change characteristics when viewed by different observers. What one expert may view as simply a variation to be expected among any population, another may see as a significant difference justifying the assignment of the specimen to another species or even another genus.

The first criticism of Louis Leakey among his peers is that he was too quick to create new taxonomic classifications, thus obscuring similarities between specimens suggestive of genetic relationships. Just such a new classification was *Zinjanthropus,* which Leakey himself came to admit seemed to be simply another species of the near-man *Australopithecus,* first discovered in South Africa. Many anthropologists believe that *Homo habilis* is also subhuman and an australopithecine, and that *Kenyapithecus,* the ape Leakey proclaimed as the father of mankind, is essentially similar to one named *Ramapithecus,* found earlier in India.

But the big disagreement between Leakey and his critics lay in his stubborn belief that modern man, *Homo sapiens,* has an ancient lineage quite distinct from that of *Australopithecus, Homo erectus,* and Neanderthal man, all of whom he regarded as aberrant growths that diverged, at different times, from the main human stem and eventually perished without issue. This belief had as its corollary the conviction that two or more kinds

8

of man or manlike creature could have existed side by side at the same period—a contention denied by most anthropologists in the past on the grounds that the particular ecological niche assigned to human evolution could be occupied by only one species at a time. In the past ten years, however, there has been evidence to show that hominids of different species and, most probably, different genera did coexist at least during the Lower Pleistocene (some 2 million to 500,000 years ago), and this evidence does much to improve the probability of Leakey's model of human evolution.

That model begins, on the basis of dental evidence, with *Kenyapithecus africanus*, a 19-million-year-old primate that Leakey believed showed the first signs of breaking away from the ancestral ape stock. It continues, past a 4-million-year gap in the fossil record, through *Kenyapithecus wickeri*, a creature that may or may not have walked upright, but that may already have been using stones to break open animal skulls for the brain and marrow.

Until recently, the trail vanished during the whole of the Pliocene (about 14 million to 2 million years ago), a time of drought, during which man's ancestors must increasingly have been forced out of the shrinking tropical forests onto the open savanna. There survival depended heavily on a bipedal posture. Walking upright vastly enlarged the field of vision and freed the hands for using naturally sharp stones as tools and weapons. Sometime during this period, perhaps 3 million years or so ago, at least one branch of the hominid line—one that had learned to eat meat as well as vegetable matter—took the crucial further step of *making* tools, an activity that encouraged the co-ordination of hand and eye and the growth of the brain. It was this branch, Leakey believed, that eventually evolved into *Homo habilis*, the first true man; other branches of this primary hominid stock took slightly different directions, to become the lightly built and robust species of *Australopithecus* known from several African sites.

Both types of australopithecine eventually died out, and Leakey believed that *Homo habilis* continued, evolving first into the primitive *Homo sapiens* types represented by discoveries at Vérteszöllos in Hungary, Steinheim in Germany, and Swanscombe in England (as well as Leakey's own Kanjera skulls), and eventually into Cro-Magnon man and other varieties of modern *Homo sapiens.*

As for *Homo erectus,* a species contemporary at one end of its existence with the australopithecines and at the other with primitive *Homo sapiens,* Leakey believed it developed specializations—anatomical peculiarities designed to combat environmental conditions—that subsequently prevented it from surviving when conditions changed. A similar fate awaited Neanderthal man, which broke away somewhat later from the common human stock.

In contrast to this view, many anthropologists today subscribe to a quite different scheme of human evolution, one that sees comprehensive stages rather than disparate lines. Only in the early subhuman stage represented by the australopithecines (among which some include *Homo habilis*) did more than one type of hominid exist, they say. Each later stage consisted of a single population whose members varied little more than modern races do today; and all of these, except, perhaps, a few extreme variants, contributed their genes to the common stock. Man first reached human status at the *Homo erectus* stage; another of Leakey's "rejects," Neanderthal man, is viewed as *Homo sapiens neanderthalensis,* different only at the subspecies level from our own kind.

The lines of battle represented by these contrasting schemes were drawn up early in Leakey's career. Although he was to acknowledge defeat in minor skirmishes (arising from his penchant for drawing dramatic but premature conclusions from his finds), he never retreated from his main position. A fair and courteous opponent, he nevertheless found it difficult to conceal his scorn for armchair anthropologists, those who, in his words, "are only prepared to devote a few months to [field] research and then return to more lucrative and comfortable work in the universities."

As this book begins, in 1932, he is soon to abandon his own comfortable position at St. John's College, Cambridge, for work in East Africa, where he was born. Nothing of that Africa remains; only the shape of the hills is the same. In August 1903, when Mary Bazett Leakey, daughter of a British colonel, gave premature birth to her first son at the Church Missionary Society's station at Kabete, Kenya, the railway from Mombasa to

Lake Victoria had only recently been completed. Nairobi was still a cluster of railroad shacks; Colonel Richard Meinertzhagen, stationed there with the King's African Rifles, noted in his diary that lions occasionally prowled through the camp and that a race meeting was broken up by an angry rhinoceros. On the Athi plains, just south of town, countless herds of eland, wildebeest, hartebeest, gazelle, and zebra roamed free, "curious but not frightened" at his approach.

The British High Commissioner, Sir Charles Eliot, had ambitious plans for this beautiful, violent country with its blue distances and vast and fertile plains. "He envisaged a thriving colony of thousands of Europeans with their families," Meinertzhagen reported, "the whole of the country from the Aberdares and Mt. Kenya to the [German East Africa] border divided up into farms, the whole of the Rift Valley cultivated or grazed. . . . He intends to confine the natives to reserves and use them as cheap labour."

But in 1903 all this was to come; Louis Leakey, growing up in the mud-and-thatch mission bungalow at Kabete, ten miles from Nairobi, had no European playmates except for his two sisters and younger brother. He learned to talk, to think, even to dream in Kikuyu. He played with the Kikuyu boys his age, learning their tribal games—spearing the hoop, throwing the club, and dueling with sharpened sticks—and in turn, coached by his father, he organized a barefoot rugby team. In preparation for his initiation into the tribe as "Wakaruigi, son of the Sparrowhawk," he sat night after night with the other boys around the fire outside a native hut while the elders taught them the history, legends, and rules of behavior of the tribe.

His Western education was in the hands of an often interrupted succession of tutors, helped out, when he had the time, by Harry Leakey. Joshua Muhia, a Kikuyu with the blood of Wanderobo hunters in his veins, took him on trapping and hunting expeditions, and Arthur Loveridge, curator of the little natural history museum in Nairobi, showed him how to skin birds, blow eggs, and classify specimens. It was Loveridge too who encouraged Louis's interest, inspired by a book he read, in collecting the stone tools and axes turned up ever more frequently by the agricultural and road-building activities of white settlers.

Louis was a strong-minded, independent boy. When he was thirteen he built his own house, as the Kikuyu boys did, and insisted on living in it, with all the paraphernalia of his many activities. Once, exploring a cave for traces of human occupation, he got stuck in a narrow airless passage and had to be rescued by his native companions. On another occasion, determined to obtain a five-pound prize offered by an English zoo, he tried raiding a nest of *siafu*, the formidable biting ant, for specimens, and was severely bitten all over his body.

Plans to send Louis to England to school were delayed by World War I; he was sixteen when he finally entered a school in Weymouth. His ambition to attend St. John's, his father's old college at Cambridge, almost foundered on his limited knowledge of foreign languages—until he convinced dubious university authorities to accept Kikuyu as one of the requirements, submitting a certificate dictated and signed by a Kikuyu chief to prove his knowledge of the language.

Then, in his second year, a football injury brought on massive headaches that required him to take a year off from his studies. With typical resourcefulness, he persuaded the directors of the British Museum of Natural History to send him on a fossil-hunting expedition to Tanganyika. The head of the expedition had never been in Africa before, so it fell to the twenty-year-old Louis to organize and lead a safari that differed little from those of Stanley and Livingstone. Supplies for the expedition were carried on the heads of porters, and news of the white man's arrival was spread by signaling drums. Once Louis narrowly escaped being caught in an elephant charge; on another occasion a leopard invaded his bedroom and carried off a pet baboon sleeping by his side.

Leakey returned to Cambridge in 1925, and the next year he obtained his degree in anthropology. By that time, his original intention to follow in his missionary parents' footsteps had been replaced by a desire to study man's origins, a quest to which he brought a missionary fervor—and a conviction that the place to work was not Asia, but the continent of his birth. Immediately after graduation, he organized what he grandly called his "First East African Archaeological Expedition" (it consisted, in its entirety, of himself and a fellow student) and set off to explore a promising site reported by a settler in Nakuru, Kenya. This site and several nearby, excavated two years later, yielded a rich harvest of Late Stone Age bones and artifacts, and provided the material for his first two books, one on the peoples, the other on the cultures of Stone Age Kenya.

It was in the same Nakuru–Naivasha area of Kenya that he carried out studies endeavoring to link the wet and dry periods of Africa's prehistoric past ("pluvials" and "interpluvials") with the similar succession of glacials and interglacials in Europe. Until the relatively recent development of radiometric and other absolute dating methods, these findings, corrected and refined by others, provided the only way to correlate discoveries in Africa with those made in Europe. (Incidentally, in the hope of helping to safeguard Kikuyu interests he sacrificed part of a crucial digging season to serve, at the government of Kenya's request, on a special committee investigating the Kikuyu system of land tenure.)

Leakey's first marriage, to Henrietta Wilfrida ("Frida") Avern, took place in 1928; their daughter, Priscilla, was born in 1930, a son, Colin, three years later. In 1931–32 came his Third East African Archaeological Expedition, the first to visit Olduvai Gorge. Hans Reck, a German geologist who had worked in the gorge before 1914 and who accompanied Louis, at his invitation, on this expedition, discouraged his hopes of finding prehistoric stone tools there. But they had been in camp scarcely half an hour when one of the African workers found an Acheulean handaxe, a type of stone tool already known from Europe. It was the first hint of what, after years of backbreaking, painstaking labor, Olduvai proved itself to be: a unique showcase not only of animal fossils, but also of tool forms and associated human occupation sites over a period of a million and a half years or more. Leaky designated one of the richest sites FLK (the letters stand for "Frida Leakey *korongo*," *korongo* being an African word for "gully"). Almost thirty years later, his second wife, Mary Leakey, was to find the remains of *Zinjanthropus* there.

In March 1932 Leakey set out for the Kavirondo Gulf area of Lake Victoria; here, near a village called Kanjera, he found fragments of four human skulls of *Homo sapiens* type, which he dated to the Middle Pleistocene, earlier than any other *sapiens* specimens then known. At Kanam, nearby, one of his

13

African workmen made an even more exciting discovery—a fossilized jaw fragment, which Leakey believed dated back to the Lower Pleistocene, hundreds of thousands of years earlier still. Back in England, he found both of these attributions bitterly disputed.

It is here, in the familiar aura of controversy that surrounded Louis Leakey throughout his life, that the present book begins.

One

In 1931, before leading my first expedition to Olduvai Gorge in what was then Tanganyika, now Tanzania (this trip was actually my Third Archaeological Expedition), my wife, Frida, and I had acquired a lovely old house in the village of Girton, a few miles outside Cambridge.

The Close was set in a large garden, and behind it stretched green fields hedged with may and brambles. On one side of us stood the village church, and just across the green there was a post office and one or two little shops. The second of the University of Cambridge women's colleges had been sited in the village, and because of this there was a frequent bus service to the university for the benefit of students—though most of them in those days, true to Cambridge tradition, used to bicycle the three miles each way, except when the weather was particularly inclement.

At that time I held a research fellowship at St. John's College, Cambridge, and had been allowed to retain my suite of rooms there while I was away in Africa. On our return from Olduvai, therefore, in the spring of 1932, I was able to take my immense collection of stone tools to the college instead of to a laboratory, where I should not have been able to study them at night as I intended. The fossil remains collected by the expedition were sent to the British Museum of Natural History to be studied by my colleague Dr. Arthur Hopwood. I kept the few precious human fossils we had found at Kanam and Kanjera, in Kenya, but since the comparative material I needed was more readily available in London than in my own university, I periodically took them with me to the Royal College of Surgeons at Lincoln's Inn Fields, where I studied them under the supervision of Sir Arthur Keith.

I was very glad to have the use of my old rooms once again, since I was able to use the small so-called "gyp room" as a combined emergency bedroom, kitchen, and dining room. The two main rooms were thus freed for use as laboratories for sorting, cleaning, and studying my specimens. The great advantage of this arrangement was that when I worked late into the night, as I often did, I could sleep in college and cook breakfast next morning, instead of having to drive out to Girton and disturb my family in the middle of the night.

Life as a fellow of St. John's College was pleasant indeed. A number of men who had been research students with me in previous years were now also fellows of the college, and conversation at dinnertime and afterwards in the senior common room, over coffee and port, was always both interesting and instructive. So many different disciplines were represented that I was forever absorbing new ideas and acquiring information outside my own research subjects.

While my time was mainly taken up with research, I also undertook a limited amount of teaching in the Department of Anthropology and supervised a few selected students from my own and certain other colleges.

I had two beautiful views from my rooms, which were right at the top of New Court. Looking out in one direction I could see Trinity and King's colleges, beyond the lovely gardens and lawns of the Backs. From the other windows I could see over and through tall oak and elm trees to the college playing fields and also—and this was more important to me—to the beautiful little patch of wild garden belonging to my college known as "the wilderness." Only fellows of St. John's had the key to the gates of this sanctuary, which was kept, as far as possible, in its natural state. Whenever I was weary from research and writing I would go out, whatever the season, to "the wilderness." There, as I sat watching the birds and little animals, or the strange aquatic life of the stream, I found, as I always can in solitude, the mental peace and refreshment I needed.

I soon found that I had to have some regular exercise; otherwise I could not keep myself sufficiently fit to work hard at my research. I discovered that the quickest way to get what I needed was an hour or so of either squash or fives (handball) in the winter and of tennis in the summer. It was hard to believe that as recently as 1926 I had been severely reprimanded and nearly sent down from the university for having dared to appear on the college tennis courts in white shorts. I had protested the objection as illogical considering that one wore shorts on the rugger, soccer, and hockey fields in the presence of women spectators. The reply had been that wearing shorts for tennis was definitely another matter; it was indecent, and I must conform to the rules or be sent down. By 1932, more than half the tennis players had adopted shorts, and a few even appeared on the courts bare to the waist without any protest from the authorities. Perhaps my 1926 gesture of defiance had not, after all, been in vain.

It makes me sad to have to admit that until our little daughter, Priscilla, was about eighteen months old I did not see very much of her. I was exceptionally busy with my research work, usually leaving home early in the morning and not returning until after she had gone to bed. But as the evenings shortened and summer turned into autumn, Priscilla reached the age when she was running about and beginning to talk, and it was fun to play with her. Instead of having a game of tennis or squash in the afternoon, I would rush back to Girton so as to have time to be with my little daughter before her bedtime. I suddenly realized how charming children—and especially my own child—could be. (At the end of the following year, on December 12, 1933, our son, Colin, was born.)

Shortly after we returned from Olduvai in 1932, a preliminary conference was organized at Cambridge by the Royal Anthropological Institute to discuss the fossil human remains we had found in Kenya, at Kanam and Kanjera on the shores of the Kavirondo Gulf of Lake Victoria. When the conference was over, I decided to make a much more detailed study of these specimens and prepare a report of my own for publication.

In order to explain the significance of the events relating to the dating of the Kanam and Kanjera finds, it is necessary for me to go back briefly to a discovery made in an earlier decade by Dr. Hans Reck of Berlin. In 1913 he had discovered a human skeleton at Olduvai Gorge. There had never been any doubt in my mind that this fossil skeleton represented *Homo sapiens* (modern man). The fact that this individual had been buried in the retracted, or so-called "prenatal," position, lying on its side with the knees drawn right up to the chin, had strongly suggested to me a relatively recent burial into earlier deposits, possibly during late Upper Pleistocene times. When referring to this discovery in an earlier book of mine, *The Stone Age Cultures of Kenya Colony*, written in 1929, I said: "Almost certainly this is not contemporary with the fossil deposits of the gorge in which it was found." I then went on to suggest that it "probably represents an intrusive burial."

In November 1931 I and a number of my colleagues had made a new and very careful examination of the site where Reck's discovery was made. Dr. Reck himself was one of the party, which included Sir Edmund Teale, director of the Tanganyika Geological Survey, Dr. Arthur Hopwood of the British Museum of Natural History, and two students of mine, "Bunny" Fuchs (now Sir Vivian Fuchs of Antarctic fame) and Donald MacInnes.

We were concerned simply with the geological evidence in connection with Reck's discovery. As a result of our investigations, it certainly seemed as though Reck had been right in claiming that the place where he had found the skeleton was in undisturbed deposits of the Bed II stratum. On the basis of this evidence, we decided to publish a report in *Nature* forthwith. This was done towards the end of 1931, and in the report we affirmed that the available evidence strongly supported Reck's claim that the skeleton was of mid-Pleistocene age. This was contrary to my earlier view that it was a more recent interment.

In 1933, with the Kanjera 1931–32 specimens strongly suggesting that man of *Homo sapiens* type had existed during the Middle Pleistocene, I felt it was incumbent upon me to go over to Munich, where Reck's 1913 Olduvai man was housed, to reexamine it and see whether it exhibited any similarities to my Kanjera human skull fragments.

Early in 1933, therefore, I traveled to Germany to see Professor Theodore Mollison in Munich. I took with me the original fragments of my two best Kanjera skulls, as well as a set of casts, so that we could compare them with Reck's 1913 specimen.

I had a delightful stay in Munich with the Mollison family, who very kindly put me up in their home. The first task that Mollison and I, with the help of his assistant, Geisler, undertook was a re-examination of the 1913 fossil skull. We soon came to the conclusion that it did not, in any way, resemble the Kanjera fragments. On the other hand, it showed many similarities to the Upper Pleistocene skulls I had excavated in 1928 and 1929 from Gamble's Cave, at Elmenteita, in Kenya. These had been found in association with artifacts of the Kenya Capsian culture. I had brought a cast of one of these skulls to Munich for comparative purposes.

As a result of our fresh examination of the Olduvai skull, the suggestion I had made in 1929 concerning its relatively recent age was strongly substantiated. As a further check, we decided to test the effect of fluorescent lighting on the 1913 skull placed side by side with genuine bones of extinct animals from Bed II. When we did this, the difference in age was immediately apparent and added strength to our view that the skull found by Reck was not of mid-Pleistocene age, but much younger. In consequence of this Munich experiment, I decided that in 1934 I would have to carry out further detailed studies at the Olduvai-man site to find out where we had made a mistake in 1931.

When I left Munich, I handed over one set of casts of the fragments of the two most important Kanjera skulls—Number 1 and Number 3—so that Mollison could experiment in making reconstructions. At Cambridge I made comparable reconstructions with another set of casts. Eventually, he and I arrived at such extraordinarily similar results that we were satisfied we had succeeded in producing something very closely resembling what the originals must have looked like before they were broken up.

Subsequently, I pooled the results of our respective reconstructions and in 1935 published them with careful drawings. These showed that the Kanjera hominids were unquestionably of *Homo sapiens* type, and also that they had had long, parallel-sided skulls with a brain capacity greater than the average of human beings today. Since a large brain capacity was at that time considered to be an ultramodern characteristic, many of my colleagues who had previously supported my interpretation of the Kanjera evidence decided to join the ranks of those who preferred to place the specimens in a "suspense account." So began the long controversy that was to rage for the next thirty-four years.

During the same field season in which we had found the Kanjera skulls, we had found a hominid lower jaw at Kanam West. This too proved to be a controversial specimen. The Kanam jaw fragment included most of the front region, where we have our chin, together with a small part on either side. Most of the teeth were missing, though a few remained on the right side. Unfortunately, both the lower margin and the hind part of the jaw on either side were missing. The jaw was heavily mineralized and had been dug out from the face of a small cliff in one of the Kanam West gullies by a member of my African staff, Juma Gitau. The discovery was accidental, since he was engaged at the time in digging out a molar tooth of an extinct type of elephant known as *Deinotherium*. In other words, this important fragmentary specimen had not been seen by any scientist while it was *in situ*—that is, in its original position.

There was never any doubt in my mind, however, that the specimen came from the deposit in which Juma said he had found it, for as soon as he noticed it—still embedded in the hard adhering rock—he summoned my student Donald Mac-Innes, who in turn called me to the spot. Juma had recognized that the specimen was of human origin because one fragment of a hominid tooth was visible.

We had not attempted to undertake any detailed cleaning of this precious specimen in the field, but had brought it back to England with most of the adhering matrix surrounding it. I had then only partially cleaned away the rock in preparation for the Cambridge conference, so that the geologists would be able to see the nature of the matrix in which the specimen had been found.

In particular, I had left a lump of what looked like matrix on the inner face of the jaw on either side of the midline. After my return from Munich I proceeded to clean this area with great care. As my work progressed, I had a very great surprise. I had thought that the lump was composed entirely of rock, but this was not the case. I found that it consisted of a strange, aberrant bony growth. I was nonplused! I took the specimen as soon as possible to Sir Frank Collier at the Royal College of Surgeons. He was then director of the Dental Department and the leading specialist in mandibular abnormalities. We spent a long time examining the specimen together and cleaning the area of the growth more thoroughly. In the end, he came to the conclusion that it was undoubtedly an ossified sarcoma, which had developed over a fracture during the process of healing. He published a report to this effect as an appendix to my book.

Because of the presence of this bony growth, it was difficult to determine whether or not the Kanam jaw had ever possessed the feature popularly known as the "simian shelf," a ledge of bone that unites the two halves of the lower jaw, on the inside. The general view of anthropologists at that time was that such a feature was bound to be present in all true primitive hominids. It was important, therefore, to determine whether it was present in the Kanam jaw.

The only way to decide this question was to cut a section through the jaw in the region of the sarcoma. A few of my colleagues supported me in my proposal to do this, but others considered it was almost sacrilege to do anything so drastic. After careful deliberation, I proceeded to cut a section, with the help of technicians at the Imperial College of Science in London. The result was that the section revealed two things clearly: the nature and extent of the bony growth, and the fact that the specimen had never possessed a simian shelf.

My announcement to this effect reinforced the view of my opponents that the Kanam jaw did not belong to the Lower Pleistocene deposits in which it had been found and that I must have been mistaken in believing that the specimen had been found *in situ*. They suggested as an explanation that a specimen of a modern man had somehow found its way down a crack into the earlier deposit.

I could not accept this view and continued to maintain that the specimen was a genuine Lower Pleistocene fossil. In my book, *The Stone Age Races of Kenya*, published in 1935, I pro-

21

posed it as the type specimen of a new species of the genus *Homo*, naming it *Homo kanamensis*.

In spite, therefore, of the detailed studies I had made of the Kanjera specimens with the help of Professor Mollison, and even though I had sacrificed part of the Kanam jaw in order to get a clearer picture of its morphology, the reaction of most of my colleagues was still disappointing. All but a few added the specimens from then onwards to their "suspense account," to await either confirmation or rejection at some unspecified future date.

Pondering the problem, I found solace again and again by reminding myself of the fact that in 1929 nearly all the scientists who had attended the meeting of the British Association for the Advancement of Science in Johannesburg had rejected my colleague Raymond Dart's view that his juvenile *Australopithecus africanus* skull was a manlike, rather than an apelike, creature. Dart had to wait for acceptance until 1947, but even in the 1930s I was certain that both his discovery and mine would one day be vindicated in the eyes of the scientific world.

The part played by prejudice in relation to scientific controversy was very strong indeed in the thirties and remains so to this day. Let me give a further example. In 1931, in Bed I at Olduvai Gorge, we found five teeth of a gigantic *Deinotherium* in direct association with primitive stone tools. This was so exciting that we quickly published a note in *Nature*. We indicated that, at least on the African continent, *Deinotherium* must have continued well into the Lower Pleistocene period, side by side with primitive man.

Within a few weeks of the publication of our evidence, two different foreign scientists published reports that many years before they too had found *Deinotherium* fossils in Pleistocene deposits in Africa. Prior to our report, they had withheld publication of their evidence. It had seemed so improbable that they had feared the criticism of their contemporaries.

In direct contrast to this skepticism was the strange acceptance by all but a few scientists of the Piltdown skull and jaw during 1912 and 1913. I believe that the Piltdown specimens were accepted with such ease because they fitted readily into the generally agreed pattern of what an ancestral human skull *ought* to look like. When, eventually, they were shown up as clever forgeries, it was clear that the perpetrators had been careful to take into account this preconceived image of early man and had modified their specimens accordingly.

I find it hard to believe that the forgers of the Piltdown hoax ever really intended to let it continue indefinitely. I suspect that their intention was to see how far the leading anthropologists of the time could be taken in by the unlikely juxtaposition of a very apelike jaw and a completely modern, even *Homo sapiens*-like, cranium. I think they hoped that the prominent anthropologists of their time—Sir Arthur Keith, Sir Grafton Elliot-Smith, and Sir Arthur Smith Woodward—would all make pronouncements accepting the Piltdown specimens as genuine. Thereafter, I believe, the hoaxers planned to produce the other half of the ape jaw and the remaining parts of the skullcap to show how inadequately physical anthropologists were equipped to interpret fossil human remains. As I see the picture, their plan failed because Charles Dawson, one of the parties to the practical joke, died before the time had arrived to tell the truth. The other man, I suspect, dared not accept responsibility for revealing what had been done when the corroboration of his partner was no longer available. I imagine that this second person was the one who had acquired the various fragmentary fossils from North Africa and America and was also the one whose knowledge of chemistry was sufficiently adept to enable him to undertake the necessary work to make the specimens look like fossils.

It is important to remember that although at the time the majority of scientists accepted the Piltdown fossils as genuine, there were a few, at the very outset, who could not accept the evidence.

In preparing the second edition of my textbook, *Adam's Ancestors*, in August 1934, I made the following remarks about the Piltdown fossils: "Undoubtedly had the skull been found without the lower jaw, it would have been regarded as a form of *Homo sapiens*." A little further on I wrote: "If the lower jaw really belongs to the same individual as the skull, then the Piltdown man is unique in all humanity." Further on again I wrote: "It is tempting to argue that the skull, on the one hand, and the jaw and canine tooth, on the other, do not belong to the same creature. Indeed a number of anatomists maintain that the skull and jaw cannot belong to the same individual and they see in the jaw and canine tooth, evidence of a contemporary anthropoid ape." I referred to the whole problem of Piltdown as an enigma. I admit, however, that I was foolish enough never to dream, even for a moment, that the true explanation lay in a deliberate forgery.

As I write this book in 1972 and ask myself how it was that the forgery remained unmasked for so many years, I have turned my mind back to 1933, when I first went to see Dr. F. A. Bather (who had taken over from Smith Woodward as curator of palaeontology at the British Museum of Natural History). I told him that I wished to make a careful examination of the Piltdown fossils, since I was preparing a textbook on early man. I was taken into the basement to be shown the specimens, which were lifted out of a safe and laid on a table. Next to each fossil was an excellent cast. I was not allowed to handle the originals in any way, but merely to look at them and satisfy myself that the casts were really good replicas. Then, abruptly, the originals were removed and locked up again, and I was left for the rest of the morning with only the casts to study.

It is my belief now that it was under these conditions that all visiting scientists were permitted to examine the Piltdown specimens, and that the situation changed only when they came under the care of my friend and contemporary Dr. Kenneth Oakley. He did not see the necessity of treating the fragments as if they were the crown jewels, but, rather, considered them simply as important fossils—to be looked after carefully, but from which the maximum scientific evidence should be obtained. In 1953, as soon as he took over the care of the Piltdown material, Oakley drilled holes into the canine tooth, the jaw, and the skull to check their fluorine content. He also allowed his colleagues, including Sir Wilfrid Le Gros Clark and Dr. J. S. Weiner, to make detailed examinations of the original material. It was found that the teeth had been filed and the bones artificially stained to make them appear fossilized. Thus the forgery was uncovered.

In 1933, when I was writing the first edition of *Adam's Ancestors*, I was lucky enough to meet Mary Nicol. At that time she was making drawings of stone tools for Dr. Gertrude Caton-Thompson, who had recently been excavating an important site in the Fayum depression in Egypt. Mary Nicol's drawings were the best representations of stone tools I had ever seen then or, indeed, have seen since. I immediately invited her to undertake the drawings for my new book, and she readily agreed. Thus began my long association with Mary, who was later to become my second wife and who is at the present time one of the leading specialists on the early Stone Age cultures of the Old World.

Although at this time I was mainly working on the Kanam and Kanjera fossils and the artifacts collected during the 1931–32 Olduvai expedition, I was also completing two books, *Adam's Ancestors*, the textbook I have mentioned, and *The Stone Age Races of Kenya*, which deals with the many Palaeolithic, Mesolithic, and Neolithic skulls and skeletons we had found during previous archaeological expeditions.

I had been laboriously drawing some of these skulls by hand—an arduous task necessitating the taking of innumerable measurements with calipers—when a mechanically minded friend of mine by the name of Harper, at St. John's, suggested that we should design a drawing machine. I knew exactly what I hoped to do with such a machine, while he provided the technical knowledge necessary to achieve our objective. The Cambridge Instrument Company gave invaluable help during the design stage and then undertook to make two prototypes for me.

Eventually, this instrument came into existence under the name of the Leakey Harper Drawing Machine. I installed one of these at the Royal College of Surgeons; the second prototype went to Japan. Later a third one was made for me and is now in the National Museum in Nairobi.

In spite of the fact that I was so closely linked with the invention of this machine, I never really became proficient in its use. Fortunately for me, one of the technicians of the Royal College of Surgeons, Edward Smith, learned to use it with considerable speed and accuracy. Before long, he was producing exact, actual-size drawings of a skull in three different views in approximately two hours. Prior to the development of the Leakey-Harper Drawing Machine, it took about three weeks to draw these skulls—with a lesser degree of accuracy.

At the close of 1933 *Adam's Ancestors* was ready for publication. I decided that it was time to return to East Africa, not only because there was a great deal of detailed work to do at Kanam and Kanjera, but also to continue our exploration of Olduvai Gorge. Accordingly, I began to make plans to take out my Fourth East African Archaeological Expedition in 1934.

Two

The consensus of scientific opinion against my evidence for the early age of the Kanam jaw and the Kanjera skulls was led by Professor P. G. H. Boswell, a senior fellow of the Royal Society. He was in charge of the Department of Geology at the Imperial College of Science in London and probably ranked as the leading Pleistocene geologist in the world at that time. Although he did not pretend to any great knowledge of human anatomy, he nevertheless had for a long time been a firm believer in the authenticity of the Piltdown finds.

When I started making plans for the Fourth East African Archaeological Expedition, which was to include further work at Kanam and Kanjera, I decided that the season's work should include geological mapping, as well as new excavations at both sites. I also hoped to be able to make an extensive collection of fossils from the early Miocene deposits on Rusinga Island, which we had briefly visited in 1931.

Since Professor Boswell was both the leader of those who disliked my evidence of the presence of the genus *Homo* in Lower and Middle Pleistocene deposits and the most prominent Pleistocene geologist in Great Britain at that time, I suggested to the Royal Society that they should invite him to participate in the work of the 1934 season at Kanam and Kanjera. This the Royal Society agreed to do, and Boswell accepted with alacrity.

Raising funds for my fourth expedition proved to be very difficult and was not achieved until nearly the middle of the year. This did not matter to me greatly, since I had much other work with which to occupy myself in Cambridge. In particular, I was in the throes of seeing *Adam's Ancestors* through the press and experiencing my first major problems in proofreading and indexing.

Mary Nicol had completed many beautiful drawings of artifacts to illustrate my book, and I now had the task of selecting photographs to indicate my ideas on human evolution, within the limits of the number of pages of plates allowed to me by the publishers. I found then, and have done so many times since, that this is a very difficult process. The author knows just what he wants to illustrate and how he would like it to be done. The publisher, on his part, is well aware from previous experience that too many illustrations may raise the costs of the book to an uneconomic level. Inevitably, therefore, there is conflict and ultimately compromise.

While *Adam's Ancestors* was in its final stages of publication, I was also completing *The Stone Age Races of Kenya* and, in particular, supervising the preparation of the illustrations of the skulls, which were being made at the Royal College of Surgeons with the drawing machine.

Although the text of the latter book was in page proof, I had decided to postpone the publication date in order to include new photographs of the Kanam and Kanjera sites. During the previous season I had used an old-fashioned concertina-type folding camera, and since we had been many miles away from any film-developing facility, it had been impossible to check whether or not the photographs were satisfactory. To my horror, every one of my pictures turned out to be a complete failure, owing to an unnoticed hole in the bellows of the camera. In preparing the site illustrations of both Kanam and Kanjera for the first draft of the book, therefore, I had had to rely on negatives of photographs taken by other members of the expedition. Ultimately, I decided to wait and get new pictures of my own. The episode of the faulty camera taught me an important lesson. Ever since then I have carried with me no fewer than two cameras, and I have always photographed anything of importance with both of them.

During the early part of 1934, Mary Nicol began to organize an excavation at a site known as Jaywick Sands, close to Clacton-on-Sea, in Essex. Previously Mary had worked only as an assistant on other excavations, mainly under the leadership of a Miss Liddell. On this occasion she planned to work on her own, but arranged with our mutual friend Kenneth Oakley, who was then on the staff of the British Museum of Natural History, that he would undertake the geological work of the program.

The planned excavation at Jaywick was destined to be one of the most important carried out in England for many years, since it was concerned with the controversy then raging over the place that should be assigned to the Clactonian culture in the prehistoric sequence.

The culture had been named by Hazzeldine Warren on the basis of a collection of artifacts he had discovered at low tide on the foreshore of Clacton-on-Sea. He was able to excavate the site only at low tide, but he succeeded in amassing an extensive collection, which he described in some detail. The site itself consisted of an old buried river channel, dating back to a time when the level of the sea in relation to the land was very much lower than at present and when the shoreline was much farther away.

In addition to the large number of stone artifacts Hazzeldine Warren recovered from his Clacton site, he found many fragmentary fossils of extinct animals and a piece of wood that had the appearance of being deliberately shaped by man, presumably for a spear point.

Because the stone tools of the Clactonian culture were quite unlike the handaxes that were then supposed to be typical of the early Palaeolithic, an immense controversy developed. Some prehistorians, led by the Abbé Henri Breuil of Paris, maintained that the Clacton specimens were unquestionably the work of man and deserved the new cultural name that had been applied to them. Many others, led by J. P. T. Burchell of London, categorically denied their human origin.

Hazzeldine Warren suggested that Mary should undertake excavations at Jaywick Sands, where the old buried river channel could be traced, before the area became completely built over by new building operations that would soon make excavation impossible. The site turned out to be part of the same channel sequence as that discovered by Hazzeldine Warren, but since it was on the mainland, work was not dependent upon the changing tides.

My personal interest in the Jaywick site arose from the fact that I had commented at considerable length on the Clactonian culture in *Adam's Ancestors*. I therefore became a frequent visitor to the excavation at weekends.

Mary and Kenneth ultimately published a very important

report on the results of their excavations, a report that placed the Clactonian firmly in its rightful place in the culture sequence of Great Britain. Before their report was published, however, I decided to conduct a brief comparable dig at the Swanscombe site, on the south side of the Thames between London and the east coast (where, in June 1935, a dentist and amateur archaeologist named Alvan Marston found the skull fragments, of mid-Pleistocene age, known as Swanscombe man). I did so because during a brief previous visit to that famous deposit I had found examples of Clactonian-type tools deriving from the lower loam and the basal gravels. I therefore recruited a small group of students from Cambridge to assist me, and we found some exceedingly interesting material. However, this added nothing to what Kenneth and Mary described in their detailed report, so my collection was stored away until such time as I could undertake a proper study of it.

By May of 1934 I had obtained sufficient funds to enable me to get my Fourth East African Archaeological Expedition under way, and accordingly I left Cambridge, accompanied by Peter Bell, a zoologist, Sam White, a surveyor, and Peter Kent, who had just qualified as a geologist at the University of Nottingham. The last two were to undertake general work for me, but Peter Bell had also promised to collect a certain number of mammals and birds for the British Museum of Natural History. Sam White was to be responsible for making a detailed map of the Kanam and Kanjera area to enable Kent to make his geological survey.

On arriving in Kenya, I was lucky to be able to recruit most of the African staff who had been with me during the previous season at Olduvai Gorge. These men were led by my old friend Heselon Mukiri (who had worked with me since 1926) and his assistant, Thairu Irumbi. Once again I took Ndekei with me as lorry driver. Having assembled the team and acquired a lorry and a car, we loaded our tents and other equipment and moved off to Kanjera, setting up our camp on a low hill halfway between the Kanjera site and the Kanam East exposures. Both these sites lie on the southern shore of the Kavirondo Gulf of Lake Victoria, between Kendu Bay and Homa Mountain.

As soon as camp was established, White and Kent began their plane-table survey and study of the geological evidence, while

Peter Bell, Heselon, and Thairu, together with a number of locally recruited men, began to dig three large trial trenches at Kanam West, in the area of the erosion gullies where the Kanam jaw had been excavated in 1932.

The Kanam area was heavily populated by members of the Luo tribe, who lived partly by cultivation and partly by fishing. I found, to my horror, that every single iron peg that, in 1932, we had set in concrete blocks to mark the site of the discovery of the jaw had been removed. Presumably these iron pegs had been converted into spearheads and harpoons for fishing. Nor was that our only setback. The area is one of very heavy rainfall— about fifty inches a year—and extensive erosion had taken place throughout the Kanam West gully area in the intervening two years. It turned out, therefore, to be impossible to relocate the exact spot where the famous, but controversial, jaw had been found, although my African staff and I could fix the position within reasonable limits.

The new excavations failed to reveal any further fossil hominid remains, but they did add considerably to our knowledge of the fossil fauna. As a result of Kent's work, we also gained a better understanding of the geology of the area and established the fact that parts of the deposits were heavily downfaulted against what we called "the Rawe fishbeds," which lay a few hundred yards to the southwest.

We had first located these fishbeds in 1932 and obtained a few interesting specimens from them, but we had not made a detailed study of the area. We had, however, photographed the contact between the fishbeds and the Kanam West deposits without clarifying their relationship. Now we discovered that in some places the fishbeds contained many mammalian fossils in addition to a wide range of fossil fish, and we obtained, among other things, a gigantic fossil tortoise more than six feet in length as well as the almost complete skeleton of an extinct giraffe with a most peculiar skull. Other finds included the skulls of two different species of extinct hippopotamus, along with some limb bones of one of them.

We had set up our camp on a ridge running down to the lake, between the Kanjera site to the east and the Kanam fossiliferous exposures to the west. Early one morning when the rest of the party left camp—some to excavate at Kanam and others to map the Kanjera exposures—I remained behind to write notes and prepare a monthly report. Suddenly my attention was distracted by a group of naked Luo fishermen wading back from their canoes through the weed belt that separated the lake proper from the inland shallows. They appeared to be very excited and were carrying something which, from the distance, I took to be a small crocodile.

I went down to the shore to have a look, and to my great surprise I found that their trophy was a large pangolin, or scaly anteater. Three species of scaly anteater occur in East Africa, the largest of which is known as the great, or Temmenick's, pangolin. We already knew that this species occurred in the Kanam area, since on several occasions we had seen the scales hanging from the belts of Luo women who came to camp to sell us milk, chickens, eggs, and vegetables. When I had inquired why their belts were adorned in this way, the women had told me that the scales were of the highest value as charms against the pains of childbirth. Apparently, any married woman of the tribe who could possibly obtain one or more of these pangolin scales did so.

The tremendous excitement exhibited by the fishermen as they came through the shallow water carrying the dead pangolin was due to the fact that their catch represented almost untold wealth for the four men who had killed it. They would be able to sell each scale for a sum of between three and five shillings, depending on its size and the place on the body from which it was plucked.

My own interest in the specimen was, of course, quite different. If I could have persuaded the fishermen to part with the whole animal I would have gladly paid them generously in return. I badly wanted to skin the creature and send the skin and skeleton to the museum in Nairobi. Nothing, however, would make the fishermen part with their booty for a lump sum. They had resolutely decided to sell each scale, one by one, not only to bring great wealth to themselves but also for the immense satisfaction of the women of their tribe.

Finally, I persuaded the fishermen to promise me the body and bones of the animal after all the scales had been plucked from it. This was certainly better than nothing, since the skeletal material was itself important from my point of view. Pangolins are rare in museum collections, and the bones are seldom available for comparative purposes. Little did I think that there was still greater excitement ahead of me.

As soon as the body was handed over, I carried it to my camp and cut open the belly in order to remove the viscera and examine the stomach contents to see what the creature had had for its last meal. According to all the books, the giant pangolin feeds exclusively on termites, but I had begun to suspect that this might not be wholly true. On the other hand, I certainly did not expect what I actually found: the total content of the stomach was a mass of water beetles. This was an exciting discovery, and it immediately explained how the creature had come to be killed by fishermen in the water. It had just been completing its breakfast.

Having established that the giant pangolin—at least, in this part of the country, where it lives near shallow, stagnant water—regularly includes water beetles in its diet, I decided to find out more about how the beetles were caught and eaten. My study revealed that frequently at dawn there were pangolin footprints going down to the shore of the lake and into the mud along the edge of the swamp. Subsequently, by keeping a close watch on the area, particularly at full moon, I was able to observe the method by which the beetles were caught.

Wading into the shallow water of the swamp or into a reedy backwater until it is far enough immersed for its lips to be level with the water surface, the pangolin puts out its long, flat, tape-shaped tongue and "woggles"—there is no other word—it over the surface of the water. Attracted by this moving object (a similar situation can be simulated by moving a stick over the water), the water beetles come swarming in from all directions. As each, in turn, comes into contact with the pangolin's sticky tongue, it is sucked into the mouth and swallowed.

I have stressed this particular incident because of the important lesson it has for field zoologists and students of natural history. Always, as a matter of routine, examine the stomach contents of any dead animal to which you have access. You never know what you may learn from doing so.

The other mammal credited in most books as living exclusively off termites is the African aardvark, or African anteater (this is not related to the South American anteater). Over the past few years I have examined the stomach contents of seven aardvarks. In six cases out of seven, the stomach contents included seeds of a plant of the cucumber family. In two cases out of seven, moreover, the last meal had been composed not of termites, but exclusively of the red biting ant, known in Swahili as *siafu* and scientifically as *Dorylus*.

Another interesting example of what can be learned by examining an animal's stomach contents concerns the African black-and-white civet. Zoologically, this creature ranks as a carnivore, and without doubt it occasionally raids farmers' fowl houses after dark and regularly eats small birds such as plovers and sand grouse, which it is able to catch at night when they are sleeping on the ground. It is recorded as also eating small rodents and lizards. Yet on the only occasion that I was able to study the stomach contents of a civet, they contained no bones or feathers, and the animal's last meal had consisted exclusively of millipedes and centipedes. Furthermore, on several recent occasions at Olduvai Gorge I was able to examine the dung of this creature. In every case, part, at least, of its food had consisted of centipedes, millipedes, and beetles.

The museum in Nairobi at that time was in the charge of Dr. V. G. L. van Someren, who had told me when I passed through Nairobi that he urgently needed a Bateleur eagle for the mounted exhibit. It is not at all easy to collect a specimen of this bird, since it spends most of its time flying high in the sky. When it does swoop to the ground, to kill a hare or some other small mammal, it usually picks up the prey in its talons and carries it off to eat it at the top of a high tree, well out of range of gunshot. So it was with great surprise that when I looked out of my tent one morning at the Kanam camp I saw a Bateleur eagle sitting on the ground about fifty yards away. Apparently it had killed a white-tailed mongoose that had proved too heavy to carry off and had been forced to feed on the ground.

Much as I dislike shooting, there are times when I consider it is justifiable for scientific purposes; I had in mind the urgent needs of the museum in Nairobi. I therefore shot the eagle, with surprising results. Within a few minutes—in fact, as I carried it back to my tent—a number of women caught sight of it in my hand and presumably passed the information on to others. In an incredibly short time several hundred Luo men and women had gathered round the tent, all insisting that I should not skin the eagle but hand it over to them intact.

It transpired that the Luo believed that for women each feather contained the same powerful magic against the pains of childbirth as did the scales of the pangolin, and for men the feathers provided protection against muscular pains. Each man and woman thus wanted to pluck at least one feather from the dead eagle. But this time the trophy was mine, and the crowd had to turn away disappointed.

In a somewhat similar fashion, the women of certain Asiatic communities regard a whisker plucked personally from the cheek of a dead lion or lioness as a complete safeguard against the pangs of childbirth. For years after I took charge of the museum in Nairobi, therefore, I arranged to have the mounted head of a lioness hung, without any protective casing, fairly low down on one of the museum walls. When all the original whiskers had been surreptitiously removed one by one by pregnant Asiatic women, I ordered fresh whiskers of nylon to be substituted. These were apparently just as efficacious, for they too regularly disappeared and as regularly were replaced by us!

After this long digression, we must return again to the problem of Kanam and Kanjera. In due course Professor Boswell announced that he was arriving from Great Britain, and I drove down to Nairobi to meet him and bring him back to our camp. I arranged, at the same time, for my friend E. J. Wayland, who was then director of the Geological Survey in Uganda, to come over by steamer from Entebbe to participate in our discussions, especially on the subject of the geological age of the deposits and the validity of my evidence as a whole.

So far as Kanjera was concerned, Boswell conceded he could find no explanation for the two *in situ* fragments of skull other than that they were genuine fossils caught up in the deposits while they were forming. He therefore accepted my view that Kanjera skulls 1 and 3 were in fact contemporary with the deposits at that site. His only doubt was whether or not the strata were really of Middle Pleistocene age, and he sought more evidence on this point. I reminded him that the mammalian fossils from Kanjera were of the same species as those we had found in Bed IV at Olduvai, and Wayland assured him that these Olduvai deposits could not be younger than the Middle

Pleistocene. However, Boswell reserved judgment on this problem until we could take him to the gorge, as we had promised.

The situation in respect of the Kanam jaw was at the same time both more important and more controversial. It had been found in direct association with Lower Pleistocene fossils such as *Deinotherium* and *Mastodon,* and the matrix adhering to it was entirely similar to that which Boswell had now seen in the Kanam West gullies. Boswell, however, remained doubtful because no scientist had seen the jaw *in situ.* He would not agree to accept Juma's statement that it had been dug out while he was working on the *Deinotherium* tooth; also, we could not locate for him the exact spot where Juma had been digging two years previously. On the other hand, as I pointed out to him, we had originally taken a level section right across the Kanam West gullies, using a Zeiss-Watts level, and could therefore locate the position to within a very few feet—and, in fact, we did so. I had brought with me a copy of the cross section, taken from a tree that could still be located on one side of the gully to another tree on the other side. On this cross section was a mark showing the point where the jaw had been recovered. I had, therefore, no doubt at all that I was showing Boswell and Wayland the right place within a few feet.

Unfortunately, as I explained earlier, the photographs I myself had taken had all failed to come out, and I had had to rely on some snapshots taken by other members of the expedition to pinpoint the place where the jaw was found. I had brought with me copies of some of these photographs. On one of them, a student had written "site of *Deinotherium* tooth" at Kanam West. I had assumed, wrongly, that the photograph illustrated the site where the *Deinotherium* tooth and the hominid jaw were found together, but when we examined the photograph carefully, this assumption proved to be erroneous. In fact, the photograph showed the area where a second *Deinotherium* tooth had been found several weeks later.

This mixup was most unfortunate because, not unnaturally, it increased Boswell's doubts about our evidence, even though it was a genuine and understandable mistake. I still had no doubt at all, nor had any of my African staff, that we had pointed out to him the place, to within a few feet, where the disputed specimen was dug out by Juma. To Boswell, however, the mistake over the photograph provided confirmation that he was right to recommend that the jaw be treated as doubtful. It is interesting to note that his view of the geology of the Kanam site coincided with both Wayland's and mine. In spite of this, so greatly was his judgment prejudiced by the evidence of the Piltdown specimens that he actually told us that were it not for the counterindication provided by the Piltdown jaw, which showed that man in the Lower Pleistocene had a simian shelf and extremely apelike characteristics, he would be inclined to accept the Kanam evidence, since the mineralization of the specimen compared closely with that of other fossils from the same deposits.

During the past few years, circumstances and new discoveries have shown that I was correct in maintaining, all along, that the Kanam jaw was genuine. First, the Piltdown specimens have been unmasked and shown to be forgeries, so the argument that all early hominids had simian shelves is no longer valid. Second, we have specimens of mandibles of *Homo habilis* from Lower Pleistocene deposits at Olduvai Gorge that have many resemblances to the Kanam jaw. Third, my son Richard has discovered several hominid jaws at sites on the northeast shores of Lake Rudolf; these are associated with fossil fauna closely resembling that of Kanam West, while the jaws themselves are definitely of *Homo* type and closely correspond to the original Kanam find. Thus, forty years later, most of my colleagues are reappraising the Kanam evidence and accepting it.

As Boswell had only a limited time to spend in East Africa, I left some of my staff behind, under Heselon Mukiri, to continue the excavations we had undertaken at Kanam West, while I set off with a lorry and car to take Boswell to Olduvai Gorge. Kent, Bell, and White all pleaded to come with us, and I agreed, since Heselon was quite competent to take charge of the excavations at Kanam while we were away. We proceeded first to Nairobi, to obtain provisions for the journey and some spare parts for the vehicles, and then set off, via Kijabe, Narok, and Loliondo.

Our journey was uneventful for the first few days, but near the boundary between Kenya and Tanganyika the car broke down, and I had to send the lorry back to Narok for spare parts. As soon as these had been fitted, we continued again until dusk, when we made arrangements to stop for the night. On this particular occasion Kent, White, and Bell were sleeping in the back of the lorry and Boswell in the car. Ndekei and I had spread a canvas tarpaulin on the ground beside the lorry and had gone to sleep in our clothes. I had removed my shoes and stockings and placed them on the lorry roof, but Ndekei had merely untied his laces, keeping his socks and boots on. It was not very cold, and we each slept with only one blanket.

In the middle of the night I woke up to hear Ndekei shouting. I switched on my torch, to find him no longer by my side but, to my astonishment, running after a large hyena, which appeared to be dragging away his blanket. I jumped up and gave chase, but although we followed that hyena for the best part of half an hour, we never caught up with it. When the chase was over Ndekei explained that it was not the blanket that was the object of the hyena's interest, but one of his leather boots, which it had seized from under the blanket! Fortunately for Ndekei, Boswell had several pairs of boots with him, and since his foot size was the same as Ndekei's, he presented him with a pair. Thereafter, Ndekei followed my example and removed his boots at night, placing them out of reach of any marauder.

We spent the first few days after reaching Olduvai explaining to Boswell our interpretation of the general geology of the gorge. He was deeply impressed by the gorge, as everyone is when he sees it for the first time, for the magnificence of the setting defies description and cannot really be captured by photography.

Boswell expressed himself satisfied with the evidence that the deposits we called Bed IV must be at least as old as the end of the Middle Pleistocene and that, consequently, this must also be true of the Kanjera deposits, which contained an identical faunal assemblage as well as tools of the same general type. In other words, he at last accepted that the Kanjera fossil skulls were of Middle Pleistocene age. But Boswell was hard to please. He then turned his attention to the reconstructions Mollison and I had made from the Kanjera fragments and expressed doubt as to whether our view that they represented a true *Homo sapiens* hominid living in the Middle Pleistocene was valid.

One problem on which I had particularly wanted Boswell's help at Olduvai was the dating of the site where, in 1913, Reck had found the human skeleton called Olduvai man. I had originally believed that this specimen had been buried *into* Bed II and was not contemporary with it. However, our excavation in 1931 had certainly made it *seem* as though the skeleton had been found in undisturbed parts of Bed II overlain by genuine Bed III. If this was so, then the skeleton clearly had to be of the same general age as the upper part of Bed II. Against this view was the evidence Mollison and I had obtained at Munich, especially that of the fluorescent-lighting test, which had thrown great doubts on the later interpretation.

It so happened that Boswell had specialized, with some of his associates at the Imperial College of Science, in heavy mineral analysis for testing the age of rock deposits. When he examined the site of Reck's find with me, he immediately suggested that an answer could possibly be found by using this technique. Consequently, he and I collected a large number of samples of Bed III from different parts of the gorge, as well as several samples of what looked like genuine Bed III overlying the stratum where Reck's discovery was made. Boswell was certain that the new heavy mineral analysis would quickly settle the question for good. He argued that the heavy minerals of genuine Bed III, no matter where they were collected in the gorge, would all be identical, and that if what was supposed to be Bed III at the Olduvai-man site was not true Bed III, then the minerals would be different.

A few months later, when the specimens were studied in his laboratory in London, the tests did give us a definite answer. The red-colored deposits that had overlain the Olduvai-man skeleton in 1913 contained heavy minerals that were never found in Bed III or even in Bed IV, but only in Bed V. The new evidence, therefore, showed clearly that the skeleton must be of post–Bed IV age and might even be younger than the main part of Bed V. (In 1970, bone from this skeleton was dated by carbon 14 to 17,000 B.P. [Before Present].)

Boswell would have liked to remain longer at Olduvai, but this was not possible, since he had to catch a plane to London. As for us, we had to return to Kanam in order to complete our excavations there, and we also had planned to make a trip to the Miocene sites on Rusinga Island. These two excursions confirmed my previous view that there were extensive and richly fossiliferous Miocene exposures in this part of Africa. In fact, it seemed likely that Rusinga would prove to be one of the most important Miocene sites in the whole African continent. We found many fossils, including additional specimens of primates, one of which was a magnificent palate of *Proconsul nyanzae*, and some remains of the fossil gibbon known as *Limnopithecus*. In 1935 I took these specimens back to London and handed them over to Sir Arthur Keith, who suggested that the former was a specimen of the genus *Dryopithecus*, which had originally been described from France, Spain, and India. However, there is no doubt at all in my mind that it did not represent *Dryopithecus*, but was a true example of the larger species of *Proconsul*.

All round the shores of Lake Victoria and its islands, including Rusinga, one can always be sure of seeing fish eagles. In fact, almost every large tree in the area seems to boast at least one pair, and occasionally two, of these magnificent birds. Since these eagles are long-lived and have few natural enemies apart from man, one would expect them to suffer a fantastic population growth, but that is not the case. I think the explanation lies in the unusually high mortality rate among newly hatched chicks. I can give no reason why this should be so, but again and again over the years I have found small, fluffy, white baby fish eagles, about the size of a tennis ball, lying dead or dying on the ground.

Three such babies came into our hands one day shortly after we returned from Olduvai. They were very newly hatched, and Peter Bell and I decided to try to rear them. We fed them small scraps of fresh lake fish and were so successful that when the day came for us to pack up the Kanjera camp, early in October, all three were of adult size, although still retaining their juvenile plumage. They had never been kept in cages, and throughout their stay in camp they had been free to fly wherever they pleased. By the time we were ready to return to Nairobi they had started to fly down to the lake shore and catch their own fish in the shallow waters. We therefore had great hopes that they would remain happily in their own habitat when we left.

But this was not to be. The three fish eagles had become so accustomed to human company that when our convoy finally moved off, heading for Nairobi, they followed us on the wing. The first part of the track ran for about ten miles along the shore of the lake, and all the way the eagles flew behind us, landing every now and again on one or other of the vehicles. When, at length, we turned inland at Kendu Bay, we hoped that we had said good-bye to our faithful friends. That night, however, already halfway to Nairobi, we found that they were still with us and very hungry. We gave them a meal and resigned ourselves to the fact that they would probably escort us all the way to Nairobi—which is exactly what they did.

We were about to begin the second half of our season's work and planned to explore the side gorge at Olduvai. But since there was little water there, and certainly no fresh fish on which to feed the eagles, they could not possibly be allowed to follow us any longer. Fortunately, the curator of the Natural History Museum in Nairobi, Dr. van Someren, had erected a large aviary behind the museum a few years earlier, and this was now empty. It was forty feet high and both longer and wider than that, providing plenty of room to house our three eagles for the time being. Accordingly, I decided to leave them in the aviary and promised Dr. van Someren that I would pay for the fish he had to buy for them while I was at Olduvai.

Before we left Rusinga, however, I had a less friendly encounter with another specimen of the area's wildlife. All the water for use in the villages on the island was drawn from the lake, mainly by the women and children, who filled their earthenware pots and tin canisters and carried them on their heads to their huts. In the ordinary course of events, fetching water from the crocodile-inhabited lake was made safe by the building of an enclosure of stakes extending out into the water about five feet from the place on shore where the water was drawn. However, one crocodile had become very cunning. On several occasions it had come out of the water, crawled along the lake shore, and made its way through the grass behind the enclosure to carry off an unsuspecting woman or child, sometimes a goat or a sheep. This had been happening at intervals for nearly two years. When we arrived on Rusinga the island's chief asked for my help in getting rid of this scourge, and I promised that if the crocodile was located while we were there, I would do my best to dispose of it.

A few days later, when we were in the middle of lunch, a messenger rushed into camp to say that a crocodile was sunning itself on a small mud bank about half a mile off. I immediately went to the spot and managed to put a bullet into the back of the crocodile's neck just behind the head, thus killing it. This is a difficult shot to make, but the only effective one. If a crocodile is hit in any other part of its anatomy it disappears into the water, even though it may be mortally wounded, and is irrecoverable. In this instance, the local inhabitants particularly wished to cut the creature open to make sure that it was, in fact, the man-eater.

The sound of the shot brought hundreds of people running down to the shore from all directions, and when they saw the dead crocodile there was great rejoicing, wild dancing, and shouting—though there were some who wept, remembering the loved ones they had lost. In a few minutes the crocodile was brought up from the mud bank onto the grass by the shore and laid stomach upwards to be cut open. It was a gruesome spectacle. The stomach contents included bracelets, beads, necklaces, and many other indisputable indications of the human meals that had been eaten. Many of the objects were identified by relatives of the victims. There was, therefore, no doubt whatsoever that the crocodile I had shot was indeed the one that had been terrorizing the people of the island for so long.

Three

During our first expedition to Olduvai in 1931, we had succeeded in taking one of the cars up the west side of Ngorongoro, right to the rim of the caldera—which is the scientific name describing the crater. (A caldera is not a volcanic crater at all, but the result of a subsidence where a volcano once stood.) It was not easy to get the car up, since we had to negotiate our way through occasional areas of rocks and boulders and over the grass-covered western slopes. We hoped, then, that it would be possible to continue along the edge of Ngorongoro and down the eastern side to join up with the main road from Arusha to Oldeani. This hope had to be abandoned because of the dense forest at the top of the eastern side of the caldera.

When we took Boswell to Olduvai, we had once again followed the road that Captain J. H. Hewlett pioneered for me in 1931, crossing the Kenya-Tanganyika border at Loliondo. On the way back, however, I had been informed by the district officer at Loliondo that plans were being made by the government to construct a road up the eastern slopes of Ngorongoro, through the forest and over the ravines to the government camp from which the Ngorongoro area was administered. On my return to Nairobi from Rusinga, therefore, I wrote to Arusha to discover more about this project. Clearly, if we could drive to Arusha and thence to Oldeani on existing roads, proceed up the eastern forested slopes to the top of Ngorongoro, and then link up with the route we had taken in 1931, it would considerably shorten the time required for the journey from Nairobi to the gorge, even though the mileage would be greater.

In reply to my letter of inquiry, I was informed that the district officer in charge of Ngorongoro, together with the Forest Department officer and the Game Department authorities, shortly planned a joint attempt to get their vehicles along the new route to the top of Ngorongoro. I decided that we should endeavor to join up with them, so that we could all make the difficult journey together.

Accordingly, in the middle of April, I sent Bell, Kent, and White, with most of my African staff, ahead with the lorry carrying much of our equipment, planning to follow next day in the car.

The lorry got through to Arusha with ease, but the next day, near the Ngong Hills, I was caught in violent rainstorms, which turned the road into a sticky mass of "black cotton" soil—black clay that seems to be bottomless when it is wet. The car stuck over and over again in this quagmire, and I spent many hours of backbreaking work before eventually reaching Arusha and joining the others in the temporary camp just outside the township.

Next morning I again sent the lorry on ahead, with instructions to follow the road to Oldeani and then to turn off along the new track that had just been cut by the Forest Department and up which the district officer and his party intended to proceed that day. Meanwhile, I planned to drive to Moshi to meet Mary Nicol and then back to Arusha to collect Sam Howard; both of them were joining us for this part of the Olduvai season. Mary had flown up from South Africa, where she had been visiting prehistoric sites, and Sam Howard had been working for the Shell Company in Tanganyika. Since the lorry was likely to travel very slowly, I thought I would easily catch up with it before it reached the summit of Ngorongoro.

It is, however, never wise to make precise plans in Africa. The lorry duly left in fine weather on the morning of April 20 and covered the whole of the 106 miles to the top of Ngorongoro before dark. We were less lucky. Mary, Sam Howard, two of my African staff, and I took no less than four and a half days to cover the same distance!

The first day, after collecting Mary and Sam, I planned to reach the Oldeani turnoff before dark. But again luck was against us. It rained so hard that by five o'clock there was nothing for it but to make camp by the roadside and trust for better weather next morning. Early next day our hopes were fulfilled; the sun rose high in a bright sky and we set off with great expectations. The previous day's rain, however, had turned the road into a quagmire, and we managed to travel only fifty miles before darkness fell and we were forced to camp at the base of the Ngorongoro range.

That night it rained again, without ceasing, with the result that it took us the next two and a half days to cover sixteen miles of the newly made track. On some occasions, Mary, Sam, the two Africans, and I practically carried the car and the equipment. Sometimes we unloaded the car and carried the luggage ahead for half a mile or so, and then returned to push and carry the car. Sometimes we took the car ahead and went back to get the luggage. An additional problem was that the lorry, which we had counted on catching up with in good time, carried all our food supplies, except for the little we had taken for the first two days! In consequence, the last part of the night-mare journey was made worse by the pangs of hunger.

Eventually, we caught up with Bell, White, and Kent, who had put up their tents a few hundred yards from the grass huts of the administrative officer's camp. They were delighted to see us; they had begun to worry, and would have come back in the lorry to look for us had the road conditions not been so terrible.

After a badly needed night's sleep, we awoke to find the sun was shining once more. The clouds had lifted, and we had a magnificent view down into Ngorongoro Crater, with its shallow soda lake at the bottom and its groves of yellow-barked fever trees, which were the home of a medium-sized herd of elephant. Through our field glasses, 2,000 feet below us we could see countless wildebeest, hundreds of zebra, and an occasional rhinoceros. I had never seen the crater from this angle before, and the others, of course, had never seen it at all. It was a most exciting moment.

We stayed with the district officer for a day and a half, in order to rest and to discuss with him the government's plans for making a graded link road from his camp, via Olduvai, to the Serengeti Plains. We then started down the track we had pioneered in 1931 and reached the mouth of the gorge in about six hours.

In 1931 we had merely cleared away boulders and cut down a few trees and bushes on this part of the journey, but the grass was now so long, owing to recent rains, that it was difficult at times to pick up our original route, and we ran into trouble again and again with hidden rocks, stones, and tree stumps. Having reached the Balbal depression, we crossed it diagonally to the point where the Olduvai Gorge debouches abruptly onto the flats, and then wound our way up the first step of the depression and camped near our 1931 site.

It is almost impossible today, as one drives from Arusha township to our present Olduvai camp in a matter of four hours, to believe that the same journey once took more than five days to complete. From the tourist point of view, the change is obviously advantageous, but I still look back with pleasure at the hardships of that pioneer trip and would gladly endure them again for the mere satisfaction of achievement in the face of so many difficulties.

My aim for the 1935 season was to spend most of our time exploring the gorge to the southwest of the point where the main and side gorges meet. I therefore intended to establish a camp as near as possible to the junction. We had made our previous camps on the open plains beyond the edge of the gorge on the north side. But I believed that near the place I had in mind there might be a chance of driving the vehicles off the windswept open plains and part of the way down into the gorge.

When we reached the area where the two branches of the gorge met, we left our vehicles and started to explore on foot.

Before long we found a place where the sheer cliffs of the gorge changed to a gentler slope, and eventually we managed to get the cars within fifty feet of the floor of the gorge. Here we established Olduvai Camp 6.

This was at the end of April 1935. The grass was green, and the whole area was teeming with herds of game. There were pools of water too, in parts of the main and side gorges. The camp stood in a clearing between two patches of sansevieria (wild sisal), just opposite FLK I, the place where, in 1931, we had found the first stone tools *in situ* in Bed I. On this occasion, however, our objective was not to explore the FLK area, but to extend our search westwards up the side gorge into an area that we had not previously prospected thoroughly.

During our first night in this new camp a number of lions came round to investigate, in the same way as they had done during our first night in the 1931 camp, when one lion had walked right through the tent in which MacInnes and Fuchs were sleeping! On this occasion the lions contented themselves with roaring at us. Inasmuch as most of the party had never heard lions at close quarters before, they experienced a great thrill.

Our arrival had been witnessed by various Masai, since there were many *manyattas*, or Masai villages, in the area, owing to the temporary availability of good grazing on the plains and water in the gorge. Early next morning a group of elders accompanied by a few *morani*, or warriors, descended on us. They were mostly men whom I had known in 1931, and they were delighted to see me. They brought us gourds of curdled milk and a fat-tailed ram as presents. I, on my part, had brought a quantity of dry tobacco leaf, and this I now gave the elders in return. The dry tobacco leaf was extremely acceptable, since, normally, the Masai could obtain it only at Oldeani or Loliondo.

After greetings had been exchanged and all the proper courtesies observed, the elders inquired whether I would, as before, conduct a daily medical clinic for their sick. I had, of course, come prepared to do so. We made a counterrequest that they supply us daily with fresh milk for as long as they remained in the area. We insisted, though, that they must milk the cows into containers we would supply and not into their own gourds. There was a good reason for this request: the Masai normally

45

rinse out their milk gourds with cow urine. This may have been satisfactory from their point of view, but we knew from previous experience that it made the milk taste strongly of ammonia. Even when put directly into our own containers, the milk had to be boiled because of the risk of bovine tuberculosis. Such freshly boiled milk was, however, much more palatable than any of the types of powdered milk available in East Africa at the time.

Because of the expense and difficulty of bringing in supplies of petrol from Arusha, we used our transport at the gorge only when it was absolutely necessary; all our exploring was conducted on foot. Our aim was to investigate the side gorge and its subsidiary gullies, pinpointing the places where fossils or stone tools were being exposed by erosion—these to be excavated in due course. Daily, therefore, while White and Kent carried out their mapping and drawing of geological sections, the rest of us were busy crawling up and down the exposures on hands and knees, looking for specimens. Peter Bell also began collecting the birds of the area so as to keep his promise to the British Museum of Natural History.

Every day we used to get up before dawn, have breakfast, and leave on foot, taking with us a little food and bottles of drinking water, together with notebooks, dental picks, brushes, and other necessary equipment. We were not, as I have said, intent on general collecting, but, rather, on locating sites for future work. However, if a rare fossil was found exposed on the surface where it was liable to be trampled on by animals or damaged by the weather, it had to be rescued and taken back to camp. When stone tools were found, a small selection was collected from the surface, marked with an index number, and taken as a sample of what that particular site could be expected to yield in the future. When a particularly rich site was found, the temptation to abandon the rule was great, but had to be resisted.

Altogether, during this period, we located some twenty good sites, of which three were particularly rich—SHK II, named after Sam Howard, BK II, named after Peter Bell, and MNK, named after Mary Nicol. The BK II and SHK II sites were, in fact, so rich that eighteen years later, in 1952, we selected them for the first intensive excavations at Olduvai.

I am frequently asked how it came about that although we started our survey at Olduvai in 1931, we did not carry out our first major excavation until 1952. The answer is simple. It lies in my determination to explore the huge area of the gorge before starting detailed excavation. This took twenty years. Had it not been for the war, the lack of funds, and the fact that I took off three whole years from my prehistoric studies to write a monograph on the Kikuyu tribe, the initial survey would not have been so drawn out.

To give a clear picture of the immense task we undertook in 1931 and 1935, I must remind my readers that we explored about 180 miles of exposures, ranging from a depth of about 300 feet to as little as 50 feet, before we undertook any major digging. Had we not worked to a plan, we might have found ourselves devoting several years to the excavation of one of the less important sites while much more significant ones remained unstudied because they had not been located. A planned program and patience are vital to satisfactory work in prehistory. The person undertaking the study must be willing to devote many years, if not his whole life, to the task, and should not aim for quick results in the field, to be followed by a comfortable armchair job at a university.

One day in November of 1935 Mary located the site we now call MNK as we crawled on hands and knees over an eroded area at the contact between Bed III and the overlying Bed IV. The surface here was scattered with Acheulean tools and flakes, as well as numerous fossil animal remains of antelope and pig. Among these Mary found two small fragments of a human skull. We spent many hours thereafter trying to locate further parts of this hominid, but without success.

The site was also of particular interest for another reason. Here, at the junction of Bed III and Bed IV, there were whole banks of fossil bivalve shells. These are fresh-water mollusks that still occur in many of the larger streams and rivers in Africa today. Most of the shells we found were intact and had undoubtedly become fossilized where we found them, through the drying up of the water in which the mollusks lived.

It is worth noting here that when we eventually began our detailed excavation of Olduvai sites, only one of the numerous fossil hominid remains came from a site not previously located and marked for detailed study during our twenty-year preliminary survey.

Within a few days of our arrival we had set up the promised

clinic for sick and wounded Masai. My usual routine was to
come back to camp late in the afternoon, quickly have some tea
and clean myself up, and then go out to attend to my patients
before darkness set in. Most of the sufferers complained of
headaches, running sores, eye infections, or tapeworm. Occasionally, there was a mother with a baby suffering from acute
diarrhea or a warrior with a fresh bleeding wound. All this was
routine.

Then, one evening, as we all came back into camp tired and
dirty, I saw a young Masai warrior and a much older man sitting
in the shade of a tree on the edge of the camp. They both stood
up to greet us as we approached, and I answered rather impatiently, suggesting that they sit down and wait; I would come to
treat them just as soon as I had had my tea. But when the old
man sat down I noticed the top right-hand side of his head. I
was utterly appalled, for there I saw a gaping, suppurating, fly-
covered, filthy wound about two inches long and one inch wide.

All thought of tea or rest was immediately put aside. I rushed
to my tent, cleaned up, and came back with the medicine box to
start an immediate investigation while the light still lasted.
Apart from complaining that he had a headache and that the
wound was hurting him, the old man claimed there was not
much wrong with him. Interrogation soon revealed that the
warrior who had escorted him to camp was his grandson, and
that the old man had been wounded at a time before he himself
was married. Apparently, during a fight some forty years previously a long, heavy Masai spear had been thrown at his head
and had penetrated the wall of the skull. As the weight of the
spear made it fall downwards, it had levered off a piece of the
bone, exposing the brain. The tip of the spear had also inflicted
some damage on the brain itself; according to the old man, "it
had bled a little." The wound had quickly become septic, and his
friends had felt certain that he would die. Somehow or other he
had pulled through, and a soft skin had formed over the wound.
It was this, for the most part, that had kept out flies and dirt. In
due course he had married, and now he was a grandfather. He
went on to say that from time to time the wound opened up and
he had severe headaches. This was one of those occasions, so he
had come to me as the *bwana mganga*, or doctor, to put him
right.

48

The whole wound was filthy and full of pus. The brain damage extended inwards, and the brain itself appeared to have either shrunk or disintegrated a little, leaving a hollow large enough to contain a few ounces of fluid beneath the surface of the bone. My first task, obviously, was to clean the wound. I clipped away the ingrowing hairs and then began the task of trying to clean the wound itself. I dared not probe into the hollow, and I wondered what I should do. Finally, I made up a weak solution of hydrogen peroxide and poured about three tablespoonfuls into the gaping hole. There was an immediate frothing, and when I told the old man to lean over to one side the peroxide solution poured out into a basin, bringing with it a lot of dirt and dead flies. After several such treatments that first evening, the wound was a great deal cleaner, and since the old man seemed rather tired, I decided to apply sterilized gauze, and then let him go to the camp and get some food and rest. I told him I would continue the treatment next morning, when the light was better. (In those days we had only wick lanterns, which burned kerosene, not the excellent Petromax lamps we use today.)

Next morning my patient reported that he felt very much better and said he no longer had a headache. This, of course, could have been due to the aspirin I had given him the previous night, but it was also, I suspect, partly psychological, from his feeling that something positive was being done for him. When I examined the wound more closely in broad daylight, I found that there was a great deal of dirt and pus remaining, and I repeated my weak peroxide treatment. I carried on with this three times a day for two days, at the end of which time the whole wound had cleared up remarkably well and looked reasonably healthy. Moreover, in one corner a thin film of translucent skin had begun to grow and cover the exposed surface of the brain.

At this point, my patient announced that he was ready to walk home. An inquiry revealed that this meant a walk of some eighteen miles to the other side of Lemagrut Mountain. I made a countersuggestion. I told him that one of my vehicles was going to collect stores in a few days and that he could travel with us to the nearest hospital, where, in all probability, the doctor would attach a light metal cap to his skull to keep out the dirt and flies.

This suggestion was strongly rejected; in the end, I simply gave the old man a beret and begged him to wear it night and day. Just before he left I carried out various tests to find out what effect this long-standing wound had had on his senses. So far as I was able to judge, he had lost none of his faculties; his sight, hearing, smell, feeling, and taste were all unimpaired. We saw no more of him after that, but a few days later his grandson arrived driving a fat-tailed ram as a thank-you gift from his grandfather.

About this time, a middle-aged man who called himself a Masai walked into camp one day. Physically, he did not look like a pure Masai, and after a few questions I discovered that he was, in fact, half-Kikuyu and spoke some of that language. He had been born in the Narok district of Kenya, but his family had long since moved to Tanganyika and was now living near Ngorongoro. He himself had transferred his flocks to a *man-yatta* on the far side of Lemagrut Mountain, not far from Laetolil.

He stayed around for several days and joined us regularly when we went fossil hunting, showing great interest in everything we were doing. On his last day, he asked whether I would like to know about another site where he had seen similar fossils, not far from where he was living. Naturally, my reply was yes. He promised to guide us in our vehicles to the spot, but warned that it would be a lengthy and difficult journey. We would have to drive westwards beyond the head of the gorge at Lake El Garja, then turn southwards to Naibadad, after which it would be an easy run to the Laetolil River. We had some old German maps with us; as far as we could see, the river that he was calling Laetolil was a stream the Germans had named Vogel Fluss.

Sanimu, for that was his name, suggested that he go home on foot and return in about ten days' time bringing with him samples of the fossils, after which he would pilot our vehicles to Laetolil. True to his word, when he returned he brought with him in a little bag some pig and antelope teeth, all of them heavily fossilized and some embedded in a hard rock matrix.

That decided me. I immediately made plans to close down the camp at Olduvai for a few weeks and leave, with Sanimu, to investigate the new area. By this time, in addition to the equipment we had brought with us from Nairobi, we had accumulated a large quantity of stone tools and fossil bones, including the complete skull of an extinct hippopotamus known as *Hippopotamus gorgops* and a pair of horn cores of the giant bovid *Pelorovis*, which we had reinforced with plaster of Paris and iron bars. Kent had also collected a large number of rock specimens, and Peter Bell had some boxes containing zoological material for the British Museum of Natural History.

Since Sanimu had stressed that we must travel as lightly as possible, I decided to leave most of our equipment and collections behind in our camp. We therefore cleared a space in the center of one of the big patches of sansevieria, a plant known to the Masai as *duvai* (it is from this word that the name Olduvai is derived). In this clearing we stacked our excess stores and equipment and the boxes of specimens and closed the gap, which was our entrance to the enclosure, with branches of thorn.

Sanimu told us that it would not be necessary to carry much water on this trip, since he planned for us to camp the first night near a spring at the west end of the gorge (where the tourist camp run by George Dove is now situated); on the following night we were to camp by Naibadad Hill, where there were several springs. The third day we were due to arrive at Laetolil, where at this time of the year there should be a beautiful running stream. In spite of Sanimu's assurances, I insisted on carrying a number of four-gallon cans of water from the stagnant pool in the gorge, since one could never be sure of reaching the proposed water points at the expected times.

So, in due course, we set off in a lightly loaded lorry and car and headed due west to Lake El Garja. I had last seen El Garja in 1931, when it was nothing but a dry soda dust bowl. Now, because of the recent heavy rains, it had become a shallow lake. Unfortunately, the water was exceedingly saline and quite undrinkable, and was not even pleasant to wash in, owing to the concentration of soda. However, as Sanimu had promised, there was a small spring of sweet water at the extreme southwest corner of the lake, and there we made our first camp late in the afternoon. While the light lasted I explored briefly round the lake basin, but did not locate any archaeological sites.

Next morning we packed up and headed southwest, after having considerable difficulty in getting the vehicles up the cliff and out of the El Garja depression. Then we had to travel very slowly over the plains, since the grass was three or four feet high—higher, in fact, than I have ever seen it in the Olduvai region in all the years since 1934. We were in constant fear that one of the vehicle wheels would hit a tree stump or fall into a hole or even a gully masked by vegetation. When the going was very rough, either Sanimu or one of our men walked ahead checking the line of advance. By late afternoon, having covered only about sixteen miles, we arrived at the granite outcrop of Naibadad Hill and established a camp beside one of the fresh-water springs that surrounded it.

The following morning, much to Sanimu's dismay, I decided that we would have to spend most of the day overhauling our vehicles, tightening nuts and bolts, and checking all the tires for thorns. While Ndekei and I spent long hours on this task, the others explored the area round Naibadad and discovered a number of small Mesolithic Wilton-type living sites, with a scatter of artifacts and potsherds. They also located several stone mounds that appeared to be prehistoric burial sites.

Peter Bell, meanwhile, was searching for birds to add to the collection he was making for the British Museum. He located a colony of green-winged, red-necked lovebirds, whose nests were in holes in the dead branches of thorn trees, and called me over to look. I was very interested in the behavior pattern of these birds; it was one I had never seen before. Whenever a mother bird left the nest—presumably containing eggs or young—she would pluck small, thorny twigs and, using her beak, stuff them into the entrance of the nest, thus barring the way to predators such as lizards, egg-eating snakes, shrikes, and small hawks. When she came back she would pull away the thorny barrier to re-enter the nest. This was the first time I had witnessed the nesting habits of these lovebirds, but later, at our camp near Olduvai site BK II, I saw exactly the same thing happen. It would appear, therefore, to be part of the regular nesting behavior of the species and not an isolated event at Naibadad.

The next day, with our vehicles overhauled and the tires free of thorns and the risk of punctures, we set out again and shortly after midday reached the banks of a beautiful flowing stream. This was the Vogel Fluss of the German mapmakers and our objective—the Laetolil valley. There were many Masai *manyattas* in the area, and cattle, sheep, goats, and donkeys were all watering as we drove up. Very soon a group of elders came over to our cars to inquire of Sanimu what it was we wanted. Sanimu told them we had come to look for "old bones and stone spears," and with his help as interpreter I tried to explain a little bit more about the object of our search. One of the elders was quick to volunteer the information that there was a site of "old bones" some fifteen miles away, while everybody agreed that about five miles upstream there were many "heavy stones that looked like bones."

Our camp on the borders of the Laetolil stream was a very pleasant one. We made a clearing and set up our tents beneath a group of large, shady yellow-barked fever trees. The Masai warned us that there were many lions in the area, as well as numerous hyenas, but they assured us that the lions were not man-eaters, so we were not unduly worried. We warned our cook, however, to place all the cooking utensils on top of the lorry cab each night, and we too were careful to keep all our stores shut up in boxes and to place anything made of leather, such as camera cases, shoes, boots, and belts, out of reach of hyenas at night.

In the early hours of the morning, while the stream ran crystal-clear, we filled all available water containers. Later in the day cattle and other livestock moved into the water upstream of our camp, so that it became increasingly clouded with mud, until by evening it was not fit even for washing.

The day after we set up our camp Sanimu guided us in our vehicles upstream to explore the fossil beds. We found an area of about two square miles of heavily eroded badlands, where residual lumps and blocks and strange shapes of rock rose out of an otherwise more-or-less flat surface. Some of the rocks were in the form of pillars, ten to fifteen feet apart, and the whole fossiliferous area was about ten feet above the existing stream bed.

Fossil remains of certain types of animal were numerous;

others were notable by their absence. For example, whereas at Olduvai remains of hippopotamus and elephant were always common except in Bed III and Bed V, there was no trace of remains of these creatures at Laetolil. Moreover, the rocks from which the fossils were eroding were not ancient lacustrine or fluvial beds, but appeared to be deposits laid down under dry-climate conditions. Fossil remains of land tortoises were common; in addition to several complete fossilized tortoise shells, we found three or four dozen fossilized tortoise eggs. Twice we found fossilized birds' eggs like those of the plover. There were also numerous rodent remains, representing seven or more species, and the bones, horn cores, and teeth of several species of antelope were common. We found a few remains of fossil pigs, but none of them of the same species as those in the Olduvai deposits. In fact, the total picture represented by the remains suggested an ecological setting wholly different from Olduvai. This was heavily underscored by the total absence of teeth or bones of any member of the horse family, which are so common in almost every layer of the Olduvai fossil beds.

When we came to review the specimens we had found at Laetolil, it was very difficult to assess whether the major difference from the Olduvai assemblage was due solely to the different ecological setting or whether it also represented a different geological age. There were several major problems to solve, one of which was the presence of a good many specimens representing jaws and teeth that appeared to be of a fossil okapi. Today, okapi are present only deep in the Congo forests, and the rest of the fauna did not suggest to us a forest habitat. (Recent work at the National Museum, Nairobi, has shown that these teeth belonged, in fact, to a miniature giraffe and not to an okapi.) Another major difference between the finds at Laetolil and those at Olduvai was the total absence of any stone artifacts here.

One day we traveled some fifteen miles with the elder who had reported seeing another series of fossil beds, but since he had not been there himself for some time, we were unsuccessful in locating the exact spot. We did, however, find a few fossils, including fragments of teeth of a very primitive type of elephant, in the general area to which he took us.

In the Serengeti, sand grouse are present in very large numbers at certain times of the year, gathering in flocks of many thousands to feed on the grass seeds on the open plains and fly to the scattered water holes to drink. Often three or four different species mix together in one flock. At Laetolil there were many sand grouse. As it was the breeding season, they were not in flocks, but in pairs, with the females busy incubating their eggs. Each day, in our walk from the camp to the fossil beds, we would put up male birds; if we then looked round closely, we would discover well-camouflaged females crouched on their nests on the ground. I suppose that we saw twenty or thirty nests each day during the few weeks we were there.

Lions, as the Masai had told us right off, were rather common, having concentrated in the area because of the huge herds of Masai cattle and sheep. A few days after we arrived an amusing incident occurred—at least, it is amusing in retrospect. We were exploring the badlands area. Mary was nearest to me, Kent and White had gone off in a slightly different direction, and Peter Bell was with Heselon. Suddenly, I noticed the pug marks of a lion or lioness, and because they looked rather fresh and I felt the lion might be quite close, I called out to Mary not to wander too far. I went on with my own search for fossils; when I looked up next, Mary was heading towards a low mound of fossiliferous deposits about 150 yards to my right. I was just about to shout to her not to go any farther when I saw her move round behind the mound. The next minute I heard two sounds—a sharp cry from Mary and a low feline growl! In a flash I saw two figures running fast in opposite directions—Mary towards me and the lioness up a grassy slope. The lioness was every bit as frightened by the confrontation as Mary was. Luckily, she had no cubs with her; otherwise, the situation might have been very tricky.

The days at Laetolil passed all too quickly, and it was soon time to make tracks back to Olduvai. Bell, Kent, and White were due to leave us shortly in order to return to England to resume their studies. I was going, with Mary and the rest of my staff, to make a brief examination of some stone-walled ruins at a place called Engaruka, on the eastern escarpment beyond Ngorongoro, since we had been asked by the Tanganyika government to write a preliminary report indicating whether or not these ruins were sufficiently interesting to justify the expense of a more detailed investigation.

I had also promised to take Mary to visit some of the prehistoric art sites in the Kisese/Cheke area, round the town of Kondoa Irangi, which I had briefly examined in 1929, during a detour in a journey to South Africa. Mary had recently come up from Rhodesia and South Africa, where she had been shown a number of famous prehistoric art sites, and she was anxious to see how the Tanganyika rock paintings compared with those farther south.

As we were packing up to leave for our Olduvai camp, Kent decided to make the trip, with two of our men, across country, over the lower slopes of Lemagrut Mountain. They intended to meet us at our Olduvai camp and expected to get there in a single day, whereas it would take the rest of us two or even three days. At first Sanimu said he would go with them on foot, but he changed his mind and decided to travel back with us—at least as far as Lake El Garja—since he feared we might lose our way. Although we expected that the journey would be slow and difficult, in fact it was so easy to follow our own tracks back —because of the way the grass had been broken down by our vehicles—that we made the return journey in a single day. Kent and his group, on the other hand, lost their way on Lemagrut and had to spend the night in a Masai *manyatta*, where they were nearly eaten alive by fleas. On their arrival next day at camp they were itching all over and looked as though they had measles.

The water situation at Olduvai had now deteriorated seriously, and our water hole near the camp was little more than a liquid, muddy swamp, in which a rhino wallowed daily and, after wallowing, added a certain amount of urine to the puddle to keep it liquid. The lions and most of the other game had moved away, and the only large wild animal sharing the water hole with us was the rhino. Not unnaturally, the water tasted very unpleasant and was not really fit to drink, but it was all we had. We devised a simple filter of charcoal and sand through which we passed all the muddy, ammonia-tainted liquid. We boiled the filtered water thoroughly and then purified it further with alum, to precipitate the remaining sediment. The resulting liquid was not detrimental to our health and was just drinkable when made into tea or diluted with orange juice. There was much better water on the far side of the Balbal, at a little spring eighteen miles away, but we had so little petrol left that we could not spare any to go and fetch it.

I was even doubtful whether the meager supplies we had left after our unexpected trip to Laetolil would be sufficient to get the vehicles back to Arusha via Ngorongoro. Since we knew that we could get petrol supplies at Loliondo, sixty-five miles to the north, we decided that the trip to Nairobi, taking Kent, White, and Bell back, would have to be made via Loliondo and Narok, rather than on the better road via Arusha. Our food too was now running very short, and I decided to divide our diminishing supplies of both food and petrol, keeping half in camp in case of an emergency and giving the rest to the party that was heading for Nairobi, in the hope that it would be sufficient to get them as far as Loliondo. If not, they would have to get as far as possible and then walk to the administrative post, purchase fresh supplies, and carry them back to the lorry. Once they reached Loliondo they would have no further trouble so far as fuel for the lorry was concerned, and the only risk was a mechanical breakdown. When they reached Nairobi, the lorry was to be taken in for the necessary repairs and overhaul, and then Ndekei and Thairu would bring it back with fresh food supplies, a stock of petrol, and our mail. I was hopeful that they could be back in about ten days, and certainly in less than fourteen, unless something went very wrong.

Those of us who stayed behind at Olduvai had the small Rugby car for emergency travel. Quite apart from the fact that our food supplies were low, there were five smokers in camp and no cigarettes at all. All of us, therefore, spent much time every evening hunting in the vicinity of the camp for old cigarette stubs, from which we made new cigarettes by rolling the tobacco in toilet paper. We rationed ourselves to two smokes a day. Most of our supplies, such as tinned milk, flour, and various tinned vegetables, were so low that we doubted they would last a week, but we still had a considerable quantity of rice, plenty of tins of sardines, a little maize meal, and a few potatoes. We also had a little tea left, to take away the taste of the foul water, but no more fruit juice.

Inevitably, as we searched for fossils over the next two weeks, we were counting the days to the possible date of return of the lorry—nine days minimum. The tenth day came and the eleventh, then the twelfth, thirteenth, and fourteenth, but still no sign of help. We held a council of war. Drastic action was indicated, because it was becoming obvious that something very serious must have happened to the lorry.

Four

At the council of war, it was agreed that if the lorry had broken down before it reached Loliondo somebody would have walked on to the administrative post or returned to inform us. In either event, we should certainly have heard by now. It therefore seemed probable that if there had been trouble it must have occurred well beyond Loliondo. It was clear that somebody must go in search of our party. The problem was who should go and who remain behind, since the small Rugby car could not possibly take all of us, as well as our equipment.

I sent Heselon off to review the stores situation. He reported that there was ample food for some time, albeit of a limited variety, while the water from the water hole, although muddy, could be counted on to last another three or four weeks. If the necessity arose, one of the staff who remained behind in camp could walk up Ngorongoro to the administrative post to seek help.

After further discussion, it was agreed that Mary, Thiongo, and I should leave forthwith with the car, loaded as lightly as possible, in search of the missing lorry, while Heselon and the other men remained behind. If we were not back by the fifth evening they were to set out on foot to Ngorongoro to alert the administrative officer. We took all the remaining petrol, a few cans of the filthy water, a little rice, and one or two tins of sardines, and set off. We made good time, following the tracks made by the heavily loaded lorry fifteen days earlier. There was still no road—in the ordinary sense of the word—from Olduvai to Loliondo, but in 1931 we had engineered crossings over some of the deeper gullies. It was necessary to relocate these, since we could not afford the time to make new ones.

By midday we were within two miles of the Loliondo administrative center. At this point, one road led east to Loliondo and the other west to Pussumuru and Narok. We took the road to the east, since it was essential to speak with the people at Loliondo, to find out whether they had any news of the lorry, and also to purchase petrol and food. We decided to leave Thiongo at the road junction, just in case the lorry should arrive while we were at the Loliondo shopping center.

Mary and I had heard that the new district commissioner at Loliondo had recently been joined by his wife; the rest of the resident officers were bachelors. As we drove the last two miles, therefore, Mary and I guessed at what the reaction of the only white woman in the district would be when she saw us arrive. We were proved absolutely right when, at lunchtime, we stopped the car outside the commissioner's bungalow. Out came a young woman in a spotless white dress and with a beautiful hairdo; she promptly said to Mary, who was in torn khaki trousers and a very dirty bush shirt, "My goodness, the first woman I've seen for months!"—more or less exactly the words we had expected to hear from her.

We were cordially received, and over drinks we explained the reason for our visit. Unfortunately, there was no news of our lorry, except that it had passed through Loliondo heading north wards. The water we drank during lunchtime tasted like nectar after the stuff, flavored with rhino urine, we had been drinking for days, and we were thankful to have the opportunity of emptying all our water containers, including those holding our water for washing, and refilling them with fresh water from a spring. The district commissioner and his wife were most anxious for us to spend the night with them, but we felt it was vital to continue our search for the missing lorry.

Before leaving we stocked up at the local shop with tins of meat, vegetables, and fruit, and then we set forth once more. When we reached the turnoff, we found that Thiongo was still at his post, but he had been joined by a number of young Masai *morani*, or warriors. None of them had news of our lorry, but they warned us to be careful as we proceeded on our journey, since there were rumors of some kind of serious political trouble in the Narok district, including one that the district commissioner had been murdered. Much worried by the news, we set off again, with Thiongo, towards Pussumuru, a small Indian trading center based on a permanent water hole on the Kenya side of the Tanganyika border. At that time, three or four Indian families were purchasing cattle hides and sheep- and goatskins from the Masai, and selling them, in return, cotton cloth, blankets, sugar, beads, honey, and occasionally such luxuries as matches, Balaklava hats, and heavy-gauge copper wire for making rings and armlets.

We pulled in at the Pussumuru *dukas,* or shops, at about five o'clock in the afternoon and were given an unexpectedly warm welcome by the Asian community. I was mystified until I learned that they too had heard rumors of the murder of a government officer by Masai *morani* farther north and therefore wanted us to stay the night at Pussumuru to give them extra protection during the hours of darkness. I explained that, regrettably, I was in too great a hurry to stop. I was beginning to wonder whether the lorry's delay might not be due to the political trouble, though I knew that even if the trouble had culminated in a murder my relationships with the Masai were so good that, in all probability, we ourselves would not be molested. Much later, we discovered that the rumors were, in fact, true. The district commissioner at Narok had been murdered by a party of young Masai warriors because he had ordered them to help with road work, which they considered to be beneath their dignity.

After such a fast drive to Pussumuru, our own luck gave out. At one point on our journey there was a seven-foot-deep channel, about five feet wide, running parallel with the road on the left-hand side. I drove a little too close to it, and the weight of the car caused the edge to collapse. Slowly, very, very slowly, the car turned over onto its side and toppled into the gully, in such a way that the rear wheels were resting on the bottom of the depression and the upper ones were almost level with the surface of the road, with the hood of the car snuggling into the far side of the ditch. The car had turned over so gently that nobody was hurt, and since the opening of the petrol tank was, fortunately, facing upwards, there was no petrol leak or fear of the car's catching fire.

Apart from this, the situation was drastic. We had no tools with which to start digging out the car, nor could we light our hurricane lamps nearby, because we could smell petrol leaking from the carburetor. However, with our fresh stores from Loliondo we were able to have an excellent meal that night, and I still remember the pleasure of eating tinned fruit and drinking clean, pure water after so many days of rice and sardines and rhino water.

As soon as it was light next morning we began our herculean task. It would have been difficult enough to accomplish with proper equipment, but all we had with us for digging was one sheath knife, two table knives, and, to act as shovels, the enamel plates from which we ate. Our only hope was to excavate the edge of the ditch facing the road and cut it away on a slope; then, when this had been achieved, to pull and push the car until all four wheels were on this slope and the car on a semieven, though dangerous, keel. Thereafter, if we dug out towards the front, it might be possible, with luck, partly to drive and partly to push the car out of the ditch.

We toiled all through the day, much to the amusement of a group of young Masai warriors who periodically came and watched and laughed and went away, only to return once more, but who utterly refused to give us any kind of help. When I asked them to assist and offered them a reward if they would do so, they said that digging was beneath the dignity of warriors, but that if, later on, we needed volunteers to push the car out, they would be willing to do that.

Towards dusk, when the main digging task was almost finished and it remained only to cut the earth away in front in order to get the car out the next morning, we suddenly heard the sound of a motor in the distance. Help of some kind was on its way. We wondered if the vehicle that was approaching would have a tow rope. If so, it would be easy to get the car out. Miraculously, the vehicle proved to be our own lorry! It was fully equipped with picks and shovels and tow ropes, and with the aid of the headlights we pulled the car out before we went to bed.

Over supper, Thairu and Ndekei told us their news and explained the reason they had been so badly delayed. The clutch had given out after they started from Nairobi, and when they set forth again further mechanical trouble developed that forced them to return to Nairobi a second time.

The first task the next morning was to repair the damage we had done to the road in getting the car out. After that, we turned round and set off in convoy back to Olduvai. We called in at Pussumuru as well as at Loliondo to pass on the news of the murder of the European officer at Narok and to assure the Asians, in particular, that there was no question of a rebellion or an uprising, so they need have no fear for their own lives.

And so, at last, we returned safely to our Olduvai camp, to be greeted by delighted cheering from the men we had left behind, who were just getting ready to tramp to Ngorongoro.

We spent a few more days completing our work and tidying up at Olduvai, and then headed over Ngorongoro to the little trading center of Mto-wa-Mbu. There we turned north onto the almost invisible and dangerous track to Engaruka, the ruined city on the slopes of the escarpment, some thirty miles away. The trip was distinctly hazardous. There were places where the road almost ceased to exist, and we had to use our picks and shovels again and again to get the car over the deeper ruts. At length we reached the Engaruka stream, drove through the ford, and then turned west along the north bank towards the rest camp. This had been set up a few years previously by an ambitious administrative officer, but it had been abandoned when he left the district and was in a very dilapidated condition. We were so tired when we arrived, however, that we were happy to use the thatched sheds instead of having to put up tents that afternoon. The next day was spent in organizing ourselves for a three-week stay in the area so that we could make a survey of the ruins.

Our camp was close to the beautiful tree-lined, fast-flowing mountain stream. The water was bitterly cold, but it was pleasant to have so much fresh water available after our privations of the previous few months. We spent part of the day discussing the ruins with the little community who lived by the stream. They told us that the ruins proper were up the face of the escarpment, about a mile and a half away. Accordingly, the next day we started out to explore.

The first task was to make a preliminary investigation of the general terrain. On the gently sloping land between our camp and the edge of the escarpment there was much thorny vegetation extending on both sides of the stream. Here and there, but mostly on the south side, we found stone mounds that looked as though they might be burials; there were also many strange patterns of stones set out mainly in rough rectangles. It was difficult to understand their significance, but we guessed they might represent some aspect of primitive soil conservation. Eventually, we reached the bottom of the escarpment, where the growth of vegetation was so much denser that the going was very difficult, but there was no doubt about the presence there of hundreds of stone ruins. These appeared to be hut platforms with low walls of an irregular oval shape, usually about thirty feet long and ten feet wide. They were built on rough terraces, and the walls, which were of dry stone without mortar, were from three to five feet high. Presumably, when the dwellings were occupied there had been some kind of upward continuation of the walls, built of perishable material, and then a roof. We estimated that there must be, in all, more than 3,000 huts set on seventeen distinct successive terraces.

We conducted a partial excavation of the floor of one of the huts and a total excavation of two of the supposed burial mounds on the sloping ground below the escarpment. The results were meager. The mounds were not burial mounds. They contained rubble—a few animal bones and potsherds—but nothing else. There was no trace whatsoever of any kind of grave goods or of human skeletons. On the floor of the hut we found a few trade beads of mediaeval appearance, a fragment of porcelain of indeterminate character, and some small scraps of iron. Nothing else was diagnostic. This did not, of course, mean that the site might not be of considerable interest to those concerned with history and protohistory, but I reported that while the site might be worth a detailed study one day, it was not something I would be willing to undertake. We left the area after three weeks, sent in our report to the government at Dar es Salaam, and moved on. My time was running short, since I had promised to take Mary to visit some of the prehistoric art sites in the Kisese/Cheke area.

While we were camped in Engaruka, Sanimu mysteriously appeared, asking that he be allowed to accompany us to Kisese. He apparently knew the area (which is on the edge of what is called the Masai Steppe) and wanted to travel in the lorry and stay with us until we went back to Kenya. Since he knew some of the local people there and would also be able to interpret for us in the Masai language as we explored for painted rock shelters, we were happy to have him with us.

Leaving Mto-wa-Mbu, we headed due west until we reached the so-called Great North Road at a place called Makuyuni; there we turned south and headed for Kisese. The going was extremely rough, and our tires by now were so very dilapidated that we had a series of punctures and, by evening, had only just managed to reach the little trading post of Babati. Fortunately for us, there was a rest camp there, for which we headed. Consisting of four thatched huts, it had all the essentials, so that we did not have to unpack any equipment, but needed to spend only a minimum of time in eating and getting to bed.

After leaving Babati, we turned off towards the Galapo Mission and then went on to the Kisese/Cheke area, where the prehistoric paintings were most common. The tsetse-fly station where I had first met a Mr. Nash in 1929 was still in operation, but all the personnel were different. Fortunately, in 1929 Mr. Nash had shown me some of the more interesting paintings and given me a rough sketch map, which I had brought with me, so that I was certain I could relocate at least some of them. The tsetse-fly research officers were very kind, and after giving us tea they told us of a good place for a camp, under a large fig tree beyond Kisese village. They also promised that if during our stay we wanted fresh vegetables and fruit, we could send a runner for them, since they had a large vegetable garden. Before we left, they warned us that at this time of year snakes were particularly prevalent and that we would be wise to watch out for mamba, boomslangs, and cobras. We left them with a cheery good-bye and a promise to call upon them for help if necessary, and they, in turn, promised to visit us one weekend. We then drove through Kisese and found the big fig tree about a mile away, where we put up our tents for the night.

Next morning, however, we saw that the site was far from ideal. It was too close to the village and was used as a general meeting place for the local inhabitants. We hastily packed up our camp and re-established ourselves in a clearing in the *miombo* trees about one mile from the main Kisese prehistoric rock shelter. The nearest water supply was back at the settlement, a mile and a half away, but the distance was immaterial because, with our transport and containers, we could fetch supplies every third day. Mangos, bananas, and huge tomatoes were in season, and the local people brought us these and other fresh fruit and vegetables almost daily.

Our African staff were quick to discover that it was the honey season and that the price of honey in this area was about one-quarter what it was in Nairobi. They consequently let it be known that they were in the market for honey and purchased vast quantities. All our extra petrol was in four-gallon cans, or *debis,* and as each one was emptied into the lorry or car it was commandeered by the staff, thoroughly cleaned, and turned into a container for honey. By the time we left for Nairobi, every can we had emptied was in use for this purpose.

Water was now so plentiful that we were able to enjoy the nightly luxury of a hot bath in a canvas tub. One evening when I was getting supper ready I heard Mary shouting for help and hurried off to see what was the matter. I found her standing up in the canvas bathtub, with a towel round her, while a garter snake circled the tub, apparently attracted by the smell of the water. This proved to be the only snake we saw during our whole three weeks at the prehistoric art sites, although, on subsequent occasions, we had exciting encounters with pythons and mambas.

Neither Mary nor I had had much experience in making tracings of prehistoric art, and none at all under the extremely difficult conditions of working in open rock shelters with a howling wind blowing all the time. Several years previously Mary had worked in France, at the site of Pech-Merle, but that experience did not help much when trying to record the art at Kisese.

We spent the first two or three days at the main rock shelter and soon realized that there were a number of very distinctive superpositions in certain art styles. These, moreover, were repeated regularly on different parts of the huge rock face. Next we began to explore along the cliffs southwards, following the edge of the escarpment. We located about a dozen new sites, but probably missed many others because of the density of the vegetation at that time. Although we were making only a provisional survey, with a view to turning to more detailed work, the results were interesting. We found that giraffe and eland were the dominant animals depicted, with a few examples of various antelope and an occasional carnivore. Human figures were common, but the human face was never drawn and was always represented by a mere blob or a circle. This was in sharp contrast to the heads of the larger animals, which were always faithfully portrayed and easily identifiable. It seemed as though there had been some kind of taboo against drawing the human features in any recognizable form. Probably this was similar to the situation that prevails today among the people of many primitive tribes, who object to being photographed because of their belief that "catching a likeness" is, in effect, "catching the soul."

At some of the sites, the paintings were on sheer cliffs with no real overhang and no real shelter or cave at the base. Other sites, especially Kisese 1, Kisese 3, and Cheke 1, were rock shelters in the true sense. We considered that these might prove to have a considerable depth of deposits buried beneath the present floor level, and that when they were excavated artifacts and animal bones might be found. We planned, therefore, to return sometime in the future to investigate the relationship between the Stone Age cultures in the deposits and the various styles of paintings on the walls.

Our lorry tires had undergone very serious wear and tear since we started out in July. At the beginning of the season they had been severely tried by the stony tracks in the Kanam and Kanjera area. After that came the trip with Boswell to Olduvai Gorge on the old road via Loliondo and back again. Then there was the second trip to Kanam and Kanjera, and the second trip to Olduvai, via Arusha and Ngorongoro. Thus, by the time we were on our way back from Kisese we were having innumerable punctures, and tire bursts were also frequent. We had started out with the four tires on the lorry and four spares. Now we had only four battered but still usable tires left. The nearest place for replacements was Kondoa Irangi, a government center to the south of us, so we decided to go there to refit and, at the same time, replenish our dwindling petrol supplies. Unfortunately, there were no tires of the size we needed at Kondoa Irangi, but the trip was not wasted, since we learned about other very important prehistoric art sites south and west of Kondoa.

Shortly after we had arrived in Kisese, Sanimu had gone to visit some of his friends on the Masai Steppe, and after that we were visited by Masai from time to time. They gave us a great deal of information about painted sites in the surrounding hills and also farther to the south, beyond the point where the Kisese road turned upwards to Kolo. They were most intrigued by the tubes of paint we had brought with us to use in the course of tracing and color-matching the paintings. One young *moran* was so covetous of a small tube of vermilion paint that he offered us in exchange a whole fat ram. Another wanted Mary's lipstick and would have given her a ewe lamb in return.

When I first came through this area, in 1929, Nash was in charge of anti-tsetse research, with a view to initiating a campaign to eliminate the fly from the district. By the end of 1934, the campaign was in full swing. One of the results, unfortunately, was that most of the larger game animals had been wiped out or driven from the area. This had merely diverted the attention of the tsetse fly to smaller creatures, such as birds, rats, hares, mongooses, and small reptiles, and had not removed the menace at all. Those in charge of tsetse control had therefore found it necessary to undertake further research and were now working on a new plan for ridding the district of the fly, by means of extensive clearing of heavily infested bush. This involved cutting down every tree and shrub in the target area, since it had been shown that tsetse flies normally lay their eggs in shady places. The possible effect on the ecology of the area had evidently been ignored, and already there were beginning to be signs of heavy erosion. Moreover, the bush clearing merely meant that the flies were driven out of the area they were occupying and into the previously uninfected steppe.

One of the major tragedies of the whole tsetse-fly campaign, so far as I could see, was the utter lack of co-ordination and proper planning. It should surely have been possible to initiate a bush-clearing program starting in an enormous ring on the periphery and moving farther and farther inwards. This would have driven the flies into the center of the circle, where they would all have perished. Clearing the bush outwards in a straight line merely enabled the flies to move on, yard by yard, as their habitat was destroyed.

As I have said, when I passed through the area in 1929 there was still a considerable amount of game, such as eland, zebra, and giraffe, but now there were no large animals left at all, except a few herds of roan antelope, and even duiker and dik-dik were very scarce. This was my first encounter with roan antelope. By day they would lie up near cliffs in the *miombo* forest and in the late afternoon move down into the glades to graze. Outline drawings of these animals were fairly numerous among the paintings in the Kisese rock shelters, suggesting that they still occupied the same habitat as they had in prehistoric times.

We were so fascinated by our preliminary work on the prehistoric art that the days passed quickly, and all too soon we realized it was time to pack up and start for Nairobi, since we had bookings on a steamer for Europe. We managed to reach Arusha with only a few punctures and no further blowouts, and there we bought a new set of tires. We drove on again and spent one night en route, camped between Kajiado and Nairobi. Next morning I went up to Limuru, where my parents lived, to pack up, pay off my staff, and settle accounts, while Mary visited friends in Nairobi.

Our major problem now was what to do with the fish eagles we had left at the Natural History Museum. Because I could think of no one willing to accept the responsibility for them and because I could not possibly afford to pay for two large fish per eagle per day at Nairobi prices while I was away, I decided that the only thing to do was to take them with us to Europe. Accordingly, I made each one a large box cage, in which they traveled to Mombasa. Once they were on board the steamer, the cages were placed in the forecastle and I opened the doors. All through the voyage the eagles flew as they wished over the ocean, catching fish and returning to alight on their cage "nests" to eat them. In this way they traveled from Mombasa, via the Red Sea and Suez Canal, to Marseilles. Here they went back into their cages again for the brief journey to London.

I hated the idea of taking the birds to the zoo, and yet I could see no other way of handling the situation. The choice was either this or to have them put away—which I was loath to do. I think I was right in my decision, for when, in subsequent years, I visited them in their commodious quarters at the London Zoo, they always recognized me and were also obviously happy and fond of their keeper.

In the ordinary course of events, I intensely dislike the idea of depriving wild animals and birds of their freedom and turning them into prisoners. It is always difficult to know what to do with orphaned birds and animals that one raises as pets to save their lives, unless one has a sufficiently large house and garden in which to give them their freedom. Mary and I have had many different such pets over the years. They have all been free to come and go at our Langata home just how and when they pleased, and the second- and third-generation offspring of some of them live free in our garden today.

When I think back over the problem of my eagles and also of the serval cat and a baboon that I had as pets in my childhood days—and that eventually I had to house in large cages—it makes me sad. It makes me sadder still, however, and also very angry, when I think of the innumerable adult animals and birds deliberately caught and locked up for the so-called "pleasure" and "education" of thoughtless human beings. I appreciate that many people cannot afford to travel to far countries to see wildlife in nature's own setting, but surely there are today so many first-class films, often in beautiful color, about almost every wild species in its natural habitat that the cruelty of keeping wild creatures in zoos should no longer be tolerated.

Five

When I arrived back in London at the end of 1935 I had to make an immediate decision as to where I was going to live for the next eighteen months. My research fellowship at St. John's College, Cambridge, which I had held since 1929, had now expired. This meant that I had to move all my accumulated collections of specimens, papers, and books elsewhere. Since I knew I would have to divide my time between working in Cambridge and at the University of London library, I began to search for an inexpensive home convenient to both places.

I was fortunate. After exploring for a few days I found a cottage in the village of Nasty (also called Great Munden), in Hertfordshire. It was almost exactly halfway between London and Cambridge, and in this respect ideal for my purpose. Moreover, it was quiet and set back from the main road by more than a mile. Seeing a "To Let" notice in the front garden, I inquired in the village and was given the address of the owner. I wrote to him immediately, and he replied offering to let the cottage, as it stood, for only twenty-five shillings a quarter, since he was not in a position to spend a great deal of money in modernizing it. I wrote back asking for a ten-year lease and requesting permission to carry out some alterations and modifications at my own expense.

And so Steen Cottage became mine for the next ten years. It was an old sixteenth-century building, which had once been divided into three cottages and later opened up again as a single dwelling. It had beautiful oak beams and a huge fireplace, but there were no modern conveniences of any kind. No running water, no bathroom, no inside lavatory, no electric light, and no telephone. The only way I could have hot water for a bath in the evening was to draw pails of water from the outside pump and heat them on the coal fire in the kitchen. Then I would bathe in a tin tub in front of the large open fireplace. It was not, perhaps, an attractive proposition, but, having been brought up in primitive conditions in Kikuyu country as a boy and having experienced the privations of our last season at Olduvai, I thought it luxury. In time I was able to modify and alter the cottage. The vegetable garden and orchard had been sadly neglected, and I developed these too, using gardening as my form of exercise.

The next problem was to get hold of a car in which to travel to London and Cambridge. Though it was somewhat the worse for wear, I was able to use the Model A Ford that V. E. Fuchs had brought back from Kenya via the Sahara. (I had left my other car in Girton, since my marriage with Frida had, regrettably, broken up, and she needed it for herself and the children.)

As soon as I had transport, I went to Cambridge and packed up everything in my rooms. I transferred all my archaeological specimens to an immense attic I had obtained in London, just off Gower Street, which belonged to University College. The Miocene fossils, with my books and papers, I took to Steen Cottage. As before, the Pleistocene material from my last expedition was taken to the British Museum of Natural History.

During the past season, I had been extremely interested by our discovery of the remains of an extinct okapilike animal at the Laetolil site. When, at last, I had time to do so, therefore, I decided to make a special visit to the Tervuren Museum, just outside Brussels, and examine the skulls and skeletons of the living species of okapi from the Congo. While I was there I met a missionary who was home on leave from the Congo, and in the course of conversation he told me that the natives living south of the Congo River in the area near his mission station regularly killed and ate the so-called "pygmy chimpanzee," *Pan paniscus.* This was a species that had recently been described on the basis of only scant material; almost nothing was known about its skull, dentition, and skeleton. I had several long discussions with the missionary, who promised that when he returned to duty he would endeavor to obtain, from Africans who had eaten the flesh of this species, examples of skulls and lower jaws and also, if possible—though he warned me that this would be more difficult—some limb bones.

True to his word, in due course he started to send specimens from the Congo, so that by the end of 1936 I had accumulated the skulls and jaws of eight of these strange primates, together with two or three limb bones, and I began to study them at the Royal College of Surgeons.

I was particularly interested in the pygmy chimpanzee because, a few years earlier, Arthur Hopwood of the British Museum of Natural History had suggested that the Lower Miocene ape we had found in Kenya—at Rusinga, Koru, and Songhor—might be closely related to the chimpanzee and, more especially, to the common species *Pan satyrus.* In fact, when he named this fossil genus *Proconsul* he did so because at that time there was a tame chimpanzee in London called Consul—hence the name *Proconsul* implied that our find was a possible ancestor. I was extremely anxious to study the little-known and very aberrant *Pan paniscus,* since I had an idea that it might stand even closer to *Proconsul* than *Pan satyrus* does.

My Miocene collection of fossil primate material was at Steen Cottage, and so I used to devote Sundays to working on it, as a change from my labors for the rest of the week—which were devoted almost entirely to writing. In fact, the whole of this period was one of intense literary activity.

I had spent most of the recent voyage from Mombasa to Marseilles working on the first draft of a new book, to be entitled *Kenya: Contrasts and Problems*. As soon as I had settled into Steen Cottage, I began work on this draft and then had it typed and prepared for the press. The book dealt with problems that had worried me greatly in recent years. In it I examined the relationship of the Kenya tribes to other races and organizations in that country.

In particular, I was concerned with problems arising out of the activities of government administrators, the police, European settlers, Asian traders, the various missionary societies, and tourists. What I had to say about each of these groups was not at all popular with the section of the community concerned, although most of its members thought that what I said about the other sections was true.

The missionaries applauded what I said about the behavior of the settlers towards their African workers and the peasants as a whole, but maintained that my views about their own work were wholly at fault. Among other things, I said, categorically, that I felt that the missionaries' view on polygamy was very misguided, since by condemning the African practice of taking more than one wife they were forcing the young Christian woman who had failed to obtain a monogamous husband onto the streets of Nairobi as a prostitute. I even went so far as to say that I believed that Christ himself would prefer such girls to be second wives in Christian homes rather than to have to earn their living on the streets. This, according to some missionaries, was blasphemy, and I was threatened with excommunication. I was also accused of "making the younger missionaries think"!

The settlers were very angry indeed at some of the things I wrote about them as a community (although I praised individuals). One result was that I lost my membership in some of the upcountry clubs.

The general view of the government officials was that I had wholly failed to understand the difficulties with which they were faced and had criticized them unfairly.

As to the Asian community—both those in Nairobi and the small traders and artisans scattered throughout the country—they found my comments alleging that they exploited the African people quite unjustified and infuriating.

Four years ago I reread *Kenya: Contrasts and Problems*, wondering whether I would write it differently in retrospect.

Times have changed, of course, and many of the conditions discussed in the book have been greatly altered since Kenya became independent. But I am certain now, as I was then, that the criticisms I made were absolutely justified. Consequently, I agreed to the publication of a new edition and contented myself with adding only a brief new preface.

After I had sent *Kenya: Contrasts and Problems* to the press, I decided to write an autobiography covering the first thirty years of my life. This book, which was eventually published under the title *White African*, was simply and solely what is often called a "potboiler." My fellowship had expired, and although my cottage was very cheap, I had to have some money to live on until my planned return to Kenya, with research funds, in 1937. Fortunately, a London publishing firm, Hodder & Stoughton, offered me a generous royalty advance if I would write a book for them, and this I readily agreed to do.

White African has recently been republished in the United States, in both hard-cover and paperback form. It is amusing to note in passing that not long ago I went round secondhand bookshops in London trying to find a first edition. I succeeded in locating only one copy, and for that the bookseller asked twenty-five pounds. Since the original price had been only seventeen and a half shillings, I reluctantly refused to pay so much more for a copy of my own book!

In the autumn of 1935, I was invited by Edinburgh University to give a series of ten lectures, known as the Munro lectures, in the spring term of 1936. I agreed, and while I was wondering what subject to choose for the series, I realized that there was no up-to-date textbook dealing with the Stone Age cultures of Africa as a whole. I therefore decided to write my ten lectures in the form of ten chapters of a book; they were published in 1936 as *Stone Age Africa*. Fortunately, Mary Nicol was again available to undertake drawings to illustrate it.

At this time, I was spending three days a week in London, in the Gower Street attic, working on the artifacts from Olduvai Gorge and trying to complete a book dealing with the Olduvai discoveries up to and including 1935. In the end, although much of the book was written, the plan had to be postponed. This first book on Olduvai was not finally published until after World War II, for reasons I shall deal with in another chapter.

As part of my preparation for the lectures I was to give in Edinburgh, I spent a whole week at the Pitts-Rivers Museum in Oxford studying Stone Age material from different parts of Africa. One evening at dinner in New College I got into conversation with some anthropologists, who suggested that since I had been born and bred among the Kikuyu, and claimed to speak their language better than English, I really should devote some time to writing a complete, detailed study of the tribe. I knew, of course, that such a book was badly needed, and the idea of doing it myself was, naturally, attractive. At the time, however, I was already making preliminary plans for the 1937–38 season of archaeological field work. I therefore explained to my dinner companions that I did not think their plan was possible, since if I were to undertake a truly comprehensive study of the Kikuyu I judged it would be necessary to devote a minimum of two, and more probably three, years to the task. I also pointed out that because there was now an ever-growing interest in my prehistoric research in East Africa, it would be relatively easy to obtain the necessary funds for it, but I did not see where money to study the Kikuyu tribe in depth could possibly be obtained.

About five months later, I received an invitation from the Secretary of the Rhodes Trust at Oxford to lunch with him and some of his colleagues. During the meal, to my utter amazement, they told me that if I were willing to undertake a detailed study of the Kikuyu, the Rhodes Trust would make me a grant of the necessary funds for expenses, as well as a salary for a minimum of two years, to start in January 1937.

The offer was a tempting one, but before making a decision I wanted to discuss it with Mary Nicol. We were hoping to get married at the end of 1936, when my divorce from Frida would be final, and then to go out together to continue field work at Olduvai Gorge. After lengthy discussions, we decided that since the opportunity to work on a Kikuyu book might never occur again, it would be wise for me to accept the Rhodes Trust offer, and we modified our plans accordingly. In order to make the best possible use of her time in Kenya while I undertook the research for the book, Mary decided that she would excavate several important Neolithic and Mesolithic sites at Kiamba and at Hyrax Hill, near Nakuru. And so it came about that I started the book about the tribe into which I was initiated at the age of thirteen—a book that, in the end, took me almost three years to complete and that, in its final draft, ran to nearly a million words.

By 1936, the Kikuyu tribe was being strongly affected by contact with European civilization and, in particular, by mission education. In the areas adjacent to Nairobi, most of the old tribal customs were changing drastically. But a number of elderly men and women—some of whom had worked for my father in my boyhood days—were still alive, and I felt confident that if I began work fairly soon I would be able to enlist their help. In another ten years many of them might not be alive to remember the detailed information I needed to augment the knowledge I had acquired in childhood, and much information about the tribe would be lost forever.

A few books dealing with the Kikuyu had already been published. One of these was written by W. Routledge at the turn of the century. It was concerned almost exclusively with the material culture of the Kikuyu—their pottery, basketwork, cultivation methods, crops, iron smelting, and so on. A second book, in Italian with an English translation, was the work of Father Cagniolo of the Catholic mission at Nyeri. His account of the tribe was written from the point of view of the Catholic church, which was said to be that the Kikuyu people were both pagan and uncivilized and greatly in need of the benefits of Western civilization as brought to them through the Catholic missions.

At a much earlier date, C. W. Hobley, who had been a district commissioner in Kenya in the early colonial days, had written a book titled *Bantu Beliefs and Magic,* which included a certain amount of information about the religion and magic of the Kikuyu, as well as of several other Bantu-speaking tribes.

Mary and I were planning to leave for Nairobi at the end of December 1936, and so I arranged to sublet Steen Cottage, which was mine for the next eight years. As a result of the improvements I had made over the past eighteen months, it was now a much more habitable place and was, of course, fully furnished. It had a telephone, and we had been promised piped water, with the consequent possibility of inside sanitation, within a few months. The garden too was in excellent shape, and finding a tenant was not difficult.

(While I was away in Africa a rather Gilbertian situation arose. The owner of the house died, and his executors put his estate, including Steen Cottage, up for sale. I was offered first refusal, but could not afford the purchase price, and so the house was bought by my tenant. He, however, had concluded an agreement with me to rent the property as a furnished house for the next six years. He therefore became the owner of the house and land, but had to continue paying me monthly rent for it!)

On Christmas Eve, 1936, Mary and I were married. Mary's mother and aunt came down to Steen Cottage for the wedding, and her mother stayed on with us until we left for Kenya early in 1937.

I could look back on the previous eighteen months as having been very rewarding. I had written three books, *White African, Stone Age Africa,* and *Kenya: Contrasts and Problems.* I had also almost completed the research necessary for my first book on Olduvai Gorge and had undertaken some exciting studies of pygmy chimpanzee skulls.

Six

Mary and I sailed for Kenya early in January. As missionaries, my parents had, naturally, been greatly upset at the breakup of my marriage to Frida, but they were marvelously understanding and welcomed Mary into the family. In fact, a warm friendship developed between Mary and my mother, for which I was exceedingly grateful. I had particularly not wanted to hurt my parents, and yet my marital situation had grown into something that made a divorce from Frida inevitable. It was very reassuring to know that my relationship with my parents would not be destroyed as a result.

Soon after getting back to Africa, I managed to buy a car and went off to visit my old friend Senior Chief Koinange to discuss the Kikuyu book with him. We had a long consultation, and I explained exactly what I wished to accomplish and asked his advice as to the best way to set about it.

Routledge's book on the Kikuyu was unknown to him, but I

had a copy with me, and Chief Koinange and I, together with one of his sons who understood English, went through it together. Both of them agreed with the view I expressed in the preceding chapter, that while Routledge's book was excellent in some respects, it was disappointing in many others. We also discussed Father Cagniolo's book and agreed that it presented a one-sided and biased picture.

(At about this same time, while a student at the London School of Economics, Jomo Kenyatta, now President of Kenya, was writing a book entitled *Facing Mount Kenya*. It dealt with Kikuyu customs in general, but many aspects of Kikuyu life were covered either too superficially or not at all.)

In due course, Senior Chief Koinange called a meeting of some hundred elders from all over the Kiambu district and asked me to tell them my reasons for planning to produce a detailed study of Kikuyu tribal customs. I explained to them that even then, owing to the rapid expansion of the educational system, many young Kikuyu had no real knowledge of the ways of their fathers and forefathers—even as recently as forty years ago. I went on to say that while now these young people had their gaze fixed only on the future and on learning the ways in which the white man lived and carried on his work, one day they would most surely want to know more about their own antecedents.

I pointed out that when my father had arrived in Kenya some forty years previously, he had found the Kikuyu way of life, as far as was known, similar to that of the British at the time the Romans invaded England 2,000 years ago. Unfortunately, the Romans had not kept any accurate record of the customs of the early Britons. Such knowledge as we have of them today was built up by excavating old forts and villages and generally piecing together such scraps of information as have become available.

With their help, I told the elders, I intended to write a detailed book about the Kikuyu, so that the young people of future generations would really know and understand how the Kikuyu had lived and developed their own country at the end of the nineteenth century and the beginning of the present one.

Having been initiated as a Kikuyu myself, with the *Mukanda* age group, I said that I already knew a great deal that was also known to other young men of my own age, but there was much more about which my generation had received no instruction. I could only learn of these things and record them accurately if I had the blessing of the elders and their active help in obtaining the information I needed.

When I finished speaking Senior Chief Koinange spoke strongly in support of my plan, but there were others who were doubtful. One of them recalled how a former British provincial commissioner had come to them seeking all kinds of information about their system of land tenure and the laws and rules under which land was occupied and cultivated. Later, this inquiry was shown to have been conducted with a view to modifying these laws and rules for the benefit of the white settlers. He and some of the others, therefore, were inclined to doubt my motives. Was I really thinking in terms of benefiting their children and grandchildren, or was I there as an emissary of the British government, wanting to obtain information that would later be used to the disadvantage of the Kikuyu people?

All I could do was to give them my solemn promise that since I too was a Kikuyu—albeit a white one—I would act only in the tribe's interest.

After consultation, the elders asked me to meet with them again, when they would give me a definite reply. They wanted time both to think about my proposals and to consult with other elders over a wider area before making their decision.

One week later, another meeting was held, and after a few brief speeches I was informed officially that my proposal was accepted and that the elders would proceed to appoint a panel of nine of their senior members to act as my advisers. Two of the very senior elders, who lived near Chief Koinange's home, were to be with me constantly as I worked. The other seven would come periodically to discuss what I had written and check the points over which there might be some disagreement. It was also agreed that when I had completed the first over-all draft a major group of some thirty or forty elders would again be convened, so that I could tell them exactly what I had put on record, for their acceptance or rejection. After this second group had gone through what I had written, I promised to make any alterations or additions they considered necessary for the sake of accuracy.

Thus the procedure was duly laid down for the long period of research and writing ahead.

Meanwhile, Senior Chief Koinange suggested that Mary and I move into a small two-room hut inside his compound in the village of Kiamba, where I could be in constant touch with my two senior advisers. He also suggested that Mary might like to make some preliminary excavations in a cave near a waterfall about a mile and a half away, where obsidian artifacts were known to be washing out. To this we readily agreed, since the cave was much more accessible than the Kiamba Neolithic sites she had planned to work.

Before getting down to any detailed study with the elders, I began to plan the way in which I would carry out my research. I decided to aim at a work in three volumes. Volume I would provide a detailed study of the general background, as well as a summary of the known historical contacts between the early British administrators and the Kikuyu at the end of the last century. Volume II would be devoted to the life of the individual from birth through infancy, childhood, young adult status, marriage, parenthood, sickness, and, finally, death. Volume III would deal with the social organization of the tribe, including such subjects as law, magic, witchcraft, religion, and, if possible, an account of the strange ceremony known to the Kikuyu as *Ituika*, or the handing over of administrative power from one generation to another.

I started my work by inviting an elder, Kavetu—whom I had known from my childhood days—to let me record the story of his life in his own words. He readily agreed, and I planned to use this as a preface for the book.

Meanwhile, Mary contacted Heselon, Thairu, and one or two other members of our Olduvai team, and set to work to cut a trial trench through the deposits at the Kiamba cave Chief Koinange had shown her.

On Sundays we usually went up to Tigoni to have lunch with my parents. My sister Gladys and her husband, Leonard Beecher, were, at that time, also living at Tigoni, so that it became quite a family gathering, with my brother, Douglas, and his wife, Beryl, occasionally coming to join us from the Nyeri forest station, where Douglas was forest officer. My elder sister,

Julia, and her husband, Lawrence Barham, were too far away to come, since they were then working in Ruanda.

Father and Mother had retired several years previously from active missionary work at Kabete Mission Station, but were still helping in a variety of ways. Father regularly preached at churches in the area and also prepared candidates for confirmation, while Mother conducted a special class for women, as well as a dispensary for children. Father was also, at that time, revising the earlier Kikuyu translation of the Church of England prayer book, helped by my brother-in-law Leonard and a Kikuyu named Matayo, son of the elder Kavetu, whose life story I was recording for my preface.

After we had been in our Kiamba home some three months, Mary was suddenly taken ill, and I fetched the local doctor from Kiambu Hospital to see her. He thought she was suffering from an attack of malaria and gave her an injection of quinine and some pills, but during the night her temperature rose sharply, and I rushed her by car to Nairobi Hospital, where she could have proper nursing. When I got her there the doctors diagnosed double pneumonia. In those days, before antibiotics were developed, the disease was often fatal. The patient's survival depended on intensive nursing and the almost constant use of an oxygen mask. The doctor felt that it was unlikely we would be able to save Mary and advised me to cable her mother to fly out to Kenya from England—which I did. One of the problems was a lack of trained staff to stand by night and day to administer oxygen, but fortunately I had some knowledge of this technique and volunteered to help. By the grace of God, Mary recovered, although for a long time her life hung in the balance.

When Mary was at last ready to leave the hospital, our friend Dr. van Someren, the curator of the museum, kindly invited us to stay at his home while she recuperated.

Later I returned to my work on the Kikuyu. It was now progressing very slowly, for I had reached Volume II, which was to cover the life span of an individual from the womb to the grave. I needed, at this stage, a great deal of information about midwifery, childbirth, infant care, and nursing, and for this purpose I recruited the assistance of several elderly Kikuyu women. Most of them, however, were quite reluctant to speak of such matters to me, a young man. Eventually, my two elders brought their own wives along with them, and Senior Chief Koinange also called in a number of older women. I found that there was a great deal of disagreement as to the correct procedures to be observed all during the period from the onset of pregnancy through birth and infancy. Custom relating to the early life of the individual was, in fact, far less clear-cut than it was for the many aspects of tribal life I had already dealt with in Volume I, such as land tenure, warfare, raiding, trading, house building, and so on.

In the end, we managed to reach a general consensus about the rules of prenatal care and the actual procedures for childbirth and midwifery, though customs appeared to differ from one area to another, and every family within each clan and subclan had its own special ideas on what a pregnant woman could and could not do with safety. As I wrote the notes for that particular chapter, I had little doubt that what I had eventually recorded on the basis of talking to thirty or forty women would be contradicted by another thirty or forty if they had access to the text. In 1938, when I came to work on the second draft of the book with a large number of elders, each sent for his senior wife in order to arrive at the truth of the matter, and I was then given so many conflicting versions of the customs involved that it was only with great difficulty that I finally arrived at an over all picture for the chapter.

Another chapter that proved immensely interesting and yet very difficult to write was the one dealing with initiation and circumcision. I had been through this ceremony myself in 1916, in a somewhat modified form; even at that time many of the more complex rules had been abandoned. In the first place, the mere fact of the coming of the white man and his introduction of work forces had meant that it was no longer possible to insist, as previously, that *all* members of a family be present when a youth or girl of that family was being initiated. Added to this, World War I had started, and thousands of young men had gone off either to what was then German East Africa, with the Carrier Corps, or to the many military camps behind the lines and could not possibly have obtained leave to attend an initiation ceremony.

Leaving aside the fact that the initiation rites by 1916 had been to some extent modified by force of circumstance, I was aware that my knowledge of them was no more than superficial, since I had been a candidate and not an elder. I did not have, and could not have had, any knowledge of the many details of the ceremony that were secret and known only to the elders and older women who organized and actively participated in the religious rites linked with initiation.

Towards the end of August 1937, I had completed the notes for my first draft of the three volumes of the book, and Mary had completed her excavations at the Kiamba waterfall site. Since she was now eager to start a major excavation at the Hyrax Hill Neolithic site, near Nakuru, we packed up and, taking with us my two senior advisers, Waruhiu and Mburu, built a camp at the foot of Hyrax Hill. It was mostly a tented camp, but we did construct one very large *banda*, or thatched cottage, which served three purposes. One half of it was a workroom, where Mary had tables for sorting, studying, and cataloguing material from her excavations. In one corner I had a small writing table, where I sat and wrote, accompanied by my two elders, to whom I referred as I worked from my notes. The third part of the *banda* was used as our private living room. Sleeping quarters for ourselves and for our men consisted of tents.

Mary first of all undertook the excavation of a huge mound of massive stones, many of which took four or five men to move and which looked as though they had been brought together by other than natural means. This mound proved to be an immense communal cemetery of an early Neolithic stone-bowl culture. Later Mary excavated some of the dwellings near the burial mound, and these also proved to be of Neolithic age. Towards the end of the season, she worked on some other pit dwellings on the far side of the hill—a site we called the "northeast village."

The land, including Hyrax Hill itself, belonged to old friends of mine, Mr. and Mrs. Arthur Selfe. They were most helpful all the time we were working on their land. Since their deaths their bungalow has been turned into a small museum to house some of the material from Hyrax Hill and other sites in the area, a number of which are now open to the public.

While Mary was excavating we had numerous visitors from the surrounding farms and also from the big European secondary school. Two of the teachers, Mary Davidson and Molly Paine, became particularly interested in the work and often came to help in the evenings and on weekends. In 1938, when Mary and I took time off from the work at Nakuru to excavate an exciting Neolithic site at Njoro—which I will describe later —these two joined us during their school vacation. Both proved to be valuable assistants. Mary Davidson became so interested that she began to study prehistory seriously and eventually married a former Cambridge student of mine, Bernard Fagg, who later became the curator of the museum of Jos, Nigeria, and is now director of the Pitt-Rivers Museum in Oxford.

It was during this period of work on my book that I witnessed a most interesting and practical example of the Kikuyu method of healing by psychological means—faith healing. One day Waruhiu developed an acute attack of sciatica and was in great pain. Nothing that I could do for him seemed to help, nor did the doctor at Nakuru Hospital, to whom I took him, succeed in improving his condition. After several days of enduring the doctoring of the white man, Waruhiu asked me to do him a special favor. He begged me to go down to the African section of Nakuru township, find a woman who had recently given birth to twins, and bring all three back to camp. A fee was promised for her services. On questioning Waruhiu about this strange request, I was told that he would presently show me what the woman would have to do in order to make him well. I asked no more questions, but hurried to the headman in Nakuru. A mother was found who was willing to return to my camp with her twins, and it was not long before I was able to watch a most exciting "cure."

Waruhiu dragged himself out of bed and came slowly from his tent to lie down on the ground in the sun. First he questioned the woman, to make certain that she was, in fact, the real mother of the twins. Once he was satisfied on this and other matters, he turned over on his stomach and told her to stand by his right side. This she did. She was then asked to place her right foot over the area of his sciatic nerve, take it off again, and repeat the movement seven times. When this had been completed, he instructed her to walk round him counterclockwise seven times, after which she must stand in the same place again and repeat the performance with her left foot. Once this was done he slowly got up from the ground, stretched himself a little, started to walk, and in a few minutes was running round the camp full of joy, completely well. The woman duly received her fee of twenty shillings, and I took her and her twins home.

The incident reminds me of a story that was told me by my old friend Dr. E. J. Wayland, the former director of the Geological Survey of Uganda. Out on a very long foot safari, he too was troubled with acute sciatica. It became so bad that during the course of his geological traverses he was forced to rope poles to the sides of a camp chair and get four men to carry him along from place to place. Whenever he saw an outcrop of rock that required studying, he painfully got out of the chair, made his notes, and then returned.

One day he was being carried through some rather long grass when there was a sudden hurried movement, the sound of trampling and crashing, and then a snort. It seemed clear that some large animal was charging towards them. Wayland's men quickly put down his chair and ran for their lives—from a buffalo! Wayland himself got out of the chair as fast as he could and shinned up a tree. After a few minutes, when the panic was over, he climbed down and suddenly realized that he was walking normally. His sciatica had completely vanished! So far as I know, it never came back again.

Another of our adventures at Hyrax Hill was less pleasant. In those days, outside towns and cities stealing was almost unknown. This was due to the fact that, by African tradition, stealing was supposed to be punished by supernatural powers from whom there was no escape, and therefore it did not pay.

One evening, in the pale half-darkness of an African starlit night, we saw three seminaked men running from our tent with their arms full. We looked quickly inside the tent and by the light of our torches saw that it had been ransacked. Sheets and blankets had been taken off the beds and suitcases forced open, and clothing was lying all over the place. We called to our men to come and help us, and gave chase through the darkness.

The thieves, as they ran, dropped nearly everything they had collected, and next morning we were able to recover most of our belongings, but certain small items we never found—presumably because the thieves put them safely in their pockets. We were lucky, however, to discover a distinctive red handkerchief that was not ours. We took this to the police, and they tracked down the owner of the handkerchief, searched his premises on a neighboring farm, and found some of our missing property.

As a result of this episode, Mary and I acquired a young Dalmatian from Major Pirie, the senior breeder of these dogs at Limuru. Our choice was a charming puppy, and we decided to breed her and eventually exhibit her at shows. Hyrax Hill was the name prefix we chose for our dogs.

Towards the end of 1937, my two elders announced that they wanted a holiday, so Mary and I decided to take time off from our work at Hyrax Hill for a brief visit to Olduvai Gorge. On our way back, we called in at the home of Count Davico, an Italian living at Monduli, near Arusha, with whom we had become very friendly in 1935, and I learned from him that a German, Dr. Ludwig Kohl-Larsen, had been on a big expedition to the area round Lake Eyasie. He had also examined some of the prehistoric art sites (which we had already recorded) around Kondoa Irangi. Then, instead of going on to Olduvai from Oldeani, he had turned off and gone down to the east shore of the lake. Here he was reported to have discovered parts of a fossil human skull. Davico went on to say that Kohl-Larsen was reported to have carried out some excavations at a cave near the northeastern shore. He had also located some interesting prehistoric burial mounds. Subsequently, he had gone to the west, to the Laetolil deposits we had studied in 1935. Here too he had made some important discoveries.

Shortly after this, I received a number of confirmatory reports from Germany about some of the finds Kohl-Larsen had made. I therefore applied for a small grant from the Royal Society in London to enable Mary and me to go down there in 1938, with a member of the Tanganyika Geological Survey, to examine some of the sites. We were particularly anxious to visit the place where Kohl-Larsen claimed to have found a fossil human skull, on the northeast shore of Eyasie.

Mary's excavations at Hyrax Hill gradually attracted more and more attention from the local public. European farmers from the surrounding area came to see what we were doing, and this led to our meeting some charming people. Sometimes we were invited to spend a Sunday at one of the farms, sometimes a weekend, and frequently we were told of possible prehistoric sites that we might like to investigate at some later date.

One of our visitors was the Honorable Mrs. Nellie Grant, from Njoro. She told us of an exciting cave near the banks of a stream in the forest reserve behind her farm, where she had found some bits of bone washed out on the cave floor and also some obsidian flakes, pieces of pottery, and a rather amazing flat disc bead of opal. These she brought to show us. As soon as it was possible, we arranged to spend a weekend with her and visit the cave. It turned out to be a site of major importance.

That first weekend we dug a very small trial trench to check the situation and immediately found the remains of a human cremated burial with stone artifacts and more beads. We therefore decided to leave the site until we had time for a prolonged and proper excavation. In April we spent three weeks at the site, helped by Molly Paine and Mary Davidson, and in October we went back for a four-week stay. In between I was hard at work on my Kikuyu study.

The task of writing the first draft of the book was proving far more difficult and taking much longer than I had anticipated. Again and again, when making preliminary notes at Kiamba, I had recorded the Kikuyu name of some plant, herb, tree, or creeper used by the Kikuyu people for medicinal or economic purposes. Now that I was actually writing the book, it was essential to locate each and every one of these plants, and to collect and press flowering specimens to take to the botanical department of the Coryndon Memorial Museum in Nairobi for scientific identification.

The majority of the plants were comparatively easy to find, but every now and then neither the elders nor I could find some particular plant in flower. From time to time, Peter Bally, the botanist at the museum, used to come up and spend a weekend with us in order to help in the search; he, of course, was often able to identify plants though they were not actually in flower at the time. In this way we identified the vast majority of the plants I had recorded as being made use of by the Kikuyu tribe, in one way or another, in the course of their lives.

Another task I had to carry out at this time was to build a model of a Kikuyu hut, with the help of my two elders. It had to be constructed in the correct traditional method, so that I could record every detail of the techniques employed by the Kikuyu in the days before nails, wire, and other modern building aids were introduced.

Mary's excavations at Hyrax Hill were proving very exciting. The main stone mound turned out to be, as I have said, a communal cemetery with numerous individuals buried in it. Each female skeleton lay on its side, in the prenatal position, and with it were a pestle and a stone bowl, probably to be used as a mortar, and sometimes a grindstone as well. These were grave goods, to be taken by the woman into the next world. The male skeletons, on the other hand, were accompanied by only a few scattered obsidian tools and no domestic wares.

While exploring behind our camp, we found two large horseshoe-shaped enclosures lying against the foot of Hyrax Hill. In front of them were the remains of two hut circles, both of which, as well as the large enclosures, were constructed of stones loosely piled one on top of the other. Near them we located a burial mound of an entirely different type. All this appeared to belong to a much younger period than the Neolithic communal cemetery. Eventually, it was proved to be a part of a late Iron Age settlement.

At the Hyrax Hill camp, our nearest source of water was almost two miles away, but our investigations led to the identification of an old post-Pleistocene beach of Lake Nakuru, 145 feet above the present level of the lake and only about a quarter of a mile from our site. It became clear that this had been the source of water for the Neolithic population of the encampment. Unfortunately, in the years before World War II the carbon-14 dating technique had not yet been invented, and therefore, although we found a good deal of charcoal, we could not date this site except by means of the stone artifacts and the pottery. The grave goods as a whole were very interesting and included pottery of types we had never seen before—in particular, some peculiar beakers.

All round Hyrax Hill there were signs of human occupation. The whole area had, in fact, been inhabited again and again in the past, and there were examples of many different cultures to be studied. Once Mary's excavations were progressing satisfactorily, she left the workmen to carry on and undertook a careful plane-table survey of the whole area, mapping all the ruins, pits, and mounds. While doing so she located evidence of the ancient, widespread African game called, in different tribes, by such names as *mbau* or *giuthi* and often referred to in anthropological literature as *mankala*. (I have described the Kikuyu version of this game in great detail in my earlier book *White African*.) The general theory in anthropological circles has always been that this game was introduced into Africa by the Arabs when they penetrated the continent in slave-raiding expeditions. But here, on Hyrax Hill, was evidence that the game had been played in Africa during the late Stone Age, some 2,000 years ago. It now seemed much more likely, therefore, that the game had been taken from Africa to Arabia by African slaves and that it was of African, not Arab, origin. This idea has since been substantiated by the finding of evidence of the game, in a primitive form, in many other Neolithic sites in Africa.

The month of October 1938 saw Mary and me, accompanied by some of our staff, back at Njoro, on Mrs. Grant's farm, where we continued our excavations at the Njoro River Rock Shelter. This proved extremely interesting, being a Neolithic cremation site that yielded the remains of more than seventy-six different individuals. There were also many fragments of pottery and numerous stone tools of obsidian, as well as the charred remains of wooden bowls, basketwork, fiber cords, and even some well-preserved burnt gourds. Most exciting of all, we discovered hundreds of stone beads and pendants. These were made of amazonite, green quartzite, opal, and a variety of other semiprecious stones. Altogether, it proved to be an interesting and exciting site, and we eventually published a lengthy report about it.

Seven

Towards the end of 1938, I decided that the time had come for us to leave the Hyrax Hill camp and return to Kikuyu country. The first draft of the book was now taking shape, and, quite apart from my promise to discuss it with the elders of the tribe,

I was anxious for their help in connection with some additional research that I felt was necessary at this stage. In particular, I needed a great deal of additional information about Kikuyu marriage customs.

While I was writing the first draft of the chapter on marriage, at Nakuru, I found myself continually getting into problems that I had not anticipated when preparing my notes at Kiamba. I suppose that this was chiefly because my approach to anthropology was too much conditioned by my training at Cambridge University. There I had read a number of studies on African tribes written by various social anthropologists. But I had not realized how superficially many of them dealt with African marriage customs.

Most Kikuyu marriages, like those of nearly all Bantu-speaking tribes at that time, were arranged on the basis of *ruracio,* or what is commonly described by anthropologists as the "bride price." Under this system, the bridegroom's family transfers wealth, in the form of livestock of one kind or another, to the family of the bride-to-be. This transaction, referred to by most Europeans as "buying a wife," is, in fact, a highly complex and well-planned arrangement having several major objectives. The first of these is to ensure the security, welfare, and proper upbringing of any children arising from the marriage and to make divorce, once children have been born from a union, very nearly impossible. The second is to make sure that no widow is ever left without proper maintenance for herself and her children. The third objective is to impress upon young men and women the seriousness of entering into a marriage contract. The object of Kikuyu marriage is emphatically not—and I repeat *not*—the legalization of a sexual relationship between two people, but a means of founding a stable family unit that will be a credit to the tribe.

All this, of course, I had known ever since my own initiation into the tribe in 1916, but I had not realized that though most Kikuyu marriages were arranged within this highly evolved system, there were several other lawful forms of marriage still in use. These were probably the relics of some former stages in the evolution of the Kikuyu marriage system.

When we returned to Kiambu, Senior Chief Koinange reassembled the nine advisers I had had with me during the first note-taking sessions at Kiamba, and we went into the subject of Kikuyu marriage in great detail. It was during these discussions that I first learned of the strange but fully accepted and recognized Kikuyu custom whereby, in certain clearly defined circumstances, a married woman (usually one who already had several children of her own and who either was a widow or had proved by her steadiness that she was able to control a family) was encouraged to take upon herself the legal status of a man. Thereafter, such a woman was entitled—nay, encouraged—to "marry" a number of young women who otherwise, for one reason or another, would not have been able to have legitimate children.

As I have explained, Kikuyu marriage was not regarded as a means of legalizing sexual relations between two people. And most emphatically, the legal recognition of certain females as males had nothing whatever to do with any kind of sexual behavior between them and their so-called wives. Lesbianism, like male homosexuality, was regarded by the Kikuyu as utterly wrong and was usually punished—on the rare occasions when it was discovered—by death.

The whole object of giving certain middle-aged women male status had an entirely different purpose. Clearly, in any community—and the Kikuyu were certainly no exception in this respect—there are always a certain number of young girls who do not attract offers of marriage easily. This is partly because in nearly all communities females are more numerous than males, making it difficult for the less attractive girls to find husbands. But there are also other reasons. Some girls are so flighty that men do not want them as wives—even (in polygamous households) as second or third wives, let alone first ones. This is particularly true in households where the first wife helps to decide whether or not her husband should take another wife and who she is to be. The custom of encouraging a number of responsible, respectable middle-aged women to adopt legal male status and thereby gain the ability to "marry" the tribe's unmarriageable girls enabled every female to achieve the social status of a married woman, with all the benefits this brought within the social organization of the tribe. It also meant that no child would lack a "father" to provide for it and care for its needs.

Female fathers had exactly the same responsibilities to the

children born of their wives as ordinary husbands in other circumstances did. But the wife had the absolute right to take any man she wished as *physical* father of her offspring. In point of fact, then, Kikuyu custom was so organized that no woman was ever condemned to a life of spinsterhood, or to one in which she had no husband responsible for the support of herself and her children. Even the most wanton nymphomaniac, whom no man would accept as a wife, could achieve the full social status of a wife by accepting marriage to a female who was legally a male and who thereupon became her legal husband. At the same time, she could sleep with any man she liked and produce children by him.

In practice, this custom has led to much misunderstanding among non-Bantu people. Until recently—the custom died out in about 1920—someone asked to go and fetch his father might return with a woman! I have known a number of cases where this has caused considerable confusion. In one case, a white man actually assaulted an African for daring to produce a woman as his father. But in point of fact the woman concerned *was* his father under Kikuyu law.

This custom of giving certain women legal male status and the ability to marry young women (remember, there was absolutely no sexual implication—lesbianism was completely ruled out in such marriages) was not uncommon in Bantu societies in other parts of Africa. In fact, the more inquiries I have made, the more widespread I have found it to be. It was first recorded in anthropological literature, so far as I know, by a friend and fellow Cambridge student, Hugh Stayt, who had been studying the Bavenda tribe in the Transvaal of South Africa. He reported the case of a woman who had ten or twelve such "wives." Since then, at least a dozen other such records have been published, and I have no doubt that in the not very remote past this custom was practiced by most Bantu-speaking tribes.

It is probable too that the practice gave rise to the reports made by early travelers in Africa of having met women chiefs. Having been accorded male legal status, these women would have had male rights and could be appointed to any male occupation or even promoted to the rank of chief of the tribe, clan, or subclan.

Writing the first draft of the Kikuyu book not only was very exciting, but was also exceedingly tiring. At intervals I simply had to stop working because I found that I was not concentrating sufficiently well. On such occasions, Mary and I would take a brief holiday—Mary from her excavations and I from my book. During one such interlude, in 1938, we went down to the east shore of Lake Eyasie, in Tanganyika, to investigate the site where Dr. Kohl-Larsen had found parts of a fossilized human skull.

Since one of the problems that had to be tackled at Eyasie was the geology, we persuaded Dr. W. H. Reeve, a geologist of the Tanganyika Geological Survey, to accompany us. We were anxious to find out the nature of the fossil fauna deriving from the site where the skull had been found and to discover whether the deposit contained any signs of human artifacts.

Getting to the Eyasie site proved very difficult. We traveled by car as far as Oldeani and from there, instead of turning up to the Ngorongoro Crater, headed south and then west. At length, the road we were following became less and less visible, until it was no more than a track leading through thick, long grass to a native settlement set down beside a spring. Ahead of us now lay a range of hills beyond which, so we were told, no vehicle had ever penetrated. When Kohl-Larsen made the trip, he had apparently taken porters and walked the last thirty miles down to the edge of the lake. We had no porters with us, and, anyhow, I was determined to try and get our vehicle through to the lake shore. We spent the greater part of three days in prospecting and exploring ways and means of getting over, around, or through this range. In the end, we were able to make a track over the top and down the other side. It was very rocky and the going was extremely difficult, but once we reached the far side of the hills we found that the land sloped gently down towards the shores of Lake Eyasie, some twenty miles away.

One of the Africans from the settlement, who had accompanied Kohl-Larsen on his foot safari in 1936, offered to come along and show us the exact place where the skull, or, rather, the parts of it, had been discovered. We found that the site was on the shores of the lake; it did not seem to us to be of any great antiquity. It might, perhaps, have been of Upper Pleistocene or even younger age, so far as we could judge. (Radiometric dating, undertaken recently at the University of California, has given an age of 34,000 years B.P. for the Eyasie skull.) Fossil animal remains were not numerous, and most of them were in fresh condition. Of the others, the few that were distinctly "rolled" appeared to be derived from older deposits and reincorporated at the place where the skull was found. All the specimens, with these few exceptions, appeared to represent living animal species. None represented the extinct forms we had so frequently found at Olduvai Gorge.

We also discovered a few stone artifacts that were unquestionably from the deposits where the skull was found. These, in the terminology of African prehistory, could be classified as of Middle Stone Age type. They were clearly younger than the tools from the top of Bed IV at Olduvai.

When I later saw the Eyasie fossil skull fragments in Germany, I found them very interesting, and wrote a note for *Nature* about them. I described them as representing something rather like the female skulls of the *Pithecanthropus* type from Choukoutien in China. At that time, of course, no trace of any pithecanthropine had ever been discovered in Africa, and, therefore, my colleagues were a little unwilling to accept my interpretation. Personally, I still think that there is a definite relationship between the Eyasie skull fragments and some of the specimens of *Pithecanthropus* (now called *Homo erectus*). I suspect that one day we shall establish a close resemblance between Kohl-Larsen's Eyasie specimens and the small fossil skull found a few years ago by Margaret Leakey, formerly my son Richard's wife, at Site VEK in upper Bed IV, when she was working with us at Olduvai. This skull still remains to be studied in detail, but has been provisionally referred to *Homo erectus;* it is, of course, very much older than the Eyasie skulls.

We camped at Eyasie for some three weeks, and during that time made contact with a small group of men, women, and children of the Tindiga, or Hadza, tribe. They were an exceedingly interesting people. Their language and material culture suggested that they were allied to the Bushmen of South Africa, but though some of them had markedly Bushmen features, others resembled the Bantu-speaking tribes of the surrounding area. The latter circumstance was, no doubt, due to the fact that, from time to time, some renegade member of a Bantu-speaking tribe had joined the Tindiga on the lake shore. Such an outsider would undoubtedly have been welcomed by the community on account of his advanced technical skills and would have been absorbed into the tribe.

We had come to Eyasie to discover more about Kohl-Larsen's discovery, not to make a study of the Tindiga tribe. But having been trained as a social anthropologist by Dr. A. C. Haddon at Cambridge, and being at that time intensely involved with my Kikuyu study, I naturally found out as much as I could about these fascinating people.

The principal hunting weapons of the tribe were bows and arrows, but the latter were very unusual. Many years before, I had written, on the basis of a lengthy study, a report entitled "A New Classification of the Bow and Arrow in Africa," but the Tindiga arrowheads were new to me. They bore a remarkable resemblance to the so-called barbed "harpoons" made from antler, bone, or ivory in Upper Palaeolithic times in Europe, except that they were made from hardwood. Watching the Tindiga hunters at work gave me a new insight into how those harpoons of prehistoric times in Europe were probably used.

The word "harpoon" usually conjures up a vision of hunting for seals, whaling, or fishing, but the Tindiga harpoons were used only for hunting small mammals and the larger birds, such as guinea fowl, francolin, and bustard.

The principle was simple but very effective. The hardwood arrowheads were from eight to ten inches long, with a single series of barbs carved down one side. The tip end was worked to a sharp point, while the opposite one was blunt and cut at right angles to the long axis. This end was shaped so as to fit into the hollow tip of a reed shaft. Feathers were attached to the other end of the shaft by a technique I had earlier described as "tangential feathering." A small circular groove was cut round the base of the hardwood head, and into this a thin string, made of either vegetable fiber or animal gut, was firmly tied. The rest of the string—a yard or so in length—was wound loosely round the shaft and attached at the midpoint.

When such an arrow found its target the barbs penetrated and were held tightly by the flesh and skin. The shaft fell away from the head and trailed along, still linked to the wounded animal by the string. In the case of a small mammal, the wounded creature would run away, but before long the trailing shaft would be caught among the bushes, anchoring the animal there until it could be dispatched. In the case of birds, the situation was slightly different. A wounded bird usually flew off trailing the shaft, but was soon forced to land in a bush or tree or even on the ground, where, once again, the shaft acted as an anchor.

At this time—1938—we knew of no prehistoric harpoon heads in the Upper Palaeolithic, Mesolithic, or Neolithic sites of East Africa, but I had come across some barbed arrowheads similar to the prehistoric specimens among the swamp-dwelling peoples at Lake Bangweolo, in Rhodesia, and Lake Albert, in Uganda. Since then, Dr. J. de Heinzelen of Belgium, when excavating Mesolithic sites at the southwest corner of Lake Albert, has found bone harpoons very similar in shape to the Tindiga specimens. Other scientists working at Neolithic and Mesolithic sites on the west shore of Lake Rudolf have also found bone harpoons that resemble those of the Tindiga. Consequently, I feel sure that many of the so-called harpoons used by prehistoric man in France were not, in fact, used for fishing and other aquatic purposes, but for hunting small game in the Tindiga manner.

When we were at Eyasie, the Tindiga had no tobacco and were always exceedingly glad to pick up discarded cigarette butts or to be given handfuls of the coarse-leaf tobacco we had brought down from Kamba country in Kenya. Normally, they smoked wild dried leaves, using pipes for the purpose, but I was unable to discover from which plant this substitute for tobacco was obtained.

Tindiga pipes were almost exactly the same as those used by the Bushmen of South Africa. They were made from a stone carved into a cylinder eight to ten inches long, slightly thicker in the middle and narrow at both ends, with a center diameter of about one and a half inches. At one end, a bowl about two inches long was carved out to take the tobacco or its substitute. A narrow hole was drilled through the middle of the pipe, and the end that was put in the mouth was given a slightly larger aperture. These pipes, when smoked, looked for all the world like oversized cigars. Not everyone possessed a pipe; in fact, there was usually only one per family. Often pipe smoking appeared to have some kind of ceremonial significance; on these occasions, a pipe would be filled with tobacco or other herbs and passed round among the male members of the gathering. I did not stay long enough with the Tindiga to discover in what circumstances such smoking was considered desirable or necessary.

Among the Tindiga, it was customary for men and youths to go out hunting in small groups, armed with bows, arrows, and clubs, while the women and girls and the smaller children went out gathering nuts, fruits, and edible insects such as locusts, grasshoppers, and termites. All the women who went on food-gathering expeditions carried small clubs with them, in case they came upon a baby gazelle or antelope or an adult hare trying to make itself invisible by hiding in the long grass. Then, with a quick gesture to the other women, the one who had seen the animal would attack the quarry. Between them the women would usually manage to kill it and thus return to camp with meat in addition to the various other foods they had gone out to collect.

The Tindiga were very skilled indeed in making fire by drilling, and they used a far longer drilling stick than any I had ever seen being manipulated by other African tribes. The Kikuyu—and many other tribes around Nairobi—used a short drill, and the man who was drilling squatted on the ground or sat on a stool. Moreover, in most of the Bantu-speaking tribes, in recent times, the fire drill was used only to produce ceremonial fire, while the fire required for ordinary domestic purposes was obtained by borrowing an ember from some other family. The Tindiga did not seem to have the same semireligious regard for fire drilling, and it was done not only on ceremonial occasions, but every evening when they came back to camp, simply for the purpose of lighting fires for cooking. (Although the Tindiga left their fires burning in the morning, they were not tended during the day, and so had gone out by the time everyone returned in the evening.)

The drills the Tindiga used were five or six feet long, so that the top of the stick was near the face of the man who was standing working the drill; placing his hands at the top, he would work them nearly halfway down in a twirling movement. Usually, one long continuous twirl of this sort would produce the spark necessary to ignite the tinder below. The "female" part of the fire-making apparatus—that is to say, a piece of soft wood with holes drilled in it—was held steady on a flat stone by a second person, squatting on the ground. As the drill was twirled, a small pile of charred, very dark powder formed and caught fire. The smoking powder was tipped from the stone into a small bundle of specially prepared tinder. This was blown gently and soon was aflame. I found that the Tindiga could usually start a good fire in about thirty seconds. In my youth, I had learned from the Kikuyu to use a fire drill, but I could never make fire quite as quickly as that.

There were a number of caves and rock shelters in the area near our camp, and in some of these there were traces of rather modern-looking rock paintings. Unfortunately, none of the Tindiga who were with us at the time were very old, and all of them denied that they or their ancestors were in any way responsible for these paintings. It was difficult to tell whether they were speaking the truth or were simply unwilling to admit to strangers that they had had any participation in such activities, which, for them, might well have had some magic significance. I should note here that after World War II, when Mary and I went down once more to study the prehistoric art in the Kisese/Cheke area, we found a group of Bushmenlike people of the Sandawe tribe living in the hills. They too denied all knowledge of any of the rock paintings in their area.

Once we were back again at Nakuru, I resumed work on the Kikuyu draft; I had reached the chapters dealing with magic, witchcraft, and herbal remedies. Waruhiu—famous for his skill in the arts of herbal medicine—showed me many plants that were used by the Kikuyu and explained their purposes. These included general antiseptics, remedies for the reduction of inflammation of the eye, and various types of vermifuges. He also gave me a demonstration of suturing a serious wound.

One of my staff had accidentally cut himself, leaving a fairly deep tear, about four inches long, on the calf of his leg. Waruhiu first applied the antiseptic juices of the plant *Mukengeria*. (Incidentally, it was the juice of this plant that was applied to the wound on the prepuce of a youth after the circumcision ceremony.) He then swiftly inserted five long thorns across the wound—rather like darning a hole in a sock—but left each needle in position, so that the five thorns ran through the skin on both sides of the wound. Next, he took a small piece of fine fiber, knotted it to the end of one of the thorns, and proceeded to lace it backwards and forwards over the ends of the thorns, drawing the two edges of the wound together. The result was that the wound looked as if it had been stitched by a surgeon. Waruhiu then applied more antiseptic juices. About six days later he pulled out the thorns and removed the fiber, when it was seen that the edges of the skin had joined and the wound was healing perfectly. It was a most interesting lesson in Kikuyu surgery.

Waruhiu also spent some time showing me how to find two very different but similar-looking plants—one used in white magic and religious ceremonies, and the other in black magic and witchcraft.

One of these plants, known as *muthakwa mwega,* normally has a single strong woody stem growing to about five feet above the ground and then dividing into five or, at the most, six subsidiary branches, all emerging more or less from the same point on the stem but in different directions. The botanical name of the plant is *Vernonia auriculifera.* When in flower it has striking heads of pale mauve blossoms. This is a good plant, used in white magic, healing, and many religious ceremonies.

The other plant, a close relation scientifically and similar in appearance, is known as *muthakwa muuru*—the bad *muthakwa.* It has the same single woody stem extending about five feet from the ground, but this then divides into seven— occasionally more, but never fewer—subsidiary branches, which spread out radially from the same point. The leaves of this species are, incidentally, a darker shade of green than those of the good *muthakwa.*

In Kikuyu folklore, the number seven is regarded as dangerous and very unlucky, to be avoided at all costs except in special circumstances. The finding of such a *muthakwa muuru* stem is always taken to be an ominous sign because of its association with black magic. It was essential, by Kikuyu custom, to have one of these seven-pronged *muthakwa muuru* stands on which to place the *githathi* stone when swearing a solemn oath—in much the same way as a Christian swears on the Bible.

In the olden days, no Kikuyu with a guilty conscience would

have dared to swear an oath on a *githathi* stone properly set up on the fork of a seven-stemmed *muthakwa muuru*. If he had done so, he would have been perfectly sure in his own mind either that he would die or that some awful catastrophe would come upon himself or his family. Consequently, he would do anything rather than risk such supernatural punishment.

As an elder of the second grade of the Kikuyu tribe, I was fortunate enough to participate twice in such oathing ceremonies—with the *githathi* stone set in the fork of a *muthakwa muuru*. I remember one of the ceremonies extremely well. A certain Kikuyu elder who was a member of a tribunal that used to hear minor criminal cases in Nakuru had been accused, on a number of occasions, of taking bribes to decide cases in the bribers' favor. Other elders had been called in from outside the district to look into the matter, and their investigations had convinced them that the accusations against this elder were justified and that he had been taking bribes over a long period. They therefore proposed that the *githathi* oath be administered to him.

The accused was informed of their decision and readily agreed to participate, on condition that his eight fellow members on the tribunal submit to the same judicial test and the same oath. All nine were told to appear on a certain day, the *githathi* stone was sent for, and Chief Koinange, Senior Chief of the whole Kikuyu tribe, made a special hundred-mile journey to administer the oath.

The *githathi* oath stone is a strange object that is kept hidden, wrapped in leaves, in a cave all the year round, by a man who is known as its guardian. The secret of its whereabouts is known to two other men, so that the stone can always be quickly found if its guardian happens to meet with sudden death. Whenever it is moved from one place to another, it is carried in the leaves of the good *muthakwa*, the *muthakwa mwega*. On the occasion I am writing about, the guardian elder brought the *githathi* stone from its hiding place. He was accompanied by another elder, who brought with him the stem of a *muthakwa muuru*, the bad *muthakwa*, which had been cut off close to the ground. The tips of the seven subsidiary stems had been lopped off.

This stem of *muthakwa muuru* was set up in the center of a grassy lawn where the ceremony was to be held. Several hundred second- and third-grade elders gathered to watch the proceedings, but no younger people and no women were allowed to be present. The guardian of the *githathi* stone very carefully unwrapped it and handed it, still on the leaves of the good *muthakwa*, to Senior Chief Koinange. He, in turn, placed it in the middle of the seven-forked stick. Having done so, he stood up and made a careful and lengthy speech explaining the significance of the ceremony, which was to culminate in his asking the nine judiciary elders to swear they had not accepted any bribes that could have influenced the decisions they reached while sitting on the tribunal.

As far as I could see—I was not allowed to handle it—the *githathi* stone consisted of a piece of consolidated ash with seven holes of different dimensions penetrating it from different directions, all meeting at the center. The holes were, I am quite sure, artificially made, although the Kikuyu always maintained that they never manufactured *githathi* stones, but found them as natural objects.

After Chief Koinange concluded his address he called on the nine men to approach close to where the *githathi* stone was set up, and he again explained the consequences to them—not through any human action, but through the anger of God—if they swore falsely during this ceremony. The first and senior of the nine elders then came forward and put his right forefinger into each of the seven holes in turn. Each time he did so, he said, in the Kikuyu language, "If I have ever taken bribes in any way from any person and as a result of the bribes have not administered justice, may this stone cause my death." He then stepped back and another elder came forward. This man was called upon to do likewise, but as he approached the stone he became afraid and would not put his finger into even the first hole; instead, he confessed that he had, on one or two occasions, accepted bribes. The third elder was called and swore that he had never taken bribes. Then it was the turn of the man over whom all the trouble had started and who had denied over and over again that he had accepted bribes. Now he came forward to the *githathi* stone and was called upon to make his oath. Instead, he suddenly stepped back, declaring that he would not, in any circumstances, take the oath. One other elder also refused to take the oath, so that, in effect, three out of the nine confessed to having taken bribes.

It is interesting to note that the very definite claims of the Kikuyu that they themselves found the *githathi* stones and did not make them, have recently been strengthened by the discovery of many of these stones in a cave on Mount Elgon. Neither the reason for such a collection nor the identity of the people who either made or collected them is known.

The significance of the seven holes, or openings, in the stone is that these are supposed to represent the seven apertures of the human body—the mouth, two nostrils, two eyes, the anus, and the urinary canal. (The ears do not count as openings, since it is considered that nothing ever comes out of them; sound merely goes into them.) Thus, swearing on the *githathi* stone is like swearing an oath on the human body.

In connection with this mention of the number seven, it is worthy of note that in my boyhood days no Kikuyu would ever work seven consecutive days on the same job. Nor would he travel on seven consecutive days, or roast seven potatoes or seven bananas, or eat seven of anything. Six or eight were permissible, but seven was always unlucky. Similarly, women were taught to regard the seventh month of pregnancy as far and away the most dangerous for them. They consequently took extra precautions against a possible miscarriage all through the seventh month.

In the eyes of the Kikuyu, and of many related tribes who speak one of the Bantu group of languages, the number seven is so special that it is not even treated as an ordinary numeral from the point of view of grammatical structure. The numbers one, two, three, four, five, six, and eight are adjectives and must always agree with the nouns they modify, just as ordinary adjectives do. Seven, nine, and ten do not agree, but for different reasons. In the case of seven, the Kikuyu word is a contraction of a verbal clause that never changes, no matter what word it is modifying in any of the noun groups. The form is always *muqwanja*. The meaning of this contraction (short for *mweri mugua nja*) refers to the concept that the seventh month of pregnancy is one in which a woman is liable to fall down and faint in the courtyard.

Eight

At the beginning of 1939, Mary and I decided to go to Njoro River Rock Shelter once more, to continue the excavations in the cave, and we invited Mary Davidson and Molly Paine to join us for the rest of their school holidays.

On this occasion, we did not stay in Mrs. Grant's home, but were lent a small, empty farm bungalow about two miles away, while the men who were to work with us had a tented camp on the edge of the forest reserve, close to the point where the Njoro River entered the farming area. Our earlier preliminary excavations had been carried out almost entirely at the back of the main area of the rock shelter, but we knew from our previous work that there was a long and narrow cavern extending back from the rock shelter proper.

During these excavations we were able to interpret in greater detail the method of the cremated burials. The bodies had been buried in shallow graves on the floor of the shelter; since space was necessarily limited, each had been compressed as much as possible. The body had first been folded into the prenatal position and then fastened with cords so as to make it as small as possible. It had then been wrapped in an animal skin, placed in the grave, and covered with a shallow layer of soil. It seemed that a large fire had then been lit on top, so that the flesh and bones of the body baked—but did not burn, as they would have if exposed to flame. When, as often happened, another grave was dug some time afterwards through one or more of the existing graves, the bones were, of course, disturbed. Nevertheless, several more or less whole skeletons were recovered, especially from the outer perimeter of the shelter.

Another surprising fact was the presence of numerous beads made from peculiar seeds with hard siliceous coverings, as well as others made from semiprecious stones.

I was, at this stage, working on my third draft of the Kikuyu monograph, having again spent a few weeks at Kiamba with a group of elders going through the second draft and clearing up certain points.

I was disturbed that I had not been able to record a really good account of the ceremony of *Ituika,* which should have formed an important part of the third volume. *Ituika* was a Kikuyu ceremony that formerly took place at roughly thirty-year intervals. It consisted of a formal handing over of the reins of authority by one generation of elders—usually between sixty and seventy years old—to the generation of thirty- to forty-year-olds. This new group was then responsible for ruling the tribe until they, in turn, reached sixty or seventy and relinquished their authority.

The last time a full and complete *Ituika* ceremony had taken place over the whole of Kikuyu country was reported to have been around 1897 or 1898. In 1929 an attempt had been made in the Fort Hall area to arrange an *Ituika,* but this had not been achieved, and by the time I began working on my book, the forces of so-called "civilization" had changed the Kikuyu way of life and disrupted so many of the old ideas that there was no likelihood of an *Ituika* ceremony's ever taking place again. There were, however, a number of very old men still living who had been junior members of the generation that took over in 1897 or '98. A few of them volunteered to describe for me, in detail, the ceremony as they had seen it. This offer was conditional on my being able to get full tribal authority from the chiefs and elders.

I consulted Senior Chief Koinange, and he promised to make every possible effort to persuade the elders throughout Kikuyu country, from Embu, Nyeri, Meru, Fort Hall, and Kiambu, to agree that I should be allowed to have a panel of their senior members give me a full account of the *Ituika.* He did not succeed, and, in the end, the only information I was given was very incomplete. This was a matter of great regret to me personally, and a major loss to anthropology. It was also a misfortune for the Kikuyu themselves, who, in years to come, will look to my monograph to find out more about their ancient ways of life. When they come to the chapter on *Ituika* they will regret, as I do, that it is so incomplete. But since the elders in possession of the knowledge I required were not allowed to impart it, I was forced to let the matter drop.

Early in 1939 Mary and I moved back to Nairobi and rented a house belonging to a Mr. Clark of the Kenya Game Department. There I continued my work on the third and final draft of the book, with the assistance, once more, of the two elders who had been with me at Hyrax Hill. Meanwhile, Mary was preparing her report on the Njoro River Rock Shelter excavations.

Two things happened at about this time that had an important bearing on our lives for the rest of the year. First, my grant from the Rhodes Trust, which had been made for a two-year period, expired, so that there was no more money coming in from that source. Second, together with ugly rumors that war might break out in Europe, it was becoming clear that there were certain subversive elements in Kenya moving about the country and trying to persuade Kenya tribesmen to work against the British government.

Since I could speak Kikuyu better than I could English and also knew the country so well, I was asked whether, in return for a small traveling allowance, I would spend the summer attempting to find out who the people were behind these fifth-column activities. This I agreed to do.

The arrangement helped me out of my financial difficulties, since, with a travel allowance to pay for my car, I was able to set up a small wholesale distributing service for the many village shops that were beginning to appear everywhere in Kikuyu country. Most of the owners of these shops could not afford to buy large quantities of any commodity from the main wholesalers in Nairobi. On the other hand, if they bought their wares from the bigger retail stores they could not resell them at a price sufficient to make a worth-while profit. I bought goods such as soap, household medicines, tea, sugar, coffee, canvas shoes, and sandals at wholesale rates in Nairobi and went round the country delivering them to the small Kikuyu shops. After paying me a commission, the shop owners were still able to sell their goods at the usual retail price and so discourage their customers from going farther afield to do their shopping.

It became clear to me during my travels that propaganda against the British was indeed being spread throughout the country—presumably in preparation for the possibility of war.

One widespread rumor suggested that the British were deliberately adding a drug to all the maize meal that was being marketed to Africans, in order to make them sterile. In due course, it was said, there would be no more babies born, and then, when all the tribes had died out, the British would take over the African lands. Another absurd but nonetheless dangerous rumor claimed that the British were about to "take the people's blood." (A blood bank had been set up at one of the hospitals in Nairobi for transfusion purposes.) The rumor stated that the British intended to use this blood to make a very powerful black magic against the local tribes and thus eliminate them. Yet another rumor warned that the British were sending out veterinary officers, ostensibly to inoculate African-owned cattle against rinderpest, but in reality to inject a poison that would decimate the herds.

At this time the Kenya government was engaged in an active antierosion campaign in Kamba country, where the soil of the hills was being washed away so badly that there was a serious threat of famine. But the underground movement assiduously spread word among the Kamba people that after the tribe had undertaken the building of dams and the use of contour cultivation to improve the land, it would be taken over and given to white British immigrants.

These rumors were causing the government great anxiety and had somehow to be checked. My assignment was to discover who was responsible for them.

Another task also engaged my attention. I had, once again, joined the committee of the Natural History Society, which was then responsible for the running of the Coryndon Memorial Museum in Nairobi. At this time the committee was engaged in lengthy and sometimes difficult negotiations concerning the possibility that the museum's government-appointed board of trustees might replace it in running the museum.

The history of the museum—now the National Museum—is, I think, of sufficient interest to be worth recording here.

In 1910–11 a small group of keen amateur naturalists formed the East Africa and Uganda Natural History Society. (East Africa in the title applied only to what is now the Republic of Kenya. German East Africa, which today is Tanzania, was not included in the scope of the society's activities.)

My father, Canon Harry Leakey (a Church Missionary Society worker at Kabete, some ten miles from Nairobi), and Canon Kenneth St. Aubyn Rogers, also of CMS, and at that time stationed in the Teita Hills, halfway between Mombasa and Nairobi, were among the founder members of the Natural History Society, which also included a number of government administrators, such as C. W. Hobley and John Ainsworth; medical and dental practitioners, like the two van Someren brothers; various big-game hunters; and a number of gentlemen farmers.

Towards the end of 1911, the society decided to set up a small museum and library, to be run by an honorary curator. Fortunately, the project attracted the interest of Aladina Visram, an Asian businessman, who became the museum's first benefactor. Having provided the money for a small two-room, single-story building, he then rented it to the society for a "peppercorn" rent of one rupee (about one shilling and four pence) per year.

By 1914, the society had gained so much ground and received so many donations, in addition to the subscriptions from its members, that it could afford to engage a full-time paid curator. Advertising for one in Great Britain led to the appointment of Arthur Loveridge, a keen general zoologist with a specialized interest in snakes. Early in March 1914 he reached Nairobi and took up his post. (Many years later, he was to gain international fame as the leading expert on the snakes of the world, and in particular those of Africa. He eventually became a professor at Harvard University.)

Canon Rogers had by this time been transferred from the Teita Hills to the mission station in Nairobi, and he devoted a good deal of his spare time to helping Loveridge build up the collections in the little museum. The same was true of the van Someren brothers, particularly Vernon, who was a dentist in Nairobi. Allen Turner, whose name was to be associated with the museum for a long time to come, was also a keen voluntary worker. Allen had come out to East Africa some years previously with the Theodore Roosevelt expedition and had afterwards decided to stay in the country and do taxidermy for various big-game safaris.

The outbreak of World War I seriously curtailed the development of the little museum and the activities of the society. Loveridge had to join up and go with the army to German East

Africa, but thanks to the splendid work of Canon Rogers, the van Someren brothers, and other volunteers, the museum was kept alive.

When the war was over Loveridge returned to take charge of the museum for a short time and then left for America, and A. F. J. Gedye was appointed as his successor.

By 1923, the society had raised sufficient funds to embark on a more ambitious program. The government granted it a plot of land at the corner of Government Road and Kirk Road, and late that year the society opened its new museum building; the old one was taken over by an enterprising businessman and turned into a dairy. Gedye remained curator and had the voluntary assistance of Canon Rogers, Dr. van Someren, Allen Turner, and others.

The recently appointed Governor of Kenya, Sir Robert Coryndon, was not only an enthusiastic and ardent sportsman, but also a keen naturalist. He became a member of the society, assisted it in every way he could, and became its first patron. His sudden death in 1927, while still in office, was a catastrophe for Kenya, and immediately a fund was set up to raise a memorial to him. As the fund grew, discussions took place as to what form the memorial should take. His widow, Lady Coryndon, strongly supported the society in suggesting that the best memorial to her husband would be an even bigger and better museum, named after him.

At this stage, the government offered the society one pound for every pound collected from the public for the Coryndon Memorial Fund, and by 1928 enough money had been raised to make it possible to start building the new museum. To ensure continuity, the government appointed a special museum board of trustees (which included members of the Natural History Society), in whom the land was vested and who were required to undertake all work in connection with the erection of the new building.

By 1929, the Coryndon Memorial Museum building was ready to be equipped, but the board of trustees had no collections to put in it. All the material housed in the old museum was, of course, the property of the Natural History Society, and, accordingly, the society was approached as to whether it would be willing to organize a museum within the new building. The society looked over the newly erected premises and found that in spite of its having asked the board of trustees to provide adequate workrooms and storage space, the building had no workrooms or storage space of any kind. The society therefore declined to develop and maintain a museum in the building until some way was found to overcome this problem.

After many discussions the government agreed to purchase the old museum and the land on which it stood, both of which were owned by the society. A sum of £2,300 was realized from the sale, and with it the society built a three-room extension onto the new building to provide workrooms and storage space. It then handed over the whole of its natural history and other collections to the museum trustees, but retained the library, since it felt that this belonged essentially to its own members. The library had recently been augmented by the presentation by Lady Coryndon of a collection of Sir Robert Coryndon's books and papers. It was now housed in the new museum, and the museum staff, as well as the members of the society, was allowed free access to it at all times, though it was still looked after by the society's librarian.

Dr. van Someren, who had acted occasionally as honorary curator of the old museum, now took up his appointment as full-time paid curator and was given a house on the museum grounds. He was fortunate in having the voluntary services of John Gedye and Allen Turner, and two new paid staff members were appointed—Donald MacInnes and Peter Bally.

However, the arrangement rapidly became unworkable. The building was owned by the trustees, and the scientific and natural history collections were also their property, but the Natural History Society was responsible both for the library and for the scientific work and the maintenance of the collections. Accordingly, the society requested the government to appoint a commission of inquiry to work out the best way of getting over these difficulties.

Sir Charles Belcher, a judge of the High Court in Nairobi and a keen naturalist, was appointed chairman of a committee of three. After lengthy discussions it was agreed that the museum trustees should take over complete responsibility for running the new museum (except for the library) and, further, that they should make a payment to the Natural History Society of a thousand pounds a year for fifteen years, in return for the exhibits and study collections that had been handed over to them. This figure, while of course it did not represent the real value of the collections, proved satisfactory to the society, since at long last it provided sufficient funds to enable the society to increase its publications.

Mary and I found the new museum's laboratory space and equipment invaluable, for we were able to use it to sort and study the Hyrax Hill material.

By this time I had begun distributing wholesale goods to shops in the Kiambu district during the day; my evenings were devoted to the task of piecing together the Hyrax Hill skull and skeletons and preparing my paper to go with the report Mary was writing on that exciting Neolithic and Iron Age site. We finally finished our joint report in the early part of 1940, and the paper was published by the Royal Society of South Africa, in Cape Town.

As soon as I began to receive back the typed chapters of the Kikuyu book from the secretary in Nakuru, I started negotiations with various publishers. It had now become possible to estimate the book's approximate length, and it was quite clear that this was going to be in the neighborhood of over 700,000 words. I sent summaries, as well as synopses of some of the chapters, to publishers in Great Britain, the United States, and South Africa. Nowhere could I find anybody who was interested in publishing my book. One and all pronounced it to be far too long and asked me to reduce it from three volumes to one. This I was not prepared to do, since it was, in my opinion, the most detailed anthropological study that had ever been written on an African or any other primitive tribe anywhere in the world. Thus an impasse was reached. I refused to publish an abridged version, while the publishers refused to publish the book in full.

Eventually, I placed my finished copy in a fireproof safe, concerned that I could do nothing more about it. I even went so far as to send the chapters on marriage and initiation to anthropologist friends at various universities, asking them to help me find a publisher. All but two were of the opinion that my work was far too detailed. The one person who seriously supported me was the late Reverend Edwin Smith, who had been a missionary in Northern Rhodesia. He himself had published two volumes on the Ila tribe, and, realizing the value of a study in depth such as mine, he tried very hard to help. I also, naturally, approached the people who had subsidized my two years' work —the Rhodes Trust in Oxford. They felt, however, that since the trust had already spent a great deal of money on making it possible for me to prepare and write the book, it was up to some other organization to pay for the cost of publication.

In due course, I interested a wealthy Kenya landowner, the late Colonel Ewart Grogan, a romantic figure who, in his youth, had walked the length of the African continent, from the Cape to Cairo, since his fiancée had made this a condition of her marrying him. Colonel Grogan, hoping that some publisher would accept the book for publication if it were subsidized, promised to provide £500 if someone else would provide an equal sum. However, I was unable to find anybody to match his offer. Then war broke out, and so the book, which had taken two and a half years to write, remained locked in a safe, unavailable to students and anthropologists alike.

As the war clouds of World War II gathered, Mary and I had to decide whether to return to the United Kingdom or to remain in Kenya. Her family very much wanted her to come back, but before we reached any decision the Kenya government set up a manpower committee, and all men between the ages of eighteen and fifty were required to register immediately. I did so and was at once given an appointment in the CID, in what was called the Special Branch, Section 6, concerned with civil intelligence.

On September 3, 1939, the day war was declared, a colleague and I were on our way home from an assignment we had carried out in the area round Mount Kenya. We were approaching the Sagana railway bridge, about fifty miles from Nairobi, when we noticed a small group of people crawling through the bush towards one end of it. Since we had been warned that sabotage might be attempted against some of the Kenya railway bridges, we immediately decided to investigate. Leaving our car by the side of the road, we set off on foot, fully expecting to find a small group of fifth columnists preparing to blow up the bridge.

When our quarry realized that we were stalking them, they immediately assumed that *we* were coming to blow up the bridge and set an ambush to catch *us!* Suddenly we and they came face to face and, in the moment of recognition, felt very sheepish about our strange antics. The people we were stalking turned out to be British settlers who had been sent to provide protection at both ends of this important railway bridge. Following orders from the commissioner of Fort Hall, they were moving down to the bridge as quickly as possible to defend it against possible saboteurs until such time as the police or the military could provide a proper guard.

Soon after war was declared, in addition to my other duties in connection with intelligence I was called upon to provide a weekly broadcast to African tribes in four languages—Kikuyu, Swahili, Luo, and Kamba. Of these four, I spoke Kikuyu and Swahili fluently, Kamba fairly well, and Luo not at all. I was given four men to assist me in this task. My job was to select the news items that were to be translated into these four languages and to organize listening points all through the country, at chiefs' villages and public market places, where the population as a whole could hear a simple version of the war news, to counteract any rumors that might be going round the countryside. The task of selecting the news was not an easy one, and the necessity of putting it into language that would be intelligible to those who listened was even more difficult. It is not a simple matter, in any circumstances, to translate English into a Bantu or Nilotic language, and many serious confusions can arise from overliteral translations. None of the Africans attached to me had ever undertaken translation work, although they did understand the English language. I had, therefore, to be very careful to guard against careless wording of news items.

There was also a suggestion around this time that the government should issue a weekly newspaper or newssheet in the Swahili language, to augment the news that was going out on the wireless and keep the Africans better informed of the war situation.

The late Colonel Oscar F. Watkins and I were asked to draw up plans for a possible government-sponsored newspaper, but eventually it was decided that it would be better to allow the existing privately owned newspaper organization, the *East African Standard,* to plan an extra weekly issue in the Swahili language. This newssheet for Africans was started at the outbreak of war. Today that same paper, *Baraza,* has become a regular feature of the East African newspaper scene, in a full-fledged newspaper format.

Another of my duties at the time was to visit outlying areas and persuade the chiefs to call *barazas,* or meetings, of the elders in order to give them the latest war news and to encourage their young men to volunteer for service in the King's African Rifles or some other military or paramilitary department.

The situation then existing in northern Tanganyika was a curious one. Between the two wars a large new German colony had been established there with the permission of the British government, which held a mandate to govern the country under the League of Nations. Fortunately for Kenya, its intelligence service was highly efficient, and it was well known that many of the immigrants were of the Nazi persuasion and that Nazi cells were being organized to take action upon the outbreak of war. In fact, the whole situation was so closely watched by intelligence that when war was declared nearly all the Germans who had been indulging in subversive activities were quickly picked up before any serious incidents could occur.

It now began to seem certain that Italy, under Mussolini, intended to join Hitler in the war against the Allies. This, from the Kenya point of view, constituted a real menace. On our northern borders, Italy then occupied Abyssinia (now Ethiopia) and Italian Somaliland.

We knew that in both places they had strong military installations and air bases. Consequently, a great deal of time had to be spent in organizing an intelligence network throughout the Northern Frontier District of Kenya, to check on the possible infiltration of fifth columnists. We also intensified our checkup on the large numbers of Italians, Somalis, and others living in Kenya who had Italian contacts. All this involved a considerable amount of detailed investigation, since we had been ordered to compile a complete record for each individual. Though in the end most of this vast accumulation of information turned out to be superfluous, it is a necessary part of the routine work of an efficient and well-organized intelligence service.

Despite the preparations for the impending conflict, the Kenya government, at long last, was persuaded by a number of us that steps must be taken quickly to give real protection to wildlife. There were, of course, game reserves under the control of the Game Department, but this merely meant that, in certain areas, hunters could not get licenses and poaching was controlled to some extent. Many of us felt that the situation could not be left as it was. Encroachment was taking place all the time; there was a movement to reduce the size of the reserves, and there was clamor from Africans for the government to kill even the animals in the reserves, because of the competition for fodder between the plains game and domestic stock and because of the depredations of lion prides, which were getting larger and more numerous.

The Kenya government therefore set up a committee of inquiry to formulate a sounder game policy. Mervyn Cowie was active in stirring up public opinion for the project, and he was strongly supported by men like Archie Ritchie, Alan Tarlton, Donald Ker, and Syd Downey. I was also very much behind his efforts, as was the whole Natural History Society.

Thus began the attempt to take the protection of wildlife out of the hands of government departments and deliver it into those of an independent board of trustees, which would be able to accept support from international organizations in a way that a government department could not.

Dr. van Someren, who was then the curator of the Coryndon Memorial Museum, and his friend "Bus" Browne were also exceedingly active in support of the scheme. They had, at long last, succeeded in photographing and filming lion and rhino in the Lone Tree area, in what is now the Nairobi National Park, and were anxious that the first national park in East Africa should be on the site of what was then the Nairobi Commonage.

When I was a child, an outing to the commonage was one of the highlights of a visit to my Uncle George and Aunt Sibbie in Nairobi. Father and Uncle George would arrange to take Mother, my sisters, and me out to the plains just beyond the Nairobi railway station. We went in rickshaws, and that was where my love of wild animals and of all nature was born.

After the interruption of the war, and the temporary break in all such activities as wildlife preservation, the committee reassembled, and at the end of 1946 our objective was achieved. Colonel Cowie was chosen as the first national parks director, and many of us who had been his supporters in the campaign became founder trustees.

Nine

Soon after war was declared, it became clear that I could not possibly carry out all the different activities that were expected of me in Special Branch 6 of the CID. In addition to its other duties, the branch was now responsible for a good deal of censorship work. This meant that there had to be someone in authority permanently on duty at the headquarters in Nairobi to decide such matters as whether a letter of dubious content should be destroyed or excised in part, or whether the writer and the recipient should be put on a "suspect" list and kept under observation.

I put my problem before the head of the department, and as a result he appointed P. Wynn-Harris, the famous Himalayan mountain climber, to take charge of the work in Nairobi.

I had, in the meantime, trained a number of intelligence men and stationed them at strategic posts throughout the country. Selecting people for this work was not easy, but in the end I had ten full-time workers I could count on. The new arrangements gave me the time I needed to travel all over the country keeping up contact with this intelligence network. In addition, I had selected and appointed a number of what we called VIOs—voluntary intelligence officers. These were unpaid people who carried on their normal duties, whether as farm workers or secretaries, while at the same time keeping their ears open in bars and other public places in order to report anything that seemed to need investigation.

Early in 1940, I was also involved in helping to solve a crisis that developed at the Coryndon Memorial Museum. At one stage, it seemed possible that we might be forced to close the museum for the duration of the war.

At the beginning of the year, we still had the services of Peter Bally, the Swiss botanist, Donald MacInnes, the Cambridge zoologist, and Allen Turner—who had previously worked voluntarily but was now a full-time technician—all under the direction of the curator, Dr. van Someren. It was not long, however, before MacInnes was called up to join the armed forces, with special duties as a mosquito controller in military camps.

The crisis was now brought to a sudden head by an ultimatum presented to the trustees by Dr. van Someren: unless they asked Bally to resign forthwith, he himself would resign. The trustees, of whom I was one, told Dr. van Someren they could see no valid reason for terminating Bally's services. In consequence, Dr. van Someren tendered his resignation, and the trustees were left with no alternative but to accept it. Some members of the board now felt strongly that we should close the museum, since the staff was reduced to Bally and Turner, neither of whom had had any administrative experience whatsoever. Some of us were equally determined to try to keep going, especially because so many military personnel were moving into Kenya from other parts of the world and we felt that it was important for them to have access to a place where they could learn something of the natural history of their new surroundings.

After much discussion, I ultimately offered to resign from the board of trustees if I could be appointed honorary curator of the museum. I laid down two conditions: one, that I could occupy the curator's house in the museum grounds that had been vacated by Dr. van Someren, and, second, that I be permitted to find a suitable voluntary secretary, since we could not afford to pay one on a full-time basis. In this I was lucky. Kay Attwood, who was then the full-time paid secretary to the director of Veterinary Services in Nairobi and was a keen naturalist, volunteered to work with me in this capacity five evenings a week, from six to eight o'clock.

Thus, we were able to keep the museum open and even to develop it considerably during the war years. One of the changes I introduced was to open the museum to all members of the public. Previously, there had been an entry fee so high that it virtually excluded all Africans and most Asian members of the community. The museum, in fact, had virtually been "for whites only." I therefore suggested to the trustees that this situation should be altered forthwith, by allowing African adults to enter the museum for a fee of ten Kenya cents and Asians for a fee of fifty cents, while Europeans should pay a shilling. This proposal was accepted by the trustees, but at first there was a considerable outcry from the white population of Nairobi, followed by a temporary fall-off in the number of European visitors to the museum.

This was partly due to a feeling of pique. The museum was the first public institution to be opened to nonwhites, and the Europeans disliked the idea of viewing the exhibits side by side with Africans, who, they claimed, were "smelly," or Asians, who were "overscented." This situation, however, did not last long, and since we made the museum exhibits more attractive, we soon had more European visitors than ever before. This was mainly due, I believe, to my deliberate policy of arranging at least one new temporary exhibit every week of the year, an exhibit advertised in the local press by means of a small nature note. This note explained the special points of interest to be seen and studied in the week's special show at the museum.

I was very lucky with my staff, in that Peter Bally and Allen Turner both recruited a number of volunteer workers from among their friends, and this enabled us to attempt many innovations.

Extra troops, particularly from England and South Africa, were being moved into Kenya at this time as a precautionary measure against the possibility of the Italians' entering the war on Hitler's side. I made a special effort to encourage members of these forces to make use of the museum. To help them, we arranged for groups to be shown round by one of the staff whenever a special request for a guide was made.

In order to stimulate greater interest in the exhibits in the museum, I also arranged a monthly competition. For two days at the end of each month, we took ten exhibits that had been on view during the month in their own sections and placed them together in a case near the entrance of the main hall *without labels*. The object of the competition was to identify each of these ten specimens in as much detail as possible. Whoever submitted the best entry was given free admission to the museum for the whole of the following month.

It surprised me how few people could identify the unlabeled exhibits, in spite of having seen them on previous visits. It revealed a remarkable lack of observation. Gradually—and this was our objective—visitors to the museum began to read the labels more carefully and to remember the exhibits so that they could enter the competition with some hope of success. For example, many learned the difference between land crabs, shore crabs, and free-swimming crabs, or between a bird such as the spectacled weaver and a rather similar black-headed oriole. Consequently, they began to give more correct identifications, and some even earned bonus marks for giving the scientific names as well.

Once the Asian and African population of Nairobi came to realize that they were welcome at the museum, their numbers increased by leaps and bounds. This was very satisfactory. At first, although we made every possible effort to encourage schools of all races to bring their children on free museum tours, we found that they were not doing so. I therefore let it be known to teachers of all the schools in the neighborhood that they themselves could, by arrangement, be accompanied round the museum by a member of the staff, in order to learn about the exhibits before a class tour. They would then be in a much better position to answer the questions their pupils might ask them. This we found was a satisfactory arrangement, since we could not afford to employ a special school lecturer.

At about this time, Peter Bally married a young Austrian woman who was a musician by training, but also exhibited artistic talents. Naturally, she started going along with her husband on botanical collecting safaris, and I suggested that she learn to paint flowers, so as to initiate a collection of paintings of the flowering plants of Kenya for exhibition in the museum.

She was enthusiastic about this and began to teach herself to paint. In a remarkably short time she became an excellent botanical artist. In fact, she was so proficient that in due course she earned a gold medal from the Royal Horticultural Society— one of the highest available botanical awards—for her flower paintings. This artist, Joy Bally, will be known to most readers as Joy Adamson, who became famous for her books on lions, *Born Free, Living Free,* and others, which she wrote after her later marriage to game warden George Adamson.

Joy painted not only hundreds of flowers for the museum, but also a large collection of marine fishes, water colors that are now housed in the city hall at Mombasa. Later she undertook the task of painting hundreds of studies of the indigenous peoples of Kenya. These not only represented different types of Africans, but also were clearly recognizable portraits of named individuals wearing the traditional headdress and garments of their tribes. This collection of ethnographic paintings provides a wonderful record of the culture, clothing, ornaments, and way of life of the tribes of Kenya—a record of cultures that are fast disappearing as more and more of the country is overtaken by so-called civilization.

The museum suffered a great loss when Joy ceased to be its artist, but she has since done magnificent work in other fields and has made a great contribution to wildlife conservation through the books and films that commemorate her work with lions and cheetahs.

In 1940, I learned, accidentally, that the railway authorities were planning a realignment of the track to the east of Naivasha station. This meant that huge earthworks would be undertaken right along the edge of a cliff where we had located a number of sites in 1929. We had also discovered many Pleistocene beach levels in that area. I went immediately to see the general manager of the East African Railways and tried to persuade him to hold up the work, so as not to destroy these important sites. He was unable to accede to my request, since work had already started on other parts of the new alignment and had to be linked up through this area. However, after some discussion, he agreed that the railway would provide a sum of £400 for a rescue excavation before the bulldozers and other machinery were brought into the area.

I myself could not spare the time from my war work, but Mary at once undertook the task, and we managed to gather together sufficient members of our trained staff to work with her. The next problem was to find a base camp in the Naivasha area. Luckily, our museum technician, Allen Turner, had a small cottage on the shores of Lake Naivasha, which he immediately put at Mary's disposal. She was then able to live near the site, which became known as the Naivasha Railway Rock Shelter.

Owing to the limited amount of money available and the short time left to us before the bulldozers were due to come in, we were able to undertake only one very long trial trench. From the flats in front, this extended up the slope and into one of the

Louis Leakey at
Cambridge as an
undergraduate in
1926, when he was
reprimanded for
playing tennis
in this indecent
attire

In the 1930s

Louis with the man-eating crocodile he shot on Rusinga Island

An expedition in camp en route for Olduvai Gorge

The Masai elder whom Louis successfully treated
at Olduvai for an unhealed skull injury inflicted
by a spear many years before

A stone-walled dwelling with fireplace and circular seat in the
ruined town of Engaruka—a site the government had asked Louis to
investigate, but which proved to be of no great age

Prehistoric rock paintings in the Kisese/Cheke area of Tanzania—
Louis and an African assistant prepare a tracing of a painting

Steen Cottage, Great Munden, Hertfordshire, where Louis lived in
1936 while writing and doing research on his discoveries in East
Africa—at the front door, the Model A Ford brought back from Kenya
across the Sahara by Sir Vivian Fuchs

One of the female burials with pestle and mortar in the Neolithic
communal cemetery at Nakuru that Mary excavated while Louis was
working with tribal elders on his Kikuyu book

Louis with members of the first Pan African Congress on Prehistory at Olorgesailie, where the Leakeys had uncovered one of the richest known deposits of early Stone Age tools

Louis and Mary at Olorgesailie at the time of the congress

Olduvai Gorge, the 300-foot-thick lake sediments where the Leakeys have made so many important discoveries relating to early man

main shelters. In this way we were able to obtain full details of the various occupation and cultural levels that were present.

When Mary took on this assignment she had no idea what a major undertaking it was to be. That single trial trench yielded over 75,000 finished artifacts, together with over 2 million waste flakes and other *débitage!* All of this had to be classified, marked, catalogued, and later studied. Fortunately, Mary was able to enlist the help of two friends, Mrs. Madeleine Worthington and Mrs. Millicent Ellis, to help her in this gigantic task.

The lowest levels of the site yielded cultural material similar to that of the middle part of the basal occupation of Gamble's Cave II at Elmenteita, which I and my team had excavated in 1929. The upper levels were very different and represented a continuation of the so-called Kenya Capsian into later stages than we had found hitherto.

Whenever possible I went to Naivasha to join Mary and give her a hand in the evenings with the sorting of specimens.

Some months after the excavations were completed, Superintendent Poppy, of the CID, and I were in Naivasha on duty, and we took the opportunity to visit the site one evening. The railway engineers had already begun to build up the embankment and had taken the soil to do so from two large borrow pits. We were examining these when Poppy noticed some fragments of human skull in one of them. The specimen had been slightly damaged by the earth-moving machinery, but we were able to collect most of the fragments.

We were unable to persuade the railway management to stop all work, but they did agree to delay action in this one area for about ten days, so as to give us a chance to see what else could be recovered. We immediately set some of our trained staff to work, and in due course we assembled an almost complete fossilized skull and most of the skeleton of an aged female associated with the Kenya Capsian culture. The bones lay scattered over an area of about 12,000 square feet, at a single level, in shallow lake beds lying beneath an ancient beach gravel. It appeared that either this individual had been drowned or the body had been thrown into the shallow lake waters, where the bones were then dragged over a wide area by fish presumably feeding on the rotting flesh. (This skeleton has since been dated at 10,850 ± 330 B.P. by radiocarbon.)

Superintendent Poppy, who found the original fragments of skull, became very interested in our search and spent many hours helping us during those ten days. He found it refreshing to go back in time through thousands of years to look for the fossil remains of a long-deceased person. It was a change from his usual pursuits in search of clues to the cause of a more recent death.

At about this time, I became involved in a number of curious incidents linked with the King's African Rifles and other units of the armed forces. This was owing to my anthropological background and knowledge of some of the local languages. While most of the British officers who were in charge of training were first-class men in the military sense, they had little knowledge of Africans and their customs, beliefs, and psychology. Consequently, again and again they found themselves in difficulties with their men.

One of the incidents I was called in to disentangle concerned a sergeant major of the Luo tribe who had been detailed to help with the training of new recruits. He had become extremely popular with the officers at the training camp, and in the circumstances it was not surprising that when he asked for leave of absence on compassionate grounds, to "go bury his father," his request was immediately granted, in spite of the fact that it was an awkward moment to release him. The sergeant duly went off and buried his father, and then returned to duty.

He had been back for only a few days when he again went to the senior officer and asked for three more days' leave of absence, on compassionate grounds, to go to Nyanza Province to "bury his father." This request seemed wholly unreasonable, but since the commanding officer thought that there was possibly some ceremony that the man had not completed, he let him go. A few weeks after the sergeant returned from again "burying his father," he requested compassionate leave for the third time to "bury his father."

Now the commanding officer was extremely annoyed and demanded a full explanation. The man replied that his father had died two days previously and that he, as the eldest son, must take charge of the funeral rites. The officer replied, "But you buried your father six weeks ago, and then again a few days after that." The Luo sergeant tried to explain. "Yes, but that was not the father that I am going to bury now. I have to go to bury my *new* father." The officer was completely bewildered by this and concluded that the man thought he had discovered a good way of getting repeated leaves of absence to which he was not entitled. Indeed, there was thought of punishing him. However, the officer decided to seek advice before taking such action, and I was detailed by the Special Branch to investigate.

The man's claim turned out to be true. Among the Luo, as in many other tribes, as soon as a man's physical father dies another male relative becomes *de jure* his father. In the case of the sergeant major, it happened that there had been an epidemic in his home area. First of all, his real physical father had died. Then two successive uncles—who had, in turn, become his "father"—died one after the other of the same disease. Since the sergeant major was the senior "son," required by custom to take charge of the funeral rites, the family could not proceed with the ceremonies unless he was present to lead them. Fortunately, I was able to explain all this to his puzzled officer, and all was well. (So far as I know, although a fourth legal "father" took the place of the third, he did not succumb to the same epidemic as his predecessors had.)

There was another strange occasion when an officer at a military camp near Mount Kenya, exceedingly well liked by all his NCOs and men, suddenly found himself shunned and avoided. The young officer was very disturbed by this situation, but he could offer no explanation to his seniors. So far as he knew, he had done nothing that could possibly have upset his men.

The morale of the whole camp was going to pieces. The only explanation, given by one of the African sergeant majors to the commanding officer, was that Lieutenant X had "put a curse on all the men in his company," and that unless the commanding officer dismissed him, the men wished to be transferred to some other unit.

The matter became so serious that the Special Branch of CID was asked if it would send somebody to look into the problem. Strictly speaking, it was a job not for civil but for military intelligence; in the circumstances, however, I was asked if I would take on the task.

Accordingly, I arrived in the camp one evening, and after

having drinks at sundown, I dined in the officers' mess. When dinner was over the commanding officer took me aside and told me all he knew of the events leading up to the isolation of the young lieutenant, how—suddenly, with no warning, and for no apparent reason—the men in his company had turned against him and were terrified in his presence.

Next morning I asked if I could talk to some of the NCOs. I interviewed them one at a time, and in each case their evidence was the same. They all stated that Lieutenant X had most unfortunately laid a curse on members of his company. When, eventually, I gained their true confidence, they proceeded to explain in detail just what had happened.

It seemed that on a certain late afternoon, when crossing the parade ground along a footpath that ran diagonally across it, the lieutenant had stood for a short time conversing amicably with a small group of his men. While talking he had idly drawn his stick through the dust across the track and then had turned round and walked away "mumbling to himself." Here was the explanation. I knew only too well that the act of drawing a line across a footpath and then naming a person represented an extremely serious curse, which was greatly feared. From the anonymity of the curse, the lieutenant's men had presumed that he wished them all to suffer, and their faith in him had been destroyed. They had not dared to explain to the commanding officer why they were frightened, since they were sure they would be ridiculed.

Having heard and understood the full story, I explained to the commanding officer exactly what had caused the state of tension in the camp. I told him that the only way to put things right was to persuade the lieutenant to go through a ceremony that would remove the curse he had so inadvertently invoked.

Next day the troops were paraded and I spoke to them in Swahili, with the officers in charge, the NCOs, and the lieutenant all present. I told them I understood that they were all afraid a curse had been put upon them by Lieutenant X—to which they all shouted *ndio,* the Swahili word for "yes." I then took the lieutenant aside and had him come with me to point out the approximate place on the pathway where he had stood when talking to his men. I had him take the same stick that he had used before and, very solemnly, draw another line across the dust in the footpath. After this I told him to get down on his knees and deliberately wipe out the line with his hands, at the same time saying out loud, "I hereby remove the curse I put upon the people." It was as simple as that.

There was a great shout of joy from the assembled company, and from that moment the morale in the camp returned to normal and all was well again. In a brief speech, I then hastened to explain to the men that the lieutenant had never intended to put a curse upon any of them. He simply had not known that the act of drawing such a line could be taken as placing a curse, and he was most distressed to have caused them so much anguish.

At a much later date during the war, an incident occurred that was in this same general category and may as well be described here. It actually happened after the Italians had been defeated in Eritrea and Ethiopia, at the time when the men of the King's African Rifles were preparing to go overseas to fight in Burma and Malaya. A battalion drawn mainly from the Kamba tribe—which had long provided some of the best and most distinguished recruits for the KAR—had been specially chosen to be in the first contingent to fight against the Japanese, and the men had been granted three weeks' embarkation leave. Most of them came from a single small district of Kamba country. At the conclusion of their leave a large proportion of the contingent did not return to duty. Their ship was due to sail shortly from Mombasa, and there was much to do in the way of final preparations and briefings. Moreover, quite apart from the nuisance value of their failure to return, the fact that they were absent without leave during wartime constituted a very grave offense.

One of the military intelligence officers sent for an elder of the Kamba tribe who lived in Nairobi and asked him if he could offer any explanation. He merely replied that, in all probability, the wives and the parents-in-law of the men in question were responsible for their absence. It had, in the meantime, been noted that all of those who had failed to return from leave were newly married men.

I was asked by my opposite number in military intelligence if

I would go down to the area of Kamba country where the missing young soldiers lived and try to uncover the reasons behind their failure to return to duty.

I knew that in certain clans of the Kamba tribe a young man, in order to beget a first-class child, was expected to have sexual intercourse with his wife during the second half of her menstrual flow, as well as when the flow was over. The young soldiers concerned in this incident were, in most cases, educated, or at least literate, and they no longer believed in what they considered to be the old wives' tales of an earlier generation. Their brides, however, were mostly uneducated girls, as were their relatives-in-law. The latter adamantly adhered to the belief that if the wife of one of these soldiers was not already pregnant, then it was his bounden duty, before sailing away to fight in a far country at the risk of losing his life, to ensure not only that his young wife became pregnant, but, even more important, that her pregnancy would result in a child of really first-class quality. (It was known that intercourse during the latter part of the menstrual flow was not vital to conception, but it was considered essential, in order to beget a first-class child, that conception follow intercourse in which the blood of the menstrual flow of the mother was mixed with the "brain fluid" —semen—of the father.)

Consequently, those soldiers whose wives were already pregnant had returned to duty at the appointed time, as had those whose wives happened to have their menstrual period sufficiently early in their husbands' twenty-one-day leave. But in those cases where neither condition applied, both the wife and her family had insisted that the husband await her menstrual period and fulfill his obligations before going overseas. A further problem then arose. Once a young soldier had overstayed his leave, he felt that he might just as well be punished for a long absence as for a short one. He would therefore extend his leave still more, until, finally, he was afraid to return to camp at all.

Having learned all this, I returned to Nairobi and explained the situation to my opposite number in military intelligence. He, in turn, informed those in charge of the troops going overseas, and an envoy was sent to explain to the offenders that the authorities understood why they had gone absent without leave and that those who returned forthwith would not be punished. As far as I remember, all except one then returned to camp.

Yet another incident, which occurred still later in the war, is part of the same story of how easily misunderstandings can arise between white man and black man. It is linked with the return from overseas of a detachment of King's African Rifles that had been fighting in Burma and Malaya. In this case, they were young soldiers of the Kipsigis tribe, in the Nandi Hills area.

Most of these young men had seen active service. Even those who had not killed a man in a hand-to-hand engagement (and, therefore, had no proof of having taken human life) had nevertheless taken part in the fighting and so, presumably, had killed one or more of their opponents. Among the Kipsigis, at that time, a warrior who had killed an enemy in battle was not allowed to sleep with or even touch his wife, or to have any kind of sexual relations with any other woman of his own tribe, until he had undergone a two-week purification ceremony. This was an unbreakable rule, and the elders insisted that every young man returning from the war stay away from the villages and live in the fields until he had been purified.

The returning soldiers, after getting back to their base camp in Nairobi, were usually given about three weeks' leave. They had to travel, often for two days, to reach their families, where they were then informed that they must not, under any circumstances, go to their homes and visit their wives or sweethearts without first finding a witch doctor prepared to undertake the ceremony of purification. It was hardly surprising, therefore, that many of them overstayed their leaves. I imagine that most Europeans in a similar situation would have done the same. This was one of the problems I was detailed to solve. Once the Kipsigis chiefs had revealed the facts of the matter to me, I was able to explain the situation to the authorities, and special arrangements were made whereby the chiefs tried to accelerate the purification ceremony. The men were also given an extra ten days of leave to spend with their wives or sweethearts before returning to duty.

Another of my civilian pursuits proved very useful for war work. From an early age I had been interested in birds. Indeed, until I was almost thirteen my mind was made up that when I grew up I was going to be an ornithologist. Then, as I have already described in my earlier *White African,* I read two books, *Days Before History* and Lyell's *Geological Evidence of the Antiquity of Man,* and as a result I decided to become a prehistorian. Nevertheless, I have always retained a keen interest in bird life, and birds have remained my second love.

When I took over the task of honorary curator of the museum in 1940, working at night, I found to my dismay that certain groups of birds, and especially the birds of prey, were very inadequately represented in the study collections. My genuine interest in birds now proved a useful cover for my intelligence work, since whenever I took a shotgun into an area where I was involved in trying to extract information about fifth-column activities, I could quite honestly describe myself as a museum man collecting specimens. This frequently gave me an excellent reason for remaining in an area as long as I wished without arousing suspicion. By day I did my ornithological collecting, and during the evenings I made discreet inquiries among the local people. I found too that it was much easier to get people to come and talk to me about matters on which I wanted information while I was actually out in the bush collecting and observing birds than had I been making official inquiries. I was just regarded as a rather mad white man interested in birds!

It was during one of these trips that I located the first nest I had ever seen of the rare Verreaux's eagle. It was built on a towering cliff on Lukenia Hill, on the edge of Kamba country, and I watched the pair of birds it belonged to then and on many subsequent occasions. After they ceased to visit the cliff ledge, I saw some juvenile eagles—which I presumed to be their offspring—use the same rocks as a resting point. I have seen a Verreaux's eagle nest on only one other occasion—on a cliff near Lake Elmenteita.

My genuine interest in watching the eagles gave me a wonderful excuse for remaining in the vicinity—where I was also engaged in some intelligence work. I felt quite certain that someone in the area was dissuading young men from joining the army. While I bird-watched, all sorts of people, from elders to herd boys and even women collecting firewood, would come and sit near me. As often as I could, I turned the conversation round to the question of the war and the need for volunteers for the army. In this way, I finally learned why so few young men from the area were enlisting: they were being told by a woman "prophetess" of great renown that if they did so, and were sent for service overseas, they would never return. Thus she dissuaded many from joining up. Eventually, we were able to prove that the "prophetess" was engaged in subversive activities and was in the employ of a fifth-column agent in Nairobi.

As well as gathering valuable information by chatting with the local people while I watched the Verreaux's eagles, I also located a series of Late Stone Age living sites belonging to the Kenya Wilton culture. After the war, Mary and I, with the assistance of several students, excavated one of these.

Just before the Italians came into the war, the authorities decided that a show of the ostensible military strength in the country would be a good idea. A march through the city of Nairobi was therefore planned to enable the people to see for themselves what armed forces were available for their defense. We knew, of course, who some of the Italian agents were and that they would all be watching this display and making reports. The march was to include a number of units that had recently arrived from South Africa, contingents from the local King's African Rifles, and representatives of other branches of the services. It was arranged that they should all march down Government Road and then proceed down what was formerly called Delamere Avenue toward the War Memorial, where the governor would take the salute. What we did not announce was that the same units would march round the route several times.

I was among those delegated to keep an eye out for a suspected Italian agent, who would almost certainly be reporting our military strength. Sure enough, I saw him writing down notes as hard as he could while the troops marched past—completely unaware that he was recording the same units marching by several times over! Subsequently, when our forces invaded Ethiopia and the Italians were on the verge of defeat, his report was one of those that were recovered. In it he recorded a far greater number of armed forces in Kenya than we had at that time or at any future date!

Sometimes it was difficult not to feel sorry for the Italian agents. They were exceedingly gullible, and we found it was very easy to feed them all kinds of false information, which they swallowed wholesale.

Ten

As it became increasingly obvious that Mussolini would shortly declare war, a number of leading Italians began to leave their homes in Kenya and head for Mogadishu in Somaliland, which was the nearest Italian port. Or they went to Mombasa, where they boarded a small Italian steamer that was in the harbor. Ostensibly it was held up unloading cargo, but actually its departure was being deliberately delayed from day to day to enable these upcountry families to join the ship.

As soon as the British authorities in Kenya were informed that Italy had, in fact, entered the war, the Italians still remaining in the country were rounded up and brought to Nairobi. I, as well as most of my CID colleagues, was mainly concerned with locating nonwhite Italian supporters, such as Somalis deriving from Italian Somaliland, and Italian half-castes. The regular police force was responsible for bringing in the Italian families who were still in Kenya, many of whom were highly indignant at this treatment, claiming that our information must be incorrect and our actions illegal. They maintained that there were two more days before war would be declared and that they were packing up to leave for Mombasa to catch the boat. The general opinion among them was that Il Duce would never let them down by failing to give them adequate warning to get out of Kenya.

Nevertheless, in spite of their protests, they were picked up and taken to Nairobi, where our task for the next few days was to sort out those we thought were dangerous and should be held in detention camps from those we considered harmless enough to be allowed to return to their farms, on condition that they not interfere in any way with the war effort. We knew quite well that many of them were definitely so anti-Mussolini that they could be trusted not to enter into any subversive political activities. And it was, in fact, much easier to let them go back to their farms than to look after them ourselves.

For some time, even in the days before war was declared against Germany, the authorities had had reason to believe that a small element within the African political organization known at the time as the Kikuyu Central Association, or KCA, had been subverted by agents of Italian origin and was working actively for the fifth column against the British government.

As soon as the Italians entered the war, the headquarters of the KCA was raided and the organization declared illegal. Whether it was a wise move at this stage to ban the whole organization is not for me to judge, but on looking back I cannot help thinking that it was probably a mistake, in spite of the fact that the raid yielded documents of a subversive nature.

I think it is doubtful that the members of the KCA as a whole were aware of what a few were doing. If the association had been allowed to remain in being, I feel that most of its members would have remained loyal to the British. As it was, the arrest of the leaders and the closing down of the organization created a good deal of anti-British feeling in an influential section of the population. From the evidence that was obtained during the raid, however, it was clear that a small element within the KCA was trying to subvert army personnel and chiefs from their duty to the British government.

The unenviable task of sorting through the many thousands of documents that were captured during the KCA raid fell to me and a few trusted helpers. Most of the papers were quite obviously innocuous, but a few that had been found hidden away or had been accidentally left behind were distinctly incriminating.

It was at this time that it became known to the Kenya government authorities that while I was at Cambridge I had—as a sideline to my other studies—studied the elements of handwriting. This was not included in my official curriculum, but was undertaken as a matter of personal interest. At the time I was studying mediaeval French; as I have described in *White African,* during lectures on the latter subject my professor would sometimes declare that a particular emendation of a passage was not in the hand of the original author, but had been added subsequently by somebody else. I disliked having to rely on my professor's opinion in such matters and was determined to find out how I could decide the truth myself. Hence my study of handwriting. I should make it clear that I had no interest in handwriting as a possible means of character interpretation, but used it simply to identify the writer of a piece of script.

In Kenya, during the war, the study I had devoted to handwriting identification proved very useful. When we were sorting through the papers in the headquarters office of the Kikuyu Central Association, we found a number of unsigned, handwritten documents of a subversive nature, and it was part of my task to try to determine who was responsible for having written them. There were also many papers signed by members of the headquarters staff, as well as by people in charge of the countrywide system of branches. This gave me adequate comparative material to discover, on the basis of handwriting studies, who the authors of the anonymous documents were.

Before embarking on this task, I decided that it would be necessary to refresh my knowledge of handwriting. Fortunately, I still had my original notebooks, and I also obtained from the law courts library several modern textbooks dealing with the study of handwriting in relation to forgery and anonymous letters.

After bringing myself up to date, I began working on all the documents, with a view to identifying the writers of the few that interested the authorities. Eventually, I was in a position to give evidence before a government tribunal as to the authors of some, but not all, of the subversive documents.

Thus began my long career as a handwriting expert, principally with the CID, to whom I was responsible for all my examinations of suspected forgeries and anonymous letters.

In addition to handwriting identification, I also trained myself to identify unsigned typewritten documents. It is usually possible to identify any given make of typewriter fairly quickly, since there are differences in the typefaces of various makes. Over the years, moreover, most typewriter manufacturers have made minor changes in typeface at different times. It is thus possible to give the approximate date of the manufacture of the machine on which a particular document has been typed, and sometimes even the model.

Another interesting fact about typewriters is that after a machine has been used for some time it usually develops its own special peculiarities. This, in turn, makes it possible to pick out the very machine on which a particular document has been typed, once certain basic facts have been established.

Also, once an investigator has found the typewriter on which a document has been typed, it is nearly always possible to establish which of the persons having access to that machine typed the specimen in question. No two people ever exert exactly the same amount of pressure on the different keys. To identify the typist of a document, it is usually sufficient to have each of the people who had access to the machine in question type a few lines.

I can recall one particularly interesting example of an investigation of this nature that I carried out. A wealthy trader at Uplands, near Limuru, brought the CID an anonymous typewritten letter, threatening him with death if he failed to carry out certain instructions. The letter was passed to me with a request that I trace it to its origin and submit a report, so that action could be taken.

Fortunately, the threatened man had also brought the envelope in which the letter had come to him through the post. My first step, therefore, was to see what it could tell me. It was an ordinary business envelope with a transparent window, of the kind normally used for sending out statements, and had not been sealed. Examination showed that it had a typewritten address and that it had been date-stamped first at the Ruiru post office and subsequently forwarded through the Kiambu post office. I therefore had three different places to investigate— Uplands, where the letter was received; Kiambu, where it had been postmarked the second time; and Ruiru, where it had been originally mailed.

Accordingly, I went first of all to Uplands and interviewed the man who had received the threatening letter. I discovered from him that he had recently quarreled over an important business transaction with a person who lived in Kiambu. On being further questioned, he admitted that this particular person might hate him enough to threaten his life. He then gave me the name and address of the person concerned. However, I decided not to go immediately and interview this man, but to wait until I had made further inquiries.

Since the envelope had first gone through the Ruiru post

office, I went to the postal authorities there and asked for permission to examine every letter with a typewritten address currently in the post office, to enable me to check on what make of typewriter had been used in each case. It was a tiny post office, and since most of the letters passing through it were written by nonbusiness people, there were relatively few with typed addresses. After a few days, I had found several envelopes that had been addressed on the same typewriter as the threatening letter. I noted the addresses of the people to whom these letters were being sent and went to see them. I asked each of them for the name of the firm or individual from whom the letter had come. Before long I discovered that each of the letters in which I was interested had been sent from a single commercial firm in Ruiru. I felt I was making considerable progress.

My next step was to visit the managing director of this firm, explain my business to him, and ask to be allowed to examine all the typewriters in use within his organization and to type a few lines on each myself. In a very short time I was able to identify the machine on which the envelopes I had found in the Ruiri post office—as well as the envelope in which the threatening letter had been sent—must have been typed. I was making good progress.

Once I was certain I had found the incriminating typewriter, I asked the managing director to let me see the employees who had access to this machine in the ordinary course of their work. I then asked each of these in turn to type a brief statement for me on this machine.

As I expected, the sample produced by one of the employees was identical in key pressure to that of the threatening letter itself. I now knew that I had pinpointed the person responsible for the typing, at least. It was still not certain, however, that this man had actually drafted the threatening letter, since it was always possible that he had merely typed it at the request of somebody else. Only at this stage did I ask the employee's name. To my delight, but not surprise, he was the man whom the Uplands businessman had told me about.

I took my written report to the CID offices, and after the attorney general reviewed the file the police obtained a search warrant for the premises of the suspect. As the investigating officer, I accompanied them. We hoped, of course, that we might find a carbon copy of the threatening letter in the suspect's possession, or even, perhaps, a rough handwritten draft, but in this we were unsuccessful. I was so certain, however, of my findings that I recommended that the police officer give the suspect the official warning and then take a written statement from him. He denied all knowledge of the letter, but the case against him was strong enough for him to be arrested and taken to Nairobi. Next day he was brought before the courts and committed for trial. In due course, the Supreme Court found him guilty.

There was an interesting sequel to this case. A few months later, I received a very touching letter from the convicted man, then serving his sentence. He wrote to say that he wished me to know I had been correct in charging that he was the author of the letter, and he hoped I would forgive him. He also wanted me to know that he intended to earn remission of part of his sentence by behaving well in prison and that he would never again attempt to do anything so wicked or so foolish.

When he was released from prison, he actually sought me out at my home and thanked me for having prevented him from committing murder. Apparently, at one time he had genuinely intended to carry out his threat.

There are very few handwriting specialists in the world concerned with criminal investigations, and the introduction of the ball-point pen has greatly complicated their work. A few years ago, when the split-nib pen was in common use, it was possible to tell a great deal from pen pressure, pen position, and shading. Anything written with a split-nib pen reveals all kinds of information as a result of these three characteristics.

With the introduction of the ball-point pen, it was necessary to work out new methods of identification. I carried out a great deal of investigation on my own to discover what could be done when a ball-point pen had been used. The few experts in Europe and America who were also concerned with detecting forgeries and other crimes linked with handwriting were doing the same. Gradually, we realized that we must pay more and more attention to the minor idiosyncrasies that each person shows in his or her writing. This makes our work very much more difficult when we are investigating a single forged signature, but fairly easy with a longer document, such as a threatening letter or one of a subversive nature.

Among the minor idiosyncrasies of a personal nature that one looks for is the way in which the writer dots his *i*'s. The position and nature of the dot over the *i* and also how a person crosses his *t*'s and whether he crosses them in different ways according to where they occur in a word are always significant. Then again, one looks for the details of the form and method used in connecting one letter with another, as well as whether the writer uses link lines between letters in *all* words or whether he uses them only between certain letters or in certain situations. For example, some people divide longer words into two parts with a pen lift instead of a link line. Another common idiosyncrasy is using a different form of the same letter depending on whether it occurs at the beginning of a word, in the middle, at the end, or combined with certain other letters. Many people write *h* one way when it starts a word and is followed by a vowel, as in "hear," but quite differently when it is preceded or followed by a *t*, as in "thoughtful," or when it comes at the end of a word, as in "high." The same can be said about nearly every other consonant.

In order for me to use such idiosyncrasies as a means of identifying handwriting, I found it necessary to collect and classify many thousands of handwritten envelopes addressed to persons in Nairobi or other places, where the same letters, combinations of letters, and whole words were present. I also collected letters from many of my friends to see what personal idiosyncrasies gave away the identity of the writer. In the end, I discovered that the study of personal idiosyncrasies was less misleading than the old system of pen position, pen pressure, and shading—chiefly because people could disguise the latter deliberately, but seldom attempted to hide the former, of which they were unaware.

It often happens in handwriting investigations that one spends many hours working on a document, yet finally has to report that, unfortunately, it is not possible to identify the writer with certainty. Again and again, one will say it is probable that X or Y wrote a particular signature or document—but that this cannot be proved in a court of law.

A problem that complicated my use of personal idiosyncrasies for handwriting identification lay in the fact that at the time I was working out this new process, there were relatively few teachers in Kenya. In consequence, the pupils of any one school often developed remarkably similar handwriting, derived from the handwriting of their teacher. At first glance, the writing of a large number of pupils looked very much alike. In countries where literacy goes back many hundreds of years, this problem arises less often because the handwriting of most children is influenced as much by their parents as by their teachers. Children from many schools in Africa, although they can write, practically never have occasion to do so except in school.

In Kenya and elsewhere, a large number of the cases involving forgery and other handwriting crimes are investigated initially at police stations in the districts, removed from CID headquarters. Naturally enough, the officers like, if possible, to handle the preliminary investigations themselves and arrest suspects quickly, without first referring the matter to headquarters. The fact that the writing of pupils from the same school is so often superficially similar makes this a dangerous practice. On more than one occasion, I have known cases in which the police have arrested a completely innocent man because his handwriting bore a superficial similarity to that of the real offender.

The study of handwriting for legal purposes is a fascinating subject, and one with which I have been concerned since 1940. It was one of my official duties in the CID from 1940 to 1945; when I became the full-time curator of the museum in Nairobi late in 1946, the CID retained me as its handwriting expert, to be called upon whenever there was a case that required investigation. This often meant working on cases at night. I suppose that over the years I have investigated more than a thousand handwriting cases, only about a quarter of which were ever sufficiently clear-cut to take to court. When I ceased to be retained by the CID, I still continued to undertake handwriting work from time to time, especially for the civil courts. My last important case was in 1967, but as recently as 1968 I found myself investigating a case on my own account. It was important only to the accused and her husband. Owing to the faulty knowledge of the police "expert," a miscarriage of justice was imminent, but I managed to show up the mistake.

In the early part of 1941, soon after I took over the running of the Coryndon Memorial Museum as honorary curator, Mary and I spent many of our evenings in the museum. Consequently, we moved into the wood-and-iron bungalow that had been occupied by Dr. van Someren when he was curator. The building was on the land that had been made available to the museum's trustees in 1939, and it was very near the back entrance to the museum. It was one of the few remaining houses dating back to the earliest days of Nairobi. It had been put up by the administration for John Ainsworth when he was provincial commissioner of Nairobi and the adjoining districts. Later it was taken over by C. W. Hobley, who became provincial commissioner after Ainsworth and then chief native commissioner.

Both Ainsworth and Hobley had been closely linked, in the early days, with the East African and Uganda Natural History Society. It was, therefore, appropriate that the bungalow they had both used should be situated on land now belonging to the museum's trustees and adjacent to the new headquarters of the society. Ainsworth and, to a lesser extent, Hobley had been very interested in indigenous trees and had planted a large number of local slow-growing trees, such as *Podocarpus* and croton, in the grounds. Ainsworth had also planted a variety of exotic trees, such as jacaranda, pepper, and bougainvillaea. By the time Mary and I moved in, the bungalow was surrounded by trees and exotic plants. These attracted a wealth of bird life, and it was a real joy to wake up in the morning and hear their dawn chorus.

The bungalow lay within the municipality of Nairobi, and, fortunately, the museum board of trustees had persuaded the government to grant the whole fifteen acres surrounding it to them, so that the land could not be built upon except by the museum and its associated organizations.

The outside walls and roof of the bungalow were of corrugated iron, which, in the course of time, had become badly rusted and now needed a coat of paint. The inside walls and ceilings were made of half-inch match boarding six inches wide. Over the years a number of holes had developed in the walls, some at floor level, giving rats and mice access to the rooms from the gap between the outer and inner walls. There were also holes higher up the walls, in which spiders and other insects took refuge whenever we chased them.

At the time we moved in, there were two small swarms of bees living between the inner and outer walls, in two different parts of the building. There was also a much larger swarm engaged in constructing a honeycomb under the roof, above the ceiling. The floorboards had been perforated by termites in several places, and although we succeeded in freeing these areas of the pests by spraying paraffin down the holes, nevertheless the holes were still present underneath the covering of rough rush matting.

One evening, when Mary and I were having supper, we heard a buzzing noise developing in our bedroom and went to investigate. We found that tens of thousands of biting ants, known as "safari ants," or *siafu* in Swahili, had invaded the room through the holes in the floor. They had then entered the space between the outer and inner walls and were swarming up to raid the honey and grubs in one of the bees' nests. By the time we arrived on the scene, the battle was in full swing and the noise was terrific. Hundreds of bees were flying out from the holes in the upper level of the wall, carrying with them dead safari ants, which they dropped onto the floor. Meanwhile, thousands more ants were moving up between the walls to the honeycomb. We watched for a few minutes and then left the combatants to their own devices, hoping that the contest would be over by morning. Meanwhile we slept in the spare room.

In the morning, we found thousands of dead ants lying all over the room, though we could not see a single dead bee—and the battle was still going on. We were very interested in the fact that there were no dead bees. When a human being is stung, either the bee is hastily brushed off, leaving its sting and little poison sac behind in its victim—after which the insect quickly dies—or the bee is crushed against the body of the victim and killed. In either case, the sting remains temporarily in the victim's flesh. Even when one tries to pull the sting out with a thumb and fingernail, in the process the whole of the contents of the poison sac is squeezed farther into the body, which is very painful.

As a youth, I had spent a great deal of time with my friend Gicuru, who initiated me in the art of beekeeping. I learned from him never to try to pull out a bee sting with my fingers. The proper method, after lightly brushing the bee from the body, is to scrape the sting from the flesh with the flat side or the back of a knife blade. In this way, the sting can be pulled out without injecting additional poison into the wound.

Obviously, when the bees in our house attacked and stung the safari ants they must have quickly withdrawn their stings and then been ready to carry on with the work of stinging other ants.

The fantastic battle raged for two whole days, and in the end the safari ants gave up the unequal struggle. So far as we could tell, they got nothing for their pains—neither grubs nor honey— and suffered a very considerable loss to their armies. This was the only time I have seen these ants defeated. In a later chapter, I will tell how these vicious little insects returned to our house and attacked our son Jonathan.

Late in 1940 I had to visit the Venerable Archdeacon W. E. Owen's district, in northwestern Kenya, to arrange for listening points for the Luo- and Swahili-language news broadcasts we were then beginning to organize. I had let him know in advance that I would be coming, and he invited me to stay with him in his new house at N'giya. I think the circumstances that led to my friendship with Owen are worthy of record, because he became a serious fossil collector.

As far back as 1929, when we were excavating at Gamble's Cave 2 at Elmenteita, one of my students—Mrs. Cecely Creasy —went for a holiday to visit friends at Kisumu, on the shore of Lake Victoria. While there she met Archdeacon Owen. He belonged to the Church Missionary Society and, although a devout Christian, was a freethinker, who did not accept all the dogmas and doctrines of his church. One evening, when Cecely Creasy was having dinner with him and his wife, she began to tell them about our work at Gamble's Cave. The Archdeacon became more and more intrigued and gradually less skeptical of the idea that human beings had been present in East Africa some 25,000 years ago. Most of his colleagues at the table, on the other hand, maintained that Archbishop Ussher's date of 4004 B.C. for the creation was the only one a Christian was entitled to accept.

This difference of opinion presented a challenge to Owen, and he took up the cudgels on behalf of Cecely Creasy.

From that moment, he started hunting for artifacts and fossils all over the north and central Nyanza areas, of which he was the archdeacon in charge. From 1934 onwards, he acquired a considerable collection of artifacts and fossils, and he twice visited us at Gamble's Cave, and once at Hyrax Hill, to learn more about our work in prehistory.

I had a most interesting time when I stayed with him in 1940. He had discovered widespread evidence, around N'giya, of the culture that was known at the time in the Congo as Tumbian (now called Sangoan), but that had not been previously recorded in East Africa. He had also found some handaxe sites, probably of Acheulean age, on the Yala River, as well as a fossil bed at a site called Ombo, on the Kavirondo Gulf. The few specimens of fossils he showed me from this particular site suggested that the deposits might be of Lower Miocene age. He also showed me some of the fossils he had recently recovered from the island of Maboko, in the Kavirondo Gulf.

Some years previously, he had heard that there were fossils on this island from fishermen who had made a small clearing there and built a fishing village, in spite of the fact that the island was infested with tsetse flies. At the time of my visit, he had recently gone over from the mainland and collected some fossils from a small eroded area he had found in the middle of the island.

Just before the Italians entered the war, I sent MacInnes, from the museum, to join Owen and dig a small trial trench on Maboko. The fossils they found on that occasion were then brought back to Nairobi.

Among the fossils Owen had found previously was a small fragment of an elephant tooth, quite unlike the *Mastodon* teeth found by MacInnes during his later excavation. There was also a part of a femur that looked very much as though it represented a higher primate, possibly *Proconsul*. Other specimens included remains of an exceedingly interesting creature with deerlike "antlers." MacInnes found some further examples of this and brought them to Nairobi. He studied these later and described them as a new species of deerlike creature—*Climacocerus*. (But they eventually proved to belong to a relative of the giraffe.) Owen kindly allowed me to take some of his specimens to Nairobi, where MacInnes was writing a report, in his spare time, on a variety of *Proconsul* material. He would not let me have the *Proconsul* femur; eventually, he sold it to the British Museum of Natural History in London.

When Mary and I visited Archdeacon and Mrs. Owen during 1944, he drew our attention to some potsherds he had found while searching for Tumbian (Sangoan) artifacts. While we were out with him visiting one of the sites, called Urewe, where Middle Sangoan artifacts had been found, we discovered an area where quantities of potsherds were lying on the erosion slope. When we examined these we found a most interesting and unusual feature: every pot base found had a small, clearly defined hollow on the exterior, forming a central "dimple"; this feature had not been recorded in any other pottery. Archdeacon Owen then found this same pottery, associated with iron weapons and tools, at a number of other sites in the area. The same pottery has since been found widely distributed in central and eastern Africa. It has been dated by radiocarbon to the early part of the first millennium A.D. and is thought to represent one of the earliest Bantu iron-using migrations.

Archdeacon Owen's health rapidly deteriorated after 1946. Mary made a determined effort to publish a report on the pottery before his death. But although he saw and corrected the manuscript, he died before the report was printed.

Eleven

During 1941, in addition to my other duties, I found myself involved in work connected with the surveillance of large numbers of Italian prisoners-of-war, who were beginning to be brought in to Kenya from the battlefields of Ethiopia and Eritrea.

Insofar as it was possible, these prisoners-of-war were screened. Many had not been indoctrinated with Fascist ideas and were obviously harmless to our war effort. They were therefore given the opportunity to work on parole, either on farms or in some other type of labor, such as road construction or forestry.

Soon after hostilities commenced one of my opposite numbers in military intelligence told me about an Italian prisoner-of-war, Ferucio Menengetti, whom he had recently interviewed. Menengetti, it appeared, was a museum technician by training and was most anxious to work at the Coryndon Memorial Museum. Shortly afterwards we were able to take him on the staff, to help Allen Turner in the mounting of specimens and the preparation of habitat groups.

Menengetti was given accommodation in a small room behind the curator's residence, where Mary and I were living at the time, so that he was always, at least nominally, under my eye. Later on, as the war proceeded, he was joined by two other prisoners-of-war. One of them, Count Patrizzi, was a specialist in insects, particularly termites and ants; he was also an excellent ornithologist, and at the outbreak of war had been collecting birds in Ethiopia for one of the Italian museums. In fact, he was not strictly a prisoner-of-war but, like some of the others, a detained civilian on parole. He did excellent work at the museum in the ornithological department.

There were times when my work in connection with the prisoner-of-war camps involved me in amusing incidents. One large camp had been established near Naivasha. The men enjoyed a good deal of freedom, and most of them were quite content to work by day on the road construction that was being done between Naivasha and Nakuru and return to the camp at night. Indeed, the number of prisoners was so great and the number of guards so few that prisoners could easily have escaped while they were out working. A few, however, who were ardent supporters of the Fascist regime, were not allowed the same degree of freedom. Their sole aim was to find a way of escaping so as to get back to Ethiopia. They refused to believe the news on the camp radio and on the news boards that the war in Ethiopia was almost over.

Prior to the war, there had been a number of Italian missionary societies and organizations—including schools and hospitals—scattered throughout Kenya, and even after hostilities commenced most of the Italian missionaries had been allowed to continue their work. Some of the would-be escapees hoped that if they could reach one of these missions, they would be able to get help. The authorities, of course, were always on the lookout for escape attempts, and from time to time news of such a happening reached us at intelligence headquarters in Nairobi.

One small group of escapees from the Naivasha prisoner-of-war camp headed northwards over the Kinangop plateau into the forests on the Aberdare Mountains, with the intention of crossing the range and then making their way towards Mount Kenya to Nyeri. From there, where several Italian missionary societies were still functioning, they planned to proceed northwards across the desert to Ethiopia. Quite clearly, they could not possibly have realized how difficult this would be.

When this particular group escaped, I and some of my trained African intelligence workers—all of whom were well acquainted with the areas the prisoners were heading for—were called in to follow and bring them back.

On the second morning of our search we met a young African forest worker, who hurriedly approached us and asked me to come with him to rescue some *azungu* (Europeans) who were in the forest and in dire need of help. We followed him to the little group of escapees, who were huddled, very cold and hungry, under a big juniper tree. The moment they saw me, they rushed forward imploring me to rescue them!

It transpired that the night they spent in the forest had been a most terrifying experience, and they wanted nothing more than to be taken back, as quickly as possible, to the safety and comfort of the prisoner-of-war camp.

It seemed that when darkness had fallen the previous night the prisoners had made a bivouac under a big tree in the forest. No sooner had they settled down for the night than the most awful screeching and grating noise began to come from the branches of the tree above them. As the noise came closer and closer, it seemed to them as though some enormous animal were descending the tree to attack them. They were so frightened that they moved, despite the darkness, to the foot of another tree. Scarcely had they settled down again when the same thing happened. They moved once more, and for a third and then a fourth time, but no sooner did they relax each time than the terrifying noises started again. As city dwellers from somewhere in northern Italy, they were, naturally, completely ignorant about African wildlife and had no idea what was producing those loud and apparently threatening noises. Finally, even when they managed to reach a tree where they were not disturbed, they still found it impossible to sleep and were only too glad, next morning, to hear the young forest worker singing nearby.

Thus it came about that we apprehended these three men and took them back to the camp. After brief inquiries, it seemed quite clear that the tree hyrax (*Dendrohyrax*) was the creature that had shattered their peace in the night. The male of this species objects strongly to the presence of humans at the foot of a tree it is occupying and screams in protest at any such intrusion. Tree hyraxes are small, furry creatures about the size of a large cat and are quite harmless. Their screeching sounds, however, can be very alarming when heard for the first time.

I saw an opportunity in this incident to prevent further escapes from the Naivasha camp. I spread the word that the runaways were lucky to have escaped with their lives, since, without doubt, the noise they had heard in the night had been made by the much-feared Kinangop "man-eating hyraxes." As the story went round the camp—and was embroidered in the telling—incidents of attempted escape diminished considerably during the next few months. Unfortunately, this ruse was eventually foiled by the arrival of a prisoner-of-war who was a zoologist. On hearing the story, he quickly explained to the other inmates of the camp that tree hyraxes were tiny, furry animals who, despite their loud noise, were certainly not the slightest bit dangerous.

A really interesting prisoner-of-war escape was of quite a different nature. A group of Italians who were Alpine climbers happened to have the bad luck—from their point of view—to be placed in a prisoner-of-war camp at Nanyuki. From this camp, below the slopes of Mount Kenya, they could see the gleaming peaks of this wonderful mountain whenever the weather was clear. It was a challenge they could not resist, and so they set to work to assemble the equipment they needed for an attempt to climb the mountain. In due course, they made ropes, picks, and various other items and improvised warm clothes out of blankets provided by other members of the camp.

Finally, their preparations were complete, and on the chosen day they made their escape. The attempt was successful. They reached the summit of Mount Kenya, where they planted a little homemade Italian flag to prove what they had done. Once their object was achieved, they returned down the mountain and surrendered to the camp authorities. I am glad to say that their adventure was not punished with any severity, and one of the climbers subsequently wrote a book about the episode.

Among many other activities for which the Italian prisoners-of-war were responsible was the making of a magnificent all-weather road from Nairobi to Naivasha. The first part of this road was down the Great Rift Valley escarpment. The men had a camp built for them at the bottom of the escarpment, where there was a beautiful spring of fresh water. Although they lived in this camp, they had a good deal of freedom and in their spare time wandered about the area pretty much at will, talking with the Africans and buying food from them to supplement their rations. As long as they obtained permission beforehand from the camp commandant, they were allowed to engage in any other activity they thought worth while.

Today, as one descends the main road from the top of the escarpment, one comes—about twenty-eight miles from Nairobi—upon a little Italian-style church standing all on its own at the corner where the road turns from the escarpment towards the plains. It looks a most unlikely spot to have been chosen for such a building. In fact, the church marks the site of one of the road-making camps and was built, with the permission of the authorities, by the prisoners, so they could attend Mass in a proper church on Sundays and saints' days.

It was at this time, when the drive of British and South African troops into Ethiopia was taking place, that the incident occurred for which my second cousin Nigel Leakey (son of Gray Leakey, who later lost his life, in Mau Mau times) earned a posthumous Victoria Cross.

Nigel Leakey was a sergeant major with a company of the King's African Rifles that was moving northwards. According to all the available intelligence reports, they were in an area at least twenty miles from the nearest enemy camp. They had arrived, towards evening, near a swiftly running stream, and since they were tired and weary, the officer in charge gave permission for all the men and the NCOs to have a quick bathe in the stream to refresh themselves; supposedly, the enemy was many miles away. Almost every man in the company accordingly stripped, and they were all splashing about in the water when three enemy tanks came up on the far side of the river and opened fire.

Nigel Leakey, stark-naked and without a thought for his own safety, rushed out of the water on the far side and tackled the first of the tanks singlehanded. He climbed onto the top, forced open the hatch, got hold of one of the enemy revolvers inside the tank, and killed all the occupants. He then climbed down and up onto the second tank. He succeeded in opening the hatch, but at this point he was seized by the occupants and dragged inside. The tanks drove off and Nigel was never seen again.

Every attempt made by military intelligence, as well as by myself on behalf of our family, to find out from the prisoners-of-war in the various camps in East Africa what had happened to Nigel failed to yield any results. Certainly his heroic act saved the lives of a large number of the men in his company, and when it became clear that he would never be found alive, or perhaps never found at all, he was posthumously awarded the V.C. His father traveled to London and received the medal from His Majesty King George VI.

In 1941 I received a letter from Anthony Arkell, who was teaching archaeology at that time and also carrying out research work at Gordon College, Khartoum. Arkell wrote to say that in spite of the war he saw a chance of coming to Kenya for a holiday and would like, if possible, to be taken to Olorgesailie, Olduvai Gorge, and other places of interest. Since I had fourteen days' leave due me, I invited him to come down, but warned him that because of the pressures of my work he must give me as much notice as he could of his arrival date. Mary and I began immediately to save some of our meager petrol rations for Arkell's visit. Kay Attwood, Mary Davidson, and Molly Paine promised to do the same, provided they could join us, if they were free to do so when the time came. Thus it was that when Tony Arkell reached Kenya we were able to leave for Olduvai Gorge without delay.

Even though the journey took two and a half days each way, my fortnight's leave allowed us nine clear days of freedom from all thoughts of war and a real respite from the worries of the outside world. This was something we had dreamed about, but had hardly dared to believe could happen in wartime. It proved to be a most pleasant interlude. While we were there, Tony Arkell discovered in Bed IV a nearly complete skull of an extinct type of eland. We also collected stone tools *in situ* from a site of the Kenya Capsian culture that we had found in 1931. The tools were made from obsidian and chert. There were also numerous charred animal bones and teeth. The site was just above the waterfall, at what we call Black Rock, by the Second Fault. Overlying the deposit containing the tools was another, which looked like what was then known as Bed V. It seemed, therefore, that we had tools *in situ* that could be roughly correlated in time with the human skull found by Reck in 1913. This information would, we knew, prove extremely useful in solving the problem of just what Reck's find really represented. (Many years later, the living site and the skeleton were dated by radiocarbon to 17,000–17,500 B.P.)

One Sunday afternoon in 1941, when I was taking people round the museum, a member of the Game Department sought me out to ask whether I would take three Wanderobo tribesmen on a specially conducted tour of the exhibits. They had come from a place at the summit of the Mau range and were extremely anxious to be shown round. One of the three understood Kikuyu and acted as interpreter for the other two. I devoted as much time as possible to these men. As I was showing them the exhibits of animals, birds, insects, plants, and rocks, I explained that we were at present unable to display some of the more common animals, such as zebra, wildebeest, elephant, and rhino, simply because we lacked the space to do so. Our object, I told them, was to try to show people, especially children, some of the rarer creatures that lived in their own country.

The Wanderobo looked and listened attentively, and when the tour was over the one who understood Kikuyu said that, in view of what I had told them, they wondered why we did not have an exhibit of the rare animal that lived in the open glades of the forest high up in the Mau hills. From his description, it seemed clear that he was speaking of the animal I already knew from the literature as the yellow-backed duiker, which had been recorded only from parts of the eastern Congo and Northern Rhodesia. I had never heard of its existence in Kenya.

The Wanderobo insisted that a number of these creatures were to be found near their home in the forest, and at my request their spokesman promised to send me part of a skull and a piece of skin of one, which he had in his home at the time. He was as good as his word, and in due course there arrived in the museum, by special messenger, half of a skull of a duikerlike animal and parts of its skin. This showed the typical dark brown and yellow markings of a yellow-backed duiker, and the one horn belonged unmistakedly to this species. It remained to be proved whether the specimens represented the yellow-backed duiker found in the Congo and Rhodesia or a closely allied form.

As soon as possible—this was not for a good many months—I arranged for Peter and Joy Bally and Allen Turner to go to the Mau forest and try to collect an example of this animal for a museum exhibit, as well as study its habitat. They returned with a wonderful collection of the plants of the area, a few photographs, taken by Bally, showing glimpses of the animal in the distance, and one specimen for mounting. Here, then, was proof that this rare mammal was present in a small area of Kenya. The Game Department immediately placed it on the official list of Kenya mammals and gave it the status of royal game, so that it could not be shot by trophy hunters.

It was also during 1941 that I became officially involved in the first of a number of murder inquiries. On this occasion, it was the murder of the Earl of Errol, on the outskirts of Nairobi. I believe that the full story has been written up in one of the many books that deal with famous murder trials of this century, but, as I was one of those who actually participated in the investigation, I think it would be of interest to give a brief account of it from another angle.

Lord Errol had a large, splendidly equipped house in the Karen suburb of Nairobi. He was wealthy, a well-known sportsman, and also a man of considerable intelligence. In addition to this, he was unquestionably a man with immense attraction for most of the women who came in contact with him. Shortly before the war broke out, he had been chosen by the government to play a large part in the organization of "Manpower," an effort to utilize to best advantage all the labor resources of the country, and he had a headquarters office in Nairobi. At intervals, despite his many duties and the difficulties of entertaining in wartime, he managed to throw luxurious parties at his Karen house.

Early on the morning following one of these parties, a man who was delivering milk in the suburbs noticed a car overturned in a small quarry by the roadside. He stopped his own vehicle, got out, and went to see if anybody had been injured. To his horror, he found a dead body in the front seat of the car. He immediately drove to the nearest police station—Karen Police Post—and made a report.

The officer on duty hastened to the scene and was appalled to find that the dead man was no other than the Earl of Errol. There was every reason to believe, so it seemed, that the death was due to an accident; the car was lying in the quarry close to the road, and there was a small hole in the dead man's forehead that appeared to coincide exactly with a metal spike on the dashboard of the car.

In cars of that period there used to be devices for pulling out the choke and the throttle. The knob had come off one of these, exposing a metal spike about an inch and a half long on which there were definite traces of blood. The size and shape of the spike corresponded closely to the hole in the man's forehead. It seemed quite clear to the police officer that the Earl of Errol had somehow lost control of the car, it had gone off the road into the quarry, and as the car crashed the driver's forehead had jerked forward and been fatally pierced by the sharp spike on the instrument panel.

The officer immediately reported his discovery to police headquarters, and by ten o'clock that morning news of the "accident" was all over Nairobi. A special edition of the main English-language newspaper was published announcing that the Earl of Errol had met with a fatal accident during the previous night and that his funeral would take place late the same afternoon.

It was at this point that Superintendent Poppy, head of the CID in Nairobi, heard the news. I happened to be with him when it came. Although still quite a young man, Poppy had reached his high position because of his flair for "smelling out" crimes and solving them. When he heard that Lord Errol had been found dead in his car in a quarry with a hole in his forehead, he said at once that, in view of who the victim was, he felt he ought to go and make quite certain that the death was a genuine accident and not the result of foul play. He invited me to accompany him.

After some inquiries, we traced the body to the mortuary. As reported, the only injury appeared to be a tiny round hole in the middle of the forehead. The police officer who had found the car confirmed the report that there had been a smear of blood on the spike on the dashboard. But Poppy was not satisfied. Saying that he wanted to examine the hole more carefully, he produced his magnifying glass.

He carried out his examination in silence. Then, looking up, he said, quite casually, "Powder burns, I think—I must investigate further." Immediately after making this remark he sprang into action. In a moment he was at the mortuary's telephone issuing a stream of orders to his staff. The CID medical team was asked to send a portable X-ray machine. The press was to be informed that anyone who inquired about the arrangements for the funeral should be told that it had been postponed for some unknown reason. Poppy's subordinates were instructed to get in touch with Messrs. Cable and Wireless Ltd., which at that time were responsible for the midday and evening news broadcasts, and ask them to repeat several times, before and after the midday news and at intervals throughout the afternoon, that the funeral of the Earl of Errol had been postponed until the following day at the same time.

Meanwhile, Poppy waited patiently for the X-ray team to arrive. As soon as they had made their examination, they told us that their plates showed, quite clearly, a small bulletlike object right in the middle of the brain. Poppy again went to the telephone and called the police commissioner at headquarters. He told him how his suspicions had been aroused by what looked like powder burns, and how his diagnosis had been confirmed by X ray. Immediately, arrangements were made for a police surgeon to come and carry out a post-mortem, the results of which could be used as evidence in the event that a trial took place.

The car in which the "accident" occurred had, most unfortunately, already been removed from the quarry and towed to Lord Errol's home, but immediate orders were given for a guard to be placed on it and instructions issued that nobody was to be allowed to touch it. Despite the number of people who had handled the car since it was found that morning, there was a faint chance that there might be a few fingerprints that would provide a lead to the murderer. But this did not prove to be the case.

After completing the telephone calls Poppy returned to CID headquarters and ordered his entire staff to begin making inquiries with a view to finding out whether anyone had a motive for the murder and to fixing the approximate time it had taken place. (At this stage, Poppy had not yet been given the estimated time of death by the police surgeon.) Other inquiries were concentrated on the twenty-four hours immediately preceding the time when the body was discovered—with particular attention, of course, to those people who had attended the party at Lord Errol's house. We were all instructed to find out as much as we could about the people who had been present, what they had done while there, what time they had left, and where they had gone. My own special task was to make discreet inquiries of Errol's domestic and other staff.

An immediate search was also started for the weapon. It was the absence of a weapon that had made it appear to the policeman who was first on the scene that morning that the hole was the result of an accident, not of a self-inflicted bullet wound. That the Earl's death might have been murder had simply never occurred to him.

What happened to the weapon is still not known. Every conceivable place where it might have been hidden was searched repeatedly, including the various lavatory pits in the area and the lavatory pits at Lord Errol's home and at those of the people who had been at the party. The weapon was never discovered.

The bullet, of course, was recovered in the course of the postmortem, and when it was submitted for examination to the ballistics experts, they found minute scratches on it that had been caused during its passage through the barrel of the gun. The experts told us that if we could find other bullets with identical scratches that had been fired recently from the same weapon, these would provide evidence to show what gun had been used for the crime.

The list of those who had attended the party the previous evening included the name of the young and beautiful bride of a well-known Kenya settler, Sir Delves Broughton, who was much older than she. It also transpired from inquiries that this young woman had received more than usual attention from Lord Errol during the course of the evening, but this was not surprising, since it was well known that he found women attractive. What also came to light, however, was the fact that the young woman's husband had not stayed until the end of the party. So far as I know, it was never fully established whether he took his wife with him when he left or whether she stayed on and was taken home by somebody else.

This information pointed up the necessity for further inquiries about Broughton, since it seemed that he might have had a motive for the crime. Consequently, a young CID inspector and I, accompanied by some of my African intelligence staff, were sent to the area near Mount Kenya where Broughton had a country home, to see if we could gather any information there that might help the case. Others were working quietly and systematically in the area round Errol's home in Nairobi.

Inquiries among Africans in the neighborhood of the suspect's country home revealed that about a fortnight before the murder they had heard sounds of "much shooting." One of the farm employees informed us that his *bwana* had been engaging in target practice about that time.

When we returned to CID headquarters we made our report, and Poppy decided to send the same inspector back to make further inquiries among the household staff. This time he was armed with a warrant to search the premises for the missing weapon. He was also instructed to collect any spent bullets he could find in the target-practice area.

On this occasion the household staff confirmed that their *bwana* possessed a small firearm and that, from time to time, he engaged in target practice, but none of them knew the whereabouts of the gun. The inspector made a thorough search of the target area and collected a number of spent twenty-two-caliber bullets, as well as some cartridge cases. Since the weapon was never found, the latter were of little use as evidence, but the ballistics specialist who compared the spent bullets with the one extracted from the Earl's head reported that he had no doubt at all that the murder bullet had been fired from the same weapon as was used for target practice at Broughton's home.

Now, the man who had indulged in target practice at Broughton's home was almost certainly Broughton himself and the owner of the murder weapon. Also, we knew that Broughton was the husband of the woman to whom Errol had paid so much attention at the party. The evidence was beginning to add up!

There was no longer any doubt about the need to question Broughton. Poppy himself undertook the task, giving him the customary warning about what he said being possibly used in evidence against him. Broughton vehemently denied any knowledge of the murder. He said he had last seen Errol at the party some time before he himself left, to go to his club for the night. He said he had not returned to Karen that night and had never seen Errol alive again. Without any outward show of annoyance, he admitted freely that he had seen Errol flirting with his wife, but since this was known to be the man's normal behavior, he had paid little attention to it. He pointed out that his bride was by no means the only married woman who had been the object of Errol's flattery at the party. He therefore felt it was unfair to single him out as a suspect.

It became clear during the course of this interrogation that Broughton did not realize we had already made a search of his upcountry home and the surrounding grounds and had found twenty-two-caliber bullets at the place where he was alleged by his staff to have carried out target practice a week or two earlier. When he was asked point-blank whether he possessed a firearm of this caliber, he admitted it and said he sometimes used it for target practice at home. He added that recently it had been missing from its usual place in his house, and he thought someone might have stolen it. He could not, therefore, produce it for the police. He went on to say that Errol's propensity for flirting with young married women was very widely known and since it was common knowledge that he was paying special attention to Lady Broughton at this particular time, anyone wishing to get rid of him would quite naturally try to frame her husband as the murderer.

After all efforts to find the weapon were abandoned, and after our attempts to get precise information about the movements between midnight and dawn of others who had been at the party failed, the file was sent to the attorney general. He instructed the police to proceed with the case and arrest Broughton. (The police, incidentally, felt sure that certain people who were questioned had lied and that there were several who knew a good deal about what happened that fateful night, but who were deliberately keeping silent.)

Broughton engaged the services of an eminent South African barrister, a K.C., who traveled to Kenya from Johannesburg to organize his defense. The police and, indeed, most members of the public who daily packed the court or read the evidence in the press had little doubt as to the outcome of the case. But defense counsel made a brilliant closing speech reviewing the evidence to the jury. He was able to throw an element of doubt into their minds by suggesting that it was, in fact, possible for someone to have killed Lord Errol with the deliberate intention of making it appear an accident or, if this ruse failed, the act of his client.

After due deliberation, the jury returned a verdict of not guilty, and Broughton was set free. Shortly afterwards he returned to England. A few months later we learned, through the press, that he had committed suicide.

So ended the first murder trial with which I was connected. Although it was not really part of my duties with the CID to help with such inquiries, I nevertheless found them exciting. From them I learned a great deal about the criminal side of CID investigation work. Poppy was an excellent man from whom to learn. Before coming to Nairobi, he had been involved in one of the most sensational murder investigations of the immediate prewar period. Subsequent to the Errol case, I was called in again to help Poppy, in investigations of a rather bizarre nature, and even after my connection with the department ended I had occasion to help clear an innocent young man who had been falsely accused.

Mary was expecting her first child in November, but her doctor, Hope Trant, did not expect the birth to take place until nearly the end of the month. When, therefore, I was asked to go on an urgent intelligence assignment at the very beginning of the month, the doctor saw no reason why I should not do so, and Mary concurred.

We had received a report from one of my African agents at Thomson's Falls regarding rumors that some South African Dutch settlers, who were known to be Nazi supporters, were spreading Nazi propaganda. The report also said that they had secret caches of arms and ammunition. Before the Italian entry into the war, we had heard rumors that lorryloads of arms and ammunition were being brought into Kenya from Italian-controlled Abyssinia. It seemed possible, therefore, that the rumors from Thomson's Falls might be linked in some way with the earlier rumors about arms running. Since it seemed important to look into the matter as quickly as possible, I left Nairobi early on November 1.

I was out of touch with Nairobi for two whole days, without even a chance of telephoning, and when I got back to my home on the evening of November 4, I discovered that Mary had been taken into a nursing home and that we had a son. When I rushed to visit her, I found her in fine shape and learned that the baby had been born remarkably easily for a first child. We named him Jonathan Harry (after my father) and Erskine (after Mary's father). In a few days' time mother and son were back home, and long before Christmas Mary was completely fit again.

At a party in December, Peter and Joy Bally announced that they were planning to go on a safari to collect botanical specimens in the Ngorongoro Crater and that a friend of ours, Jack Trevor, who was my opposite number in military intelligence and who had some leave due him, was going with them. The Ballys suggested that Mary might perhaps like to accompany them, since she had spent many months carrying her unborn baby and it was now her turn for a change and a rest.

The trip promised to be particularly exciting from her point of view, inasmuch as the Ngorongoro Crater had burial mounds reported to be similar to those she had been excavating at Hyrax Hill before the war. Although Mary was breast-feeding Jonathan, it seemed too good a chance for her to miss, and so it was agreed that if we could find someone to look after the baby by day, while I was on intelligence duties, I would look after him by night, thus freeing Mary to go with the Ballys.

We succeeded in finding a nurse, Miss Peacock, who agreed to undertake all responsibility for Jonathan from eight in the morning until such time in the evening as I could get home and take over from her. Meanwhile, Mary switched Jonathan immediately to bottle food, so he could be left in our care by the time the safari was ready to leave. I proceeded to learn how to change nappies, mix formulas, and bring up Jonathan's wind by holding him over my shoulder and patting his little back before putting him to bed.

So ended the year 1941, with Peter, Joy, Jack, and Mary going on safari while I took over responsibility for our six-week-old baby, with the daytime assistance of Nurse Peacock. Fortunately for us, Dr. Trant was available nearby should either of us need her.

Twelve

During 1909 or 1910, several German farmers and their families who had come out to what was then German East Africa obtained farming concessions on the floor of the Ngorongoro Crater, in order to raise cattle. One of them, Herr A. Sietentopf, decided to build his home near the Munge stream, which flows into the crater on the east side, not far from where the little hut stands that was erected by the National Geographic Society for Dick Estes when he was carrying out research work on wildebeest (This hut was more recently used by Jane and Hugo van Lawick when they were studying the behavior of hyenas and Egyptian vultures.)

In those days, before World War I, the pioneer farmers living on the floor of the crater were hard put to it to find suitable material with which to build houses. One day, when searching the grassy hills near the Munge stream, a man named Arning, Sietentopf's manager, came across a number of mounds of stones, which seemed to be an ideal source of raw material for building purposes. When he started taking the mounds to pieces, he found, to his great surprise, that they were, in fact, burials of some long-forgotten Stone Age race and contained skulls and skeletons, stone bowls, stone beads, a good deal of red ocher, and some potsherds and fragments of animal bone.

In 1913, when Professor Hans Reck of Berlin made his first foot safari from Arusha to Olduvai, in order to follow up Dr. Kattwinkel's 1911 discovery in the gorge of bones of *Hipparion*, he decided to pause in the crater to rest his weary porters and replenish his stocks of food from the farmers. At the same time, he made up his mind to spend a few days investigating the discovery of Stone Age remains made by Sietentopf and Arning. Subsequently, Reck wrote a brief scientific report dealing with these discoveries. The published report was not very detailed, but the little he had placed on record tied in so exceedingly well with what I had found at the Nakuru burial site in 1926, and with what Mary had excavated at Hyrax Hill in 1937–38 and at the Njoro River Rock Shelter, that she was most excited about the chance of seeing the site for herself. She was anxious to find out whether there were still any undamaged mounds that might be excavated.

On the way to Ngorongoro, at Karatu, the Ballys and Mary recruited a number of Mbulu tribesmen to act as porters. These porters were sent ahead up the sixteen miles of road to the rim of the crater, where the rest of the party, traveling by car, joined them. After transferring the luggage to the porters' heads, they all made the steep descent into the crater on foot.

While the Ballys "botanized," Mary and Jack Trevor—he had been trained before the war as an anthropologist and was attached to Cambridge University—made preliminary excavations in two of the several burial mounds that were still intact. They found skulls, skeletons, stone bowls, and other Neolithic objects, including obsidian flakes and tools exactly similar to what had been found by the farmers and described in the earlier paper by Reck.

Unfortunately, since I was not able to go on this expedition, I cannot give a firsthand account of the exciting times they had. They hired donkeys from a German farmer for the return journey. On this occasion the donkey Mary was riding across the floor of the crater suddenly came face to face with a lion. Mary was unseated, the donkey bolted, and for a time there was general pandemonium! Scientifically, the trip certainly proved to be most worth while, from both the archaeological and the botanical points of view.

Shortly after the party returned to Nairobi, our young son, Jonathan, had a lucky escape from *siafu*, or biting ants—the same insects that had attacked the bees the year before. In the interval, we had had the corrugated iron removed from the exterior walls and roof of the house and had dealt with the bees both in the walls and in the ceiling. We had also thoroughly sealed the holes in the wooden floorboards in the spare room— now used as Jonathan's bedroom—through which the *siafu* had come to attack the bees.

In the evenings, after we put Jonathan to bed, we left the door wide open, so that we could hear if he cried or called out to us. One evening, we heard a most awful wail from Jonathan, and we both rushed into his bedroom and switched on the light. He was sleeping in a cot under a mosquito net, and we had thought him safe from any kind of attack by insects. Unfortunately, we had overlooked the fact that *siafu* will climb up the legs of furniture and find a means of penetrating almost anything! We found, to our horror, that Jonathan was completely covered with hundreds of these biting ants. They were already all over his cot, and the floor was a seething mass of insects. In a matter of seconds we got him out of his cot and into another room. Following their usual habit, an army of these ants had got into his room and up to his crib and had swarmed all over him in large numbers. Only then had they launched their biting attack. (It is not known how the order to attack is given, or which member of a raiding party gives it.)

After Mary and I had carried Jonathan to safety, out of the way of the main invading army, the next frantic minutes were spent in clearing him of hundreds of *siafu*. Those clinging to his face, eyes, and other tender parts of his body had to be taken off one by one, as carefully as possible.

It was a matter of great relief to us that Jonathan survived the ordeal so well. Once we got him clean and quieted down, I and members of our African staff attacked the ant army that had invaded his bedroom. We used quantities of boiling water, paraffin, and pyrethrum powder, and in due course we routed them and succeeded in killing the vast majority.

After Jonathan's escape, we set the four legs of his cot in wide pans, which we kept filled with water and paraffin, making it impossible for the ants to get to him that way. We also made quite sure each night that neither his bedding nor the mosquito net was trailing on the floor and thus providing a means for the ants to climb up into the cot, should they invade his room again. In spite of these precautions, we had a minor attack a few years later, when the ants succeeded in getting onto the ceiling, from where they dropped down on the net of our son Richard's cot and so down the sides and into his bed. On this occasion, we happened to go into his room quite accidentally and were able to rescue him before he was actually attacked.

These ants are a real scourge to domestic animals and livestock in Africa. They attack puppies and kittens—who are relatively helpless when they are born—sitting hens, ducks, and turkeys, and even lambs and calves. The suddenness of the attack by thousands of ants all biting simultaneously makes it practically impossible for the mother to remove her young in time to save their lives.

Horses too, when confined in a stable, are often the victims of a vicious attack. On more than one occasion, Mary and I, our staff, and our children (in the days when the children were growing up and had ponies) have been awakened in the middle of the night by sounds of frenzied kicking and neighing from the stables and have gone out to find our ponies being attacked by an army of *siafu*. When this happens the poor animals get frantic with pain, and it takes several people to hold them still while others are dealing with the ants in the same way as we dealt with those on Jonathan that night.

Although *siafu* must rank as a menace as far as human beings are concerned, there is little doubt that they are one of nature's means of controlling the population of some of the smaller creatures whose young are helpless, and even of some of the larger mammals. Marching down into dens and burrows, they attack young jackals, wild cats, mongooses, and many other creatures. I suppose several thousand young animals are killed every year in this way.

It is possible that the introduction of *siafu* might have been an answer to the rabbit problem of Australia—were it not for the fact that, having once dealt with the rabbits, they would have almost certainly turned their attention to newborn lambs and other helpless creatures.

Over the Easter weekend of 1942, Mary and I managed to get away from Nairobi for one whole day. We had been saving some of our petrol ration for just such an occasion, and on this particular Easter Monday we set off for the area around Mount

Olorgesailie, on the floor of the Rift Valley, in the direction of Lake Magadi.

We chose this spot because we knew that in 1918, right after World War I, C. W. Hobley, the provincial commissioner, and Professor J. W. Gregory, from Glasgow, had located in this area a "bank of white diatomaceous earth," in which they had found a few handaxes of the kind known to prehistorians as Acheulean. This fact had been reported in scientific journals, but the exact position of the discovery was not known to us. I had, in 1929, sent geologist John Solomon down to the area for six weeks to see whether he could locate any fossil beds or deposits containing artifacts, but he had had no success. I had always, however, been determined to continue this search, and now at last we had a whole day in which to do so.

Even on this first visit we found a few scattered handaxes in different areas, and we thought we were probably in the same locality Hobley had described. Later, whenever possible, we made further day trips to Olorgesailie. On one occasion, when we were accompanied by Mary Davidson, Ferucio Menengetti, and two of our African staff, we were supremely lucky.

We had stopped at a place about a mile off the road to Magadi, forty-two miles out of Nairobi. Having left the car under a tree for the day, we carried food and water with us and moved off on a series of quick traverses, as far as possible, keeping parallel with each other and in touch by occasional shouts. Suddenly, at almost exactly the same moment, Mary, Menengetti, and I each found exposures with quantities of handaxes and some fossil bones. Mary's was the most prolific site and she kept shouting to me to come over and see it. I, on the other hand, had found a site not nearly as rich as hers, but with plenty of fossils and some handaxes, and was calling her to come over to me! Meanwhile, in the area between us, we heard Menengetti calling excitedly to both of us that he had found handaxes.

I abandoned my site, having first tied a handkerchief to a thornbush in the middle of it, so that I could relocate it later on, and went across to Mary. When I saw her site I could scarcely believe my eyes. In an area of about fifty by sixty feet there were literally hundreds upon hundreds of perfect, very large handaxes and cleavers, as well as a few flakes and some bolas stones (round stone balls). Nearly all the specimens we found at this site can still be seen today, in the same position as when they were first discovered. We did not disturb them in any way at all, and eventually, in 1947, when the site was opened to the public as a museum-on-the-spot, we built a catwalk high above the exposure from which visitors could look down at and photograph the specimens without treading on them or handling them.

Menengetti's site was about fifty yards south of Mary's and yielded several hundred much smaller handaxes eroding from a different level in the deposits. At this spot there were practically no cleavers and not a single bolas stone.

My site was farther away towards the south and had rather fewer handaxes than either of the other two, but many more fossil bones and teeth. It was a memorable day. We were unable to stay very long because we had to get back to Nairobi, where Jonathan's baby-sitter was expecting us by five o'clock. We knew, however, that we had found a site of very great importance and one that would require prolonged investigations in the future. We occupied the time on the drive home that afternoon planning just how and when we were going to be able to work it satisfactorily.

Mary, by this time, had nearly finished her part of the report on the Njoro River Rock Shelter, although I had still not completed my part, dealing with the skulls and skeletons. With Jonathan on her hands (he was then about eighteen months old), Mary had not been called up by "Manpower" for any specialized war work. Consequently, she was able to do more or less what she wished.

We decided that the new Olorgesailie site was of such importance that the sooner we began detailed work on it, the better. We therefore purchased the necessary equipment and set up a tented camp by the edge of a small gully under some thorn trees, close to the richest of the sites, the one Mary had found.

Several of our older African employees, who had worked with me since 1926, were not engaged in war duties, and we sent for them to make up a team to work with Mary at Olorgesailie.

Mary had a big tent as a combined living room and workroom

and a smaller one as a bedroom for herself and Jonathan. She also had a tent for Jonathan's African *ayah,* or nurse, whose duties included washing the nappies and clothes. There was another tent for the houseboy and also one that served as a kitchen and scullery, plus two others for the male African members of the party.

At that time, I was busy with administrative work at the museum most evenings, but whenever it was possible, even if it meant leaving Nairobi late in the evening and returning early the next morning, I rushed to the camp to see how things were going. I also went down on all my free weekends.

The biggest problem at Olorgesailie was that of getting water, but eventually we were lucky enough to make an arrangement with an extremely kind and pleasant road foreman, who was at the time responsible to the Imperial Chemical Industries for the upkeep of the road to Lake Magadi, where the company ran a huge plant for producing soda. This man not only dropped off a few forty-gallon drums of drinking water once a week, as he passed our camp, but also acted as postman between Mary and me. He had to go back and forth two or three times a week, so the arrangement worked perfectly, especially since the ICI directors were kind enough to authorize him to give us every possible assistance in maintaining our camp.

Scientifically, from the very beginning the site proved to be exciting indeed. There were more than ten distinct "camp sites" of Acheulean man at different levels within a sequence of ancient lake deposits exposed by modern erosion. At the time we were working, the area was semiarid, and there was a dry watercourse through which floodwaters raced occasionally when there had been a thunderstorm near Mount Laisugut, about twenty-seven miles away, or when a local downpour occurred. The deposits we were working had been formed in a series of ancient lakes, by the side of which the makers of the various stages of the handaxe culture had lived in the dim past. Subsequently, these deposits had been exposed by the forces of erosion, which had cut back the lake beds, forming cliff faces. Frequently, stone tools and fossil bones could be seen projecting from these cliffs at different levels. The sequence as a whole consisted of shallow water deposits, beaches, and swamp beds, as well as a few deep-water strata. At intervals there were old land surfaces; it was on these that the artifacts and fossils occurred.

The site was in Masai country, and in the dry season the area was uninhabited by either cattle or wild animals because of the lack of surface water. When rain fell the scene changed. Grass sprang up, floodwaters raced down the watercourse, leaving rock pools in the floor of the stream bed, and the Masai moved in with their cattle, goats, and sheep to make use of the available grazing while there was still enough water. Similarly, zebra, gerenuk (a long-necked antelope of desert country), oryx, eland, and a few gazelle, as well as rhino and lion, occupied the area at such periods. One pride of five lions was much in evidence for part of the time Mary was in camp.

There was one memorable occasion when she heard lions roaring near the camp several times during the night and the dogs were very restless. (At that time she had with her our four Dalmatians, one of which was a long-haired bitch, a throwback to a type that existed several hundred years ago, before Dalmatians became carriage dogs and while they were still harriers. This little bitch, Sally, was the leader of the pack.) In the morning, as soon as the dogs were let out of the tent, Sally's hair bristled, and she led the pack, barking and growling furiously, to the edge of a small, dry gully not far from Mary's tent. When Mary followed to see what had attracted the dogs' attention, she found herself gazing down at five lions, who had apparently decided to spend the rest of the day sleeping there—less than a hundred yards from her camp! The dogs were called back immediately and had to be kept away from the gully for the rest of the day, but the lions seemed scarcely to notice the intrusion, and the work went on as usual.

Scorpions were common and troublesome, and members of our staff were stung and temporarily incapacitated on several occasions. We encountered snakes from time to time too, but most of them were harmless. Two or three times, however, when the tents were being turned out on Sunday morning (cleaning day), cobras were found curled up under a bed or beneath a ground sheet. But no one was ever harmed by them.

One Sunday morning, when I was at the camp for the weekend, a rather angry-looking rhinoceros strolled up from the stream, apparently with the intention of spending the rest of the day under our thorn trees. The staff all banged empty tins and shouted, and the rhino turned and went off in disgust with its tail held high in the air, after the manner of the wart hog—a clear sign of rhino annoyance. We could not help feeling a little sorry for it, since, quite clearly, the shady trees under which we had pitched our tents represented one of the places the rhino counted on for an occasional siesta.

When there was any water in the water holes along the stream bed and the Masai were therefore around grazing their herds, they frequently came into camp in search of medicine and other help. From time to time we would show the elders the stone handaxes we had discovered, but any reference to their extreme age produced a most skeptical reaction. The Masai were willing to admit that some of the handaxes looked rather like spearheads and some of the cleavers resembled axe heads, and that, therefore, some of them must have been made by man— but only, they thought, a few hundred years ago. They showed little or no interest in the fossil bones. While they did concede that they were not ordinary stones, they still maintained that they could not be very old.

It was only after Mary discovered and completely excavated the skull of an extinct hippopotamus that the Masai began to accept that there must be some truth in what we were telling them. They were clear in their own minds that hippopotami lived only in big rivers or lakes and never in such dry country as Olorgesailie. The presence of the hippopotamus skull, with its typical tusks, made them realize that the sites we were excavating, as well as the stone tools and the fossils, belonged to the long, long, long past—*zamani sana.*

After Mary had been working for a while, it became obvious that the site was one of such magnitude, and with so many different living floors, or camp sites, at different levels, that it would be necessary to work it on a much bigger scale than was possible at the time. Menengetti suggested at this stage that if I really needed a team to work there, I should canvass the prisoner-of-war camps for students and lecturers who had worked in Italy on archaeological sites. He felt sure that such men would be delighted to work at Olorgesailie on parole, under our supervision. Consequently, I went to see the director of the prisoner-of-war operation. He readily agreed to find out if there were any volunteers in the prisoner-of-war camps who would be suitable for work at the Olorgesailie prehistoric site.

Our first applicant was a man of about thirty named della Giustina, who, before being conscripted into the Italian army, had worked on a Neolithic excavation near Rome. When I engaged him, he helped me get together a team of nine other men, and I made him the foreman.

The POW authorities provided two portable huts for the men to sleep in, and I had a thatched hut built as their living and kitchen quarters. Weekly rations were sent down for them by the authorities, but we were responsible for providing them with water. As it turned out, their camp was a great deal better equipped than ours was, and they were really quite comfortable.

The plan worked out very well indeed, both for ourselves and for the Italians. They had a job they enjoyed, and it was much more pleasant for them to live at Olorgesailie than in a prisoner-of-war camp, behind barbed wire. We, on our part, had an excellent team to help our few Africans, under Mary's over-all supervision. The men had strict instructions to send a message to us through the chemical company's foreman, who still delivered water to the camp twice a week, if any major development took place while neither Mary nor I was there.

As the importance of the site became more and more apparent, I entered into negotiations with the government for the area to be set aside as a special scientific reserve. We then decided to fence it in, for two reasons. On the one hand, there was the danger that either wild or domestic animals might fall into our trenches and injure themselves. On the other, there was the fear that large animals, like elephant, rhino, and giraffe, would trample over the excavations during the night and damage the specimens, particularly on the living sites we were excavating. (Actually, elephant came through the area only once, but rhino and giraffe were common.) There was also the possibility that herds of cattle, moving in haste across the plains towards the stream bed when it held water, would dash over the sites, and crush and destroy the handaxes and fossils.

The provincial commissioner at Ngong, the headquarters of Masai Province, acting on behalf of the government, authorized me to call a meeting of Masai elders at Olorgesailie, at which he would be present to represent the government while I made a formal request to the Masai to allow me to fence in an area of about three quarters of a mile by half a mile.

The meeting was duly held, and authority was given us by the elders to put up a fence consisting of two electrified strands of wire, with a thorn fence around the outside. The effect of the twelve-volt electrified fence would be such that any animal touching the two wires simultaneously would get a slight electric shock, which, while not damaging it, would give it a sufficient fright to make it run away. One of our Italian prisoners-of-war was an electrician by training, and he was instructed to install the electric fence, while the other men cut down thornbushes to form the outer barricade.

The electric fence was completed long before the thorn fence, and when it was almost ready I summoned the local Masai to come with their wives and families so that I could explain how, once it was switched on, the two wires, when touched simultaneously, would give any intruder a shock that would be *kali sana*—"very fierce." I explained further that there was going to be a thorn fence around the electrified one, so that, in the ordinary way, people—especially the children—would not be in any danger of touching it. The Masai elders looked with awe at the complexities of this strange invention, as did the women and children, but one young warrior was quite certain that I was bluffing. In the middle of the proceedings, he walked up to the wire fence after I had switched on the batteries. While he was preparing to examine it, quite by accident he leaned his spear against the two wires. Instantly, he received a sharp electric shock that made him extremely frightened. Dropping his spear as if it were a red-hot poker, he took off across the plains shouting to the people, who were watching and laughing, that "the wire made my own spear bite me!" A more perfect, and entirely unplanned, demonstration of the efficacy of the wire fence could not have been devised.

We found later that the fence kept our area clear of most animals. Even a rhinoceros would turn and bolt if it touched the fence with either its horns or forelegs. The only animal that, on occasion, was not deterred was the giraffe. If one of its front legs came into contact with the wires, its normal reaction was to swing round through 180 degrees and kick violently with its back legs until it broke the wires and disconnected the whole system! Otherwise, our electric fence served its purpose extremely well.

The Olorgesailie excavations continued under our direction until 1948. As will be described in more detail later, in 1947 the site was opened to the public as a museum-on-the-spot by the then Governor of Kenya, Sir Gilbert Rennie, on the occasion of the first Pan-African Congress of Prehistory. Since then, the site has become known as the richest and most significant in the whole world of the Acheulean handaxe culture.

One of the most interesting results of our excavations concerned the fossil fauna. On one of the living floors we found the remains of more than one hundred gigantic baboons of the genus known as *Simopithecus*. This extinct baboon was larger than any other member of the family that has yet been found, and must have been about twice as massive as a very large gelada, the biggest living baboon, judging not only by its jaw but also by its limb bones. These creatures, therefore, must have been dangerous and, one would have thought, difficult for Stone Age man to hunt and kill successfully. At Olorgesailie, however, as I have said, we found many round stone balls, or bolas stones, and it is highly probable that it was by means of the bolas that Acheulean man was able to capture and kill the giant baboon.

The bolas is a very ingenious hunting weapon. It is made and used in the following manner: Two or more balls—usually of stone, but sometimes of ivory—are each enclosed in rawhide and then joined together with thongs. The heaviest ball is attached to the longest thong and the lightest to the shortest. This contraption is whirled round the head and then let fly at the legs of a running animal or the wings of a bird in flight. Because the balls are of different weights and the thongs of different lengths, the latter wind round the legs or wings of the hunted creature at different speeds and become tangled. The animal or bird is thereby brought helplessly to the ground and can be dispatched at leisure. This type of weapon is still employed by the Patagonians on the pampas, by Argentine cowboys to bring down steers, and by some of the Eskimo tribes to trap geese and ptarmigans in the subarctic regions. How such a clever device came to be invented several hundred thousands of years ago by Acheulean man is not known.

I personally tried an experiment with a bolas on one occasion, but was forced to give up after I nearly killed myself. If one does not release the thongs whirling around one's head at exactly the right moment, the result can be a blow on the head with one of the heavy balls. Obviously, practice makes perfect, because I am told that Patagonians use these contraptions from horseback!

There are two principal reasons for believing that the round stone balls found at Olorgesailie and other handaxe sites were used 200,000 or 300,000 years ago as hunting weapons. In the first place, although specimens frequently occur on the ancient living floors singly or in pairs, we found them on several separate occasions lying in sets of three. It looked as though a prehistoric hunter had put his bolas down after returning from a hunt and, for some reason, had not retrieved it. Eventually, the rawhide disintegrated, leaving the three balls lying in close association, as a set. In each of the cases when we found sets of three together, each ball of a set was of different weight, exactly as in modern bolas. Single bolas stones occur at many handaxe sites, but we found sets of three only at the handaxe site at Kariandusi and at certain places in Bed IV at Olduvai.

The second reason for my belief that the carefully made, heavy, round stone balls found at Olorgesailie must have been used for something like a bolas is that one cannot imagine a Stone Age hunter spending long hours making an artificial ball of stone merely to hurl it as a single missile. It could be argued that it is easier to aim a well-rounded sphere than a jagged lump of stone, but against this is the fact that if thrown at an animal in long grass or desert bush, a single rounded stone could be recovered only with difficulty and would hardly be worth the many hours spent in shaping it. When used as a bolas with thongs attached, the stones are almost always recoverable and can be used over and over again.

There is one other possible explanation for the rounded spheres of stone—namely, that they were used as clubheads. In my childhood days in Kenya, several tribes employed such rounded stones to make clubheads. The method was to take a strong one-half-to-three-quarter-inch-thick sapling from a hardwood tree and cut it down to about three feet long. Then, about eight to ten inches from the top, a light but very strong rawhide collar was attached and allowed to dry, whereupon it shrank, providing a very firm ring at that point. The top end of the sapling was then split into four parts and a stone ball inserted between the sections. The tips of the four sections were bound together and secured with another rawhide collar. After this, the head of the club was encased in a rawhide bag and allowed to dry. When I was young, I used to help my Wanderobo friend Joshua Muhia make such clubs more than once. But the rounded spheres we used were found, not made, by us.

During 1942, my intelligence work took me, on a number of occasions, into the Northern Frontier District of Kenya, and it was most tantalizing to see what looked like prehistoric sites of high potential and not be able to investigate them. All I could do was mark their exact positions on a map and hope to examine them at some later date. When the war was over I revisited one of these sites—beyond Mount Marsabit—and found it to be rich in early Pleistocene fossils. The site is in an area with limited water supplies and the terrain is very rough, so that it would be an expensive one to work. Most of the other sites I located in the Northern Frontier District in the latter part of 1942 and in 1943 are still uninvestigated.

The year 1942 ended with Mary, Jonathan, and me, together with our team of Italian prisoners-of-war and our African staff, spending Christmas at Olorgesailie. We were accompanied by Mr. and Mrs. Hugh Hindmarsh, who were very interested in prehistory, and their children.

Thirteen

Just as, early in 1941, we used a period of leave from war duties to make a quick visit to Olduvai Gorge, so in 1943 we used some much-needed leave from my work with the CID to make a trip to Rusinga Island and undertake further exploration of the Lower Miocene deposits there.

Our leave coincided with the school holidays, and Mary Davidson, who was becoming more and more interested in the study of man's past, asked if she could come with us—a suggestion we welcomed.

As part of the preliminary arrangements, I sent Heselon to the district commissioner in Kisii to obtain permission for us to occupy what was known on the island as "the chief's camp" during our stay. This was a necessary precaution, since if the commissioner himself, or any of his juniors, were planning to be there at the same time we were, it would have been necessary for us to take tents and full camping equipment. If permission was granted, Heselon was then to proceed to Rusinga Island to find out whether the camp was in a suitable condition for our needs.

Heselon returned with the news that the two main *bandas*— or grass-roofed huts—had recently been rethatched and that the district commissioner was happy for us to use them. The information concerning the rethatching of the huts was most welcome, since it meant that they would be reasonably water-proof. This was very important, because Lake Victoria has its own convection precipitation system and there is seldom fewer than one thunderstorm a week, and often two or three.

As everything seemed to be working out well for our visit to Rusinga, we went ahead with our plans and drove to Kisumu. The next problem was how to get ourselves to the island, some forty-eight miles distant at the mouth of the Kavirondo Gulf, and back again when our leave was over.

On several previous occasions, we had been fortunate enough to be taken out by motor launch by a Mr. Death (pronounced "deeth") of the Fisheries Service. He had dropped us off at Rusinga Island, gone on his rounds inspecting the fishing camps, and then called back for us on his return journey. This time, however, Mr. Death and his launch were not available, nor were we able to hire one of the many Asian-owned motorboats normally based in Kisumu. These are used to collect the catch of the African fishermen and bring it to Kisumu, where it is shipped by rail, in specially refrigerated containers, to the Nairobi market.

Heselon had traveled by bus to Homa Bay, via Kisii, and then to Rusinga Island by canoe, returning via Kisumu on an Arab-owned dhow. These sailing vessels, some forty-five feet in length, are used to transport freight to and from the small ports up and down the shores of Lake Victoria, from Kisumu as far south as Mwanza.

When I learned that Mr. Death's boat was not available I immediately went in search of the dhow owner and was lucky enough to find him at home. He said he was due to sail that same evening for Mwanza with his hold full of bags of maize. He was quite willing to give us a free passage to Rusinga, which was on his route, if we could be ready to sail at about 11:00 P.M. This was the time when, normally, the wind changed direction and could be expected to blow from the east, towards Rusinga Island, the full length of the Kavirondo Gulf. The dhow owner optimistically reckoned that he would be able to land us on Rusinga Island approximately at dawn the next morning.

We loaded our bedding and boxes of food before darkness fell and then went to the Kisumu Hotel for our supper. Around ten o'clock we drove down to the pier, taking Jonathan, sound asleep in a basket cot, with us and embarked on the dhow. We took along drinking water, sufficient food for Jonathan, and a snack for ourselves, which we planned to eat at dawn, on landing at Rusinga, before we walked to the chief's camp to unpack and organize the nine-day stay. It all seemed straightforward, but, like so many plans in Africa, it was too good to be true.

On the dhow, Mary, Mary Davidson, Heselon, and I settled down and tried to sleep on top of the sacks of maize, with Jonathan, in his cot, stowed in between us. Just before eleven, the wind came up as expected, the anchor was hoisted and the huge sail unfurled, and off we went. "Rusinga at dawn," promised the dhow captain with a cheerful smile.

Around 3:00 A.M. I heard a great deal of talking going on among the crew, and when I went up on deck I realized that I could no longer hear the slap, slap, slap of water against the sides of the vessel. I looked around and saw that the waters of the lake were absolutely glassy—not the faintest ripple disturbed its surface. It lay utterly still under a full moon. To the eye it was lovely, but from the point of view of our plans worrying indeed. There was, however, nothing whatsoever we could do about it, so the captain left one man on watch, in case there was a change in the weather, and we all settled down to get what sleep we could.

Dawn broke and the water was still dead calm. We ate our bread and butter and cheese, had some tea, gave Jonathan his breakfast, and waited. After a time the calls of nature began to become urgent, and one after the other the various members of the crew simply sat over the edge of the boat. Our little party held a council of war, and it was decided that two of us would hold up a blanket as a screen while the third squatted over the edge just as the crew had done. We did the same for Heselon, who, unlike the crew, had qualms similar to ours.

Around 10:30 A.M. a very slight breeze sprang up, and the captain had to decide the best thing to do. The breeze was blowing from west to east, instead of from east to west, and it was so slight that even by continual tacking we could not expect to make much progress towards Rusinga. The captain, therefore, decided not to attempt this, but, rather, to sail slowly into a little cove on Uyoma point, where there was a fishing camp. There we could cook ourselves a meal and spend the day waiting comfortably for the usual east wind to blow again towards Rusinga in the evening.

Once on shore, we collected fuel for a fire, opened some of our luggage to get out tea, milk, sugar, tinned food, and saucepans, and cooked a light snack for lunch. The crew went off and returned with some delicious-looking fish, which they grilled over the fire. These smelled so good that we asked whether we could have some for our supper that evening. When suppertime came the fish tasted just as good as they had smelled. Feeling better for having stretched our legs and eaten well, we went back on board once it was dark and waited once more for a favorable wind.

Around ten o'clock a light east wind sprang up, and the captain decided to pull up anchor and get away. We were already more than halfway to Rusinga by now, and he expected to reach the island in about three hours' time.

We arrived, as he had predicted, by the light of a full moon and anchored just beyond the narrows at the mouth of the Kavirondo Gulf. As soon as it was daylight, I took Heselon to see the chief, who at once ordered a number of his young men to help unload our luggage from the dhow and carry it to his camp. Many of these young men were people we already knew, since they had helped us on previous visits to the island.

The chief also sent a middle-aged man named Augustino to be our cook. Augustino turned out to be an excellent chef and, among other accomplishments, made beautiful bread, as well as many other dishes, which he cooked over a small open hearth. From then on, whenever we visited Rusinga Island Augustino would appear from his hut and take charge of our culinary affairs. He had, it seemed, once been a cook at a hotel in Nairobi, but had got himself into some kind of trouble (we never discovered what) with the police and had, therefore, decided to live in seclusion on Rusinga Island. He was definitely a hot-tempered man and was inclined to pick quarrels with the Kikuyu members of my staff. I suspect that his voluntary exile from Nairobi was connected with a tribal fight and that the police may have wanted him for having caused bodily harm to some other African.

Soon after we arrived at the chief's camp—which was, indeed, in fine order, with its newly thatched roofs, a new lavatory, and cleanly swept floors—the chief himself arrived to greet us and brought a young, fat ram as a gift for Mary. In return, I presented him with two brand-new hurricane lamps, since he had broadly hinted to Heselon that these would be welcome. I also gave him a four-gallon can of kerosene to keep the lamps going for at least a month or so. And because he eyed our camp beds with such obvious envy, I promised to give him one when we left. (This bed proved such an attraction to the inhabitants of the island that we were asked to bring four or five similar beds on our next visit.) The chief then sat down and told us what had been happening on the island since I was last there, in 1934 with Bell, White, and Kent.

On Rusinga, after a long, hot day exploring the Miocene fossiliferous exposures, we often felt like a swim in the lake, even though it was infested with crocodiles. My safety system was to take my shotgun down to the water's edge and, when the party were all ready to plunge in, to fire both barrels into the water just beyond the place we had selected for swimming. This was effective, because the crocodiles had been hunted for so many years for their belly skins (from which women's shoes and handbags are made) that they were extremely wary of the sound of gunfire and would swim away from the area for a period of at least ten to fifteen minutes, by which time our bathe would be over.

Every day one of us would stay in camp with little Jonathan

while Heselon and the other two, together with a number of carefully selected local people, explored the Miocene exposures. We spent many hours exploring to the west of Lunene, the highest ridge on the island, and located some very interesting fossiliferous exposures, particularly those near the base of Kiahera Hill and at Kathwanga Point. We were not so much concerned to find fossils on this occasion as to try to locate small new exposures of the Miocene deposits that might be worth studying in more detail at some future date. Many of these smaller exposures were hidden in dense bush or were in the midst of cultivated areas. On the whole, the local people were very helpful in showing us places we otherwise would never have found, and, consequently, we spent a most profitable nine days.

We had arranged with our friend the dhow captain to call for us on his way back from Mwanza and take us back to Kisumu. He did so, and we came into harbor in the late afternoon, loaded our kit into the car, and went up to the Kisumu Hotel for the night, so as to get a good rest before our journey to Nairobi in the morning.

Not very long after our return, Superintendent Poppy came into my office early one morning to ask whether I was free to go with him to the Teita Hills to help investigate an alleged murder. He said that he had had a phone call during the night from the district commissioner there, who was in urgent need of help from the CID in the investigation of a violent death.

I wanted to check whether our weekly news broadcasts to the Teita tribe were being satisfactorily received at the various listening points we had set up at market places and in chief's camps, so I approached my superiors, who had no objection to my combining this task with helping Poppy investigate his case. Poppy was in a hurry, and after a hasty telephone call to tell Mary that I was leaving Nairobi for a few days on urgent official business I left with him by car for Voi. (I always kept a small overnight bag in my office for just such emergencies.)

When we reached Voi, about 200 miles from Nairobi, we went to the police station, where we found that the inspector in charge and two of his constables had left by car in the early hours of the morning for the Church Missionary Society station at Wusi. They had gone at the urgent request of the district commissioner and had not yet returned. We therefore proceeded to the district administration headquarters in the Teita Hills, where we found the commissioner waiting impatiently for us. He gave us a quick résumé of the position as he knew it.

It appeared that late the previous afternoon a senior missionary, the Reverend Vladimir V. Verbi of Wusi Mission Station, had come to the commissioner's office in a very disturbed state to report that there had been a gun accident and that his mother-in-law was dead. The district commissioner had at once accompanied Verbi to Wusi, and on the way up to the mission station the man gave his version of what had happened.

He said that upon going into his front garden in the late afternoon he had seen some birds eating his strawberries. He had therefore returned to the house and gone to his study to load his shotgun. This was an old-fashioned double-barreled hammer gun, not a modern type with a safety catch. He had then gone back to the lawn and was just about to fire at the birds when he heard his mother-in-law call out to him. Hearing her voice, he had swung round suddenly, and the gun, which was already cocked, had accidentally gone off. The shot had killed his mother-in-law. His wife was not at home at the time. Verbi had come down immediately to the district commissioner's office to make a report.

When the district commissioner reached Verbi's house and began to look around, the first thing he noticed was that not one but *both* barrels of the gun had been fired. This made him suspicious, and he decided to leave a guard near the woman's body and station others round the house, with instructions that nothing should be removed or disturbed until the police came the next morning. He then took Verbi back with him to his own home and sent an urgent message to the Voi police station.

After we heard the commissioner's report we took him with us to Wusi, while another car followed with Verbi, since Poppy wanted to question him on the spot of the killing. At the house, we found that the police and the commissioner's men were still on guard and that nothing had been disturbed. The body was still lying where it had fallen, covered with a blanket.

As soon as we got into the house Poppy proceeded to question Verbi very closely. Finally, after giving him the customary warning, he obtained a signed statement from him.

While Poppy was interrogating Verbi I went out, with two of the men we had brought with us from Nairobi, to find out all I could about Verbi's way of life, as well as any other relevant information that could be gleaned from anyone connected with the mission. The first important fact, which emerged from more than one source, was that in the late afternoon of the previous day two distinct shots had been heard, with a marked interval between them. From the way this interval was described, it appeared to have lasted for about ten seconds. I was also told by one informant that Verbi was a very hot-tempered man, who had on one occasion fired a shotgun at his eldest son, hitting him in the buttocks. Others to whom I spoke confirmed the fact that Verbi was a man whose temper sometimes caused him to behave in a most violent manner.

When I returned to the house with the information I had gathered I found that Poppy had already sent Verbi back to Nairobi under police escort, to be detained on a provisional charge of manslaughter. This charge had been formally made before the district commissioner. Poppy was by now convinced that the incident either was the result of extreme carelessness in the handling of a loaded firearm, amounting to culpable manslaughter, or was possibly deliberate murder.

Verbi's report to Poppy was substantially the same as that he had given to the district commissioner earlier, though he added a few details. Among them was the statement that he had loaded his gun with buckshot because it happened to be the handiest ammunition available. He also said that he had cocked both barrels of his gun, and when he had swung round at the sound of his mother-in-law's voice both had gone off, one shot hitting the wall of the veranda and the second hitting her. It was a terrible accident, he said, and he was very upset. He also stated his belief that the shock of the first barrel's going off accidentally had inadvertently caused him to squeeze his finger on the trigger and produce a second shot.

Poppy's interrogation of the African household staff had put a somewhat different complexion on the afternoon's proceedings. It appeared that Verbi's wife had been invited to a dance at Voi and to spend the night with friends on a big sisal estate. (Mrs. Verbi was the missionary's second wife and was younger than two of his sons by his first marriage.) Her husband had apparently forbidden her to go. When she protested that she had already accepted the invitation and had every intention of going, there was a heated argument, and he locked her into their bedroom. (As in many Kenya houses, the bedroom windows were burglarproofed with iron bars, so escape was impossible.) According to his staff, Verbi then went off for his usual afternoon stroll.

The staff went on to tell us that while he was out his mother-in-law came to the house, found her daughter locked in, opened the door, helped her get dressed for the party, and sent her off in the car. The mother-in-law then waited for Verbi's return.

According to the staff, when he came back and found his mother-in-law in the house and his wife gone, there were loud hysterical arguments. A little later the staff heard two shots. Verbi, they said, had then called them in and gone with one of them to the district commissioner's office to report the "accident." The staff described the shots not as simultaneous, but as having had a definite interval between them, confirming what my informants in the village had already told me.

Mrs. Verbi had actually arrived back from Voi just before Poppy sent her husband off to Nairobi under police escort. She had refused to make a statement and had insisted on going with her husband in order to engage a lawyer in Nairobi to defend him. She did, however, confirm that she had gone to the party against her husband's wishes, but not that she had been locked in her room or that her mother had let her out.

Poppy now busied himself in making careful plans of the house and its surroundings, including the strawberry patch. I helped him where possible. We also collected a number of pellets of buckshot from the veranda floor beneath the spot where one of the shots had hit the wall, knocking off some pieces of plaster. When we examined Verbi's study we found a number of boxes of ammunition, mostly of bird-shot size, which suggested that when he chose buckshot to load his gun it was not with the intention of killing birds among his strawberries. We next proceeded to record a number of written statements from members of the household staff and from Africans at the mission station to the effect that they had heard two separate, distinct shots with a noticeable interval in between.

At this point, when we were nearly ready to load all the

exhibits into the car and when the body had been taken down to Voi for a post-mortem examination by the hospital doctor, the district commissioner arrived. After greeting us he astounded us by demanding that we leave everything for the time being and come immediately to the church. The Bishop of Nairobi, the commissioner explained, was arriving in a few minutes to baptize his newly born baby, and he and his wife wanted to have as large a congregation as possible. With the missionary under arrest and on his way to Nairobi, accompanied by his wife and a policeman, and with the man's mother-in-law dead, the congregation had been rather diminished. The commissioner, therefore, asked—demanded, no less—that Poppy and I go to the church and attend the service.

In an outlying district such as the Teita Hills, very little could be achieved without the co-operation of the district commissioner, and we did not wish to offend him, since it might well be that we would have to return for further inquiries in a few days' time. Consequently, there was nothing for it but to go to the church in the police car and sit quietly in the backmost pew hoping not to be noticed.

The service began; the baby was duly baptized and handed back to the godmother. Then the Bishop, still in his robes, came solemnly down the aisle straight to where Poppy and I were sitting and said, in such a loud voice that everyone in the church could hear, "I understand you have arrested one of my missionaries. Please tell me what happened." Poppy hastily made some comment about the inquiry's being incomplete, so we could not possibly make a statement at this stage. We then made our escape as quickly as possible to our waiting car.

Here we were placed in another dilemma. One of the district commissioner's young men was waiting, to ask whether we would give a lift to two women missionaries from one of the nearby mission stations, who wished to be taken to the commissioner's house for the christening party. We managed to escape this, however, by pointing out that we already had a constable in the back of our car, guarding a number of blood-stained exhibits, including the shotgun itself, and we did not feel it was really a suitable vehicle in which to take other passengers!

In due course, the case came before a magistrate's court in Nairobi for committal proceedings, and after hearing the evidence the magistrate decided that there was a prima-facie case for a charge of willful murder.

Verbi was returned to custody, and the case duly went to the Supreme Court for trial by jury. The defense put up was exactly as before, only now Verbi admitted to having locked his wife in the bedroom and forbidden her to go to the dance at Voi. Otherwise, he still maintained that the episode had been an accident. Certainly, he had been angry with his mother-in-law and had had words with her, but she had then calmed down, he said, and it was only when he returned peacefully from his usual walk and saw the birds eating the strawberries that he went to his study, loaded the gun with the nearest available cartridges—which just happened to be buckshot—and went back out into the garden to shoot the birds. He again said that just when he was on the point of firing he heard his mother-in-law calling him, and he quickly swung round and accidentally discharged both barrels of the gun, one charge hitting her and the other the wall. Again and again he reiterated that it was an accident.

His wife also gave evidence on his behalf. She admitted that she had been in disagreement with her husband about going to the dance, which she had particularly wished to attend, and that her mother *had* let her out of her bedroom, but she said that there was no question at all of her husband's having been angry enough to commit murder.

When the evidence on both sides had been heard, and after the prosecution and defense counsels had made their final speeches, the judge duly summed up the evidence, barely mentioning the defense contention that the incident had been an accident. The jury, after a brief withdrawal, returned a verdict of willful murder.

An appeal was immediately lodged with the Court of Appeal of East Africa. At the appeal hearing, the defending counsel stressed that the judge had seriously erred in his summing up and had prejudiced the defendant's case by not giving the jury a full account of the defense. In consequence, the Court of Appeal acquitted Verbi.

It should be placed on record that throughout the trial Mrs. Verbi maintained that the shooting of her mother must have been accidental. So far as I remember, as soon as Verbi was released she went away with him for a holiday and never admitted to anybody that anything but an accident had occurred.

About this time—following the Japanese attack on Pearl Harbor and America's entry into the war—we received many reports in Nairobi that a Japanese submarine was making secret landings on the Kenya coast south of Mombasa, possibly to refuel at some secret base in a mangrove swamp. We knew that before the war there had been a number of Japanese fishing craft operating up and down the East African coastal waters. It was, therefore, not impossible, though unlikely, that somewhere or other along the coast they might have hidden supplies of fuel for a submarine. As a result, I was sent down to the coast, ostensibly to collect coastal birds for the museum. I took a member of my museum staff with me, as well as a number of intelligence agents. We were completely unable to uncover any indications of illegal activities along the coast by Japanese craft.

I did, however, learn something of a very different nature, which was of special interest to me personally. At some point after the Japanese entered the war they had sunk an Allied cargo boat that was carrying bales of rubber to London from the Far East. Each bale contained about 200 pounds of rubber pressed tightly together. When the ship sank, a large number of these bales were floated to shore by the ocean currents. Two of them ended up as exhibits in the Coryndon Memorial Museum under somewhat extraordinary circumstances.

The East African coastal waters abound in swordfish, and, indeed, today the coast from Malindi in the north to Pemba Island in the south is famous for its deep-sea fishing. At that time, however, the potential of our big swordfish population was not appreciated. But we did know that there were black, blue, and striped marlin, as well as sailfish, along our coast.

The first bale of rubber sent to the museum was badly eroded by the action of salt water, but it contained, embedded clear to the roots, the bill of a marlin, probably an exceedingly large black marlin, judging from the thickness of the bill at the point where it was broken off. Consider for a moment the immense speed and force at which this marlin must have been swimming to be able to drive the whole of its bill, right up to the full length of nearly two feet, into a floating bale of rubber! (I endeavored, by means of a sledge hammer, to drive an iron bar into this same bale, but managed to penetrate only a few inches.) No wonder, then, that there are records of marlin charging small rowboats at such a speed as to drive the whole of their bills through the planks, sometimes ending up with their entire heads inside the boat, causing it to capsize. In the second of the two bales that came into our possession at the museum there was another broken-off bill, but it appeared to be that of a smaller swordfish, possibly a sailfish.

Back in Nairobi, at my office at the CID, I received a message from Captain Archie Ritchie, head of the Kenya Game Department, that he had had an inquiry the same morning from a foreign gentleman about the breeding habits of buck, which he felt that I, as honorary curator of the museum, could answer better than he could. He considered his job as head of the Game Department to consist mainly of issuing hunting licenses, controlling poaching, and running the reserves. Animal behavior did not come within his province, and at that time no animal researcher was attached to his department.

I happened to be relatively free that morning, so I took time off and drove to the Game Department, where Captain Ritchie and the foreign gentleman were waiting for me, sipping glasses of sherry. When the introductions were over I asked the visitor to tell me what it was he wanted to know. I explained that there were many different kinds of buck in East Africa—reedbuck, waterbuck, bushbuck, and many others—and I should like to know what species it was that particularly interested him. I would then endeavor to tell him as much as I could about their breeding habits.

Perhaps I should interpose here the statement that Captain Ritchie was an ex-Guards officer—tall, thin, with a white mustache and white hair and a stern and proper countenance. When on duty he was somewhat austere. He sat very erect in his chair behind his desk, listening to my questions and sipping occasionally from the glass of sherry in his hand, his whole attention fixed on the problem of satisfying the needs of his overseas visitor.

When I asked the latter what kind of buck it was that interested him, his reply was a shock to both of us. "But you do not comprehend. It is not the breeding of the horned buck that I wish to understand, but the breeding of the *bed* bucks!" As the significance of this reply sank into Ritchie's mind, he became absolutely convulsed with laughter, and his sherry glass went flying across his desk, soaking all his papers. It transpired that the foreign gentleman had found what he was reasonably sure was a bedbug in his bedding the previous evening. When he had complained the hotel proprietor had denied most vehemently that such a thing was possible, and the infuriated guest had come to the Game Department to try to find out more about the habitat and breeding habits of these insects so that he could confound the hotel manager and claim compensation!

Towards the end of 1944, I became involved in yet another murder inquiry. Again it was Superintendent Poppy who sent for me one morning; he urgently needed someone to make plaster casts of two separate series of footprints in the sand by a small stream where a girl had been found murdered that morning. Poppy knew that I had had considerable experience in making plaster casts as a result of my work in the museum, and he thought I would be the best person to help him identify the owners of the footprints, one set of which appeared to have been made by a man in army-type boots, the other by a woman (presumably the victim) in stocking feet.

I had not attempted this type of casting before. Therefore, since the footprints might well be of major importance in solving a nasty murder, I felt I ought to get some practice first. Accordingly, I took my plaster of Paris and everything else I needed to the site and surveyed the situation carefully. The stocking-feet footprints, in the sand on the edge of the stream, had been made by a small person. The other footprints, which were deeply impressed in the sand, had been made by someone wearing heavy boots, on which the hobnails were worn down, indicating the boots were old. Before I started work on these footprints, I carefully covered them, went a few hundred yards farther downstream, well away from the scene of the crime, and made footprints of my own, first with my shoes on and then with them off. I now experimented in making casts of both sets of impressions.

When I was satisfied that I could make a reasonably good cast of both types of footprint, I returned to the scene of the crime and made casts of the suspicious footprints. There were about eight prints of two large boots and about five fairly clear, smaller prints of feet wearing stockings. I also took a number of photographs and made notes, in case I should be called upon later to give evidence in a murder case.

When I finished this part of the work I was taken by police car to the mortuary, where the police doctor was undertaking a post-mortem on the dead girl. I had to wait while he completed his examination to determine whether or not she had been raped, whether she was pregnant, and whether there were any signs of bruises or other indications of a struggle's having taken place before she was murdered. He also had to determine the exact cause of her death. When he had finished his task, I asked to have her stockings, which had been removed. I put them back on the body and made casts of the stockinged feet. When I compared these with the casts of the footprints in the sand I had no doubt at all that they were identical.

The next problem was to locate the wearer of the military-type boots that had made the other set of footprints. This was not part of my job, but I did suggest that if the police found a likely suspect, they should examine his trousers or shorts for plant seeds. Indications at the scene suggested that after the murder was committed the assailant moved off through a swampy area where there was a variety of grasses and other plants, and it seemed to me likely that their seeds would adhere to his clothing.

After several days, the police located a suspect—an army lorry driver—under whose bed they found a pair of boots the same size as those that had made the prints at the scene of the crime. Hidden in a cupboard was a still-damp pair of khaki trousers.

I took the boots, made casts from their soles, and then made a careful comparison between these casts and those I had taken from the river bed earlier. Bally, the museum botanist, mean-while received the trousers and very soon found the seeds of a number of different swamp plants adhering to the cloth and in the cuffs. One seed, in particular, was that of a very rare plant. He and I then jointly visited the scene of the murder and paid close attention to the place where the tracks had led from the body through a patch of swamp and out onto the road. Among the plants growing in that limited area we found an example of the rare plant in question. This was an added, valid piece of evidence that was brought before the court at the murder trial.

The casts of the boots from the lorry driver's room showed minor variations in the stud pattern on the left and the right foot, which corresponded exactly to variations on the casts I had made from the prints in the sand. Indeed, the total circumstantial evidence built up so thoroughly that there was no doubt at all in the minds of the police that they had found the murderer. He was duly brought before a magistrate's court, remanded to the Supreme Court, and found guilty; he eventually paid the penalty for his crime. In those days, an African on trial for murder was judged not by a jury but by a judge working with three African assessors, who, on this occasion, all agreed that the man was guilty.

During this period Mary had been very busy completing her study of the Njoro River Rock Shelter archaeological material and making drawings of the tools and plans of the site. In what spare time I had, I had been similarly occupied in studying the skulls and jaws we had brought from that site.

Mary was pregnant at the time, and on Christmas Eve 1944 our second son, Richard Erskine Frere Leakey, was born.

Fourteen

One evening early in 1945, John Williams, a young ornithologist who had worked for the National Museum of Wales before being called up for the war, came to see me at the museum. He had become fascinated by East Africa, he told me, and was anxious to know whether there would be any chance of an opening for him at the Coryndon Memorial Museum when the war came to an end. I asked him to let me have some specimens of study skins made by him, as well as proof of his ability to mount birds for exhibition purposes. He satisfied me on both counts, and I felt that he would be the ideal person to take over and expand our bird collection when the time came.

Having asked John Williams to keep in touch with me, I notified the museum board of trustees that when the war was over I should be requesting additional funds for new staff and, in particular, for an ornithologist, John Williams. John eventually became a member of the museum staff and has since become well known in ornithological circles.

We had no exhibit dealing with marine biology in the museum at this time, and so I asked Allen Turner to begin preparing a whole series of casts of fishes from the Kenya coast. At the same time, I asked several friends in Mombasa to collect and send me various crayfish and crabs, so that we could also prepare exhibits of these two groups of *Crustacea*.

Only three species of crayfish were known in East African coastal waters at the time, all of them to be found in the fish market. We eventually managed to assemble seven entirely different species, all of the single genus known as *Panulirus*. Later an eighth species was sent from the coast. This was of a kind I had never seen before. After checking in various books on biology, I concluded that it was a specimen of *Paraibicus*, and, moreover, a very peculiar species known as *Antarcticus*, which had previously been collected only close to the antarctic region. Yet it had turned up in the coral reef at Mombasa. I took photographs and measurements and sent these, together with a detailed description, to the British Museum of Natural History in London, asking them to check whether my identification was correct.

They confirmed my diagnosis from the photographs and descriptions; two or three months later, final confirmation was obtained when I took the actual specimens back to England for further investigation. Since then, so far as I know, only two other specimens of this species have turned up along the Kenya coast.

The crabs that were sent to me by various friends were most interesting, and ranged from enormous swimming crabs with shells the size of soup plates down to small hermit crabs and shore crabs. One of the most unusual specimens was an example of the relatively rare coconut crab. This is a strange, overspecialized species of land crab closely related to the hermit crab. For food, it climbs up a coconut tree and nips off an unripe green coconut with its huge main claw. Then it "listens" as the coconut hits the ground. If the sound indicates that the coconut has been cracked open the crab scuttles down and eats the meat. Usually, a crab has to pick off four or five coconuts before it "hears" the right sound. When I say "listens" and "hears" I do not mean that the coconut crab has ears. What he does is to erect his peculiar antennae, which then act as a kind of radar device enabling him to tell whether or not a coconut has cracked when hitting the ground.

At the Olorgesailie prehistoric site, our Italian prisoners-of-war had been doing magnificent work, under Mary's supervision, and she and I now began to plan our museum-on-the-spot. We decided, first of all, to leave a part of each and every excavated area, or living floor, exactly as we had found it, protecting the specimens from being damaged by rain and excessive sun with a thatched roof. We also decided to put a pig-wire fence around each area to prevent visitors from touching the specimens.

We were fortunate at this time to have a brother of della Giustina, our Italian foreman, join the team from another prisoner-of-war camp. He turned out to be an exceedingly fine handyman and carpenter. We gave him the task of planning the roofs and building shelters over each of the sites. We also decided to erect a *banda*, or large thatched structure, near the entrance as a resthouse and to house a series of exhibit cases, round the walls, where the public could examine some of the specimens from the sites more closely.

Olorgesailie is situated in the floor of the Rift Valley and can be very hot. We felt that visitors who had wandered around the two-mile site would appreciate a cool place to rest and have a picnic, especially if we provided them with tables and benches. Our plan was to construct the *banda* on a really large scale, since we hoped, even at that early stage, to turn Olorgesailie into a major tourist attraction after the war was over. We sincerely hoped too that many overseas scientists would come to see what was unquestionably the richest site of handaxe man anywhere in the world.

The Italians at Olorgesailie were a most resourceful group of men. They had learned to make a slightly alcoholic brew from pineapples, the juice and rind of which were fermented. The addition of the dry centers of the stems of certain species of aloe gave the drink a slightly bitter taste, as hops do to beer. They also established a small vegetable garden, and saved all the waste water from their personal ablutions and the washing of their clothes and cooking utensils for it. In this small patch they

185

grew both melons and the most magnificent tomatoes I have ever seen.

In 1944 we had given the Italians a white mongrel puppy, and by 1945 it had grown into a sturdy, pugnacious, and very brave dog—brave sometimes to the point of rashness. Its name was Bobbie. Early one Sunday morning, Mary and I went down from Nairobi to Olorgesailie to see how the work was progressing and learned that the previous evening Bobbie had had a terrible fight with a large male baboon. The noise of their combat had been so loud that the men had heard it from at least half a mile away and had rushed over to find the baboon and Bobbie locked in mortal combat, both of them severely wounded and bleeding badly. The men had killed the baboon and carried the dog back to camp, to tend his wounds as best they could. They had had no means of contacting us that evening, but fortunately we arrived early the next morning and immediately took the dog back to a vet in Nairobi, who stitched up his wounds and gave him a general overhaul. We all hoped that this episode had taught Bobbie a lesson and that in the future he would refrain from attacking creatures too large and dangerous for him. But this was not to be.

One morning not long afterwards, when the men were about a hundred yards from the camp, they heard an appalling noise coming from inside the earth lavatory, known locally as a "choo." By the time they arrived on the scene both Bobbie and the cheetah he had cornered were so badly wounded that the latter died almost immediately from throat wounds. Bobbie died a few hours later in della Giustina's arms. So ended the life of a very courageous dog.

It was at Olorgesailie that I saw my first striped hyena by daylight. While driving at night I had from time to time glimpsed striped hyenas crossing the road in the glare of the headlights, but on this occasion Mary and I were exploring a small side gully in the cliffs about a mile to the south of the camp when, suddenly, our long-haired Dalmatian, Sally, rushed into a clump of bushes and drove a pair of striped hyenas out into broad daylight, where we could see them clearly. These are the true hyenas, known scientifically as *Hyena hyena*. They have a wide geographical distribution, ranging from India through the Near East and all along the North African coast as well as most of Africa south of the Sahara. They seldom occur in forested areas, except in a small corner of the eastern Congo. Striped hyenas were known to science long before spotted hyenas and earned themselves the reputation, in North Africa and in India, of being cowardly scavengers, who would venture into villages at night and steal whatever refuse they could find but run away at the first sight of man.

As exploration in Africa increased, the much larger spotted hyena, known to science by a different generic name, *Crocuta,* became confused by laymen with the striped hyena and, consequently, earned the same reputation as a cowardly scavenger and thief. When I was a boy, this view was widespread among Europeans. But it was mistaken. My Kikuyu friends used to warn me against the dangers of being attacked by the spotted hyena, which they called *hiti,* while the striped hyena, known as *kibubui,* was not feared at all. Spotted hyenas often hunt in packs. Recent scientific studies undertaken by Dr. Hans Kruuk and the van Lawicks have revealed that they quite frequently kill large animals, like wildebeest and zebra. On occasion, they will even attack lions on a kill or a baby rhinoceros that is being defended by its mother.

I vividly remember three incidents in my childhood days involving attacks by spotted hyenas. In the first, a big bull accidentally left out at night on Gray Leakey's farm near Nyeri, on the slopes of Mount Kenya, was found and killed by a pack of spotted hyenas.

The second attack involved a young girl of about fifteen near my home at Kabete. Fortunately, her screams were heard, and the villagers rushed out and drove off the hyenas, but she suffered a severe bite in the buttocks. Although it healed eventually, she was left with a permanent hollow where the flesh had been torn out.

On the third occasion, also near Kabete, two bullocks that had been left in a paddock by my friend Miss Olive Collier were killed and eaten by spotted hyenas.

As I have recounted in my earlier book, *White African,* Ndekei, my driver, and I were once attacked on the Balbal, near Olduvai, by a clan of about seventeen of these animals and managed to escape only by driving them off with shotguns and killing two of them. These two were then eaten by the rest of the pack. Such cannibalism is rare among spotted hyenas; these must have been very hungry indeed.

Unlike the spotted hyena, which has been the subject of at least two detailed studies and is likely to be studied again, we still know extraordinarily little about the habits of the striped hyena, partly because it is so completely nocturnal that it is seldom seen.

It was also at Olorgesailie that I saw a sand-boa for the first time. This is a small snake, seldom exceeding two feet in length, which is a close relative of pythons and boa constrictors. Because of its small size the sand-boa is harmless to man, but it kills little rodents by squeezing them, as boa constrictors kill a goat or a calf. When I saw my first specimen, I confess I had no idea what it was. I had never seen a snake like it and thought I had found a new species. However, when I got back to the museum and looked up the books on snakes I quickly found that it was well known. Like the striped hyena, the sand-boa is a completely nocturnal creature and is, therefore, very seldom seen. I doubt if there are more than a few hundred people in Kenya, of any race, who have seen one alive.

The war was now drawing to a close, but before it ended I was twice called on by the military authorities to use handwriting analysis to help resolve criminal cases. The first was a blatant and relatively simple affair involving a lance corporal who had decided to increase the money he received by altering his paybook. He did this not by overstating sums due to him, but by erasing sums drawn by him and substituting lesser amounts, so that his credit balance was apparently greater than it really was. Clearly he himself was responsible for the alterations, but I had to prove it before a court-martial by showing that the alterations were in his handwriting. This was not really difficult to do, but it involved a great deal of time, since I had to work mainly with figures and not with letters.

The other handwriting investigation I carried out for the military was of a much more serious nature and took a very long time to resolve. The army had been receiving reports from Great Britain that a number of wives and other dependents living there were not receiving their full monthly allowances from their husbands or sons overseas. At first, the authorities thought that possibly the men themselves were responsible, but as the complaints increased in number an investigation was made and it became clear that this was not so. Obviously, a major fraud, involving many accounts, was being perpetrated.

After checking in England, the military authorities became certain that the trouble was to be found somewhere within the Kenya Pay Corps, and the CID in Nairobi was asked to take a hand in discovering the truth of the matter. Although the amount of money involved in each separate case each month was not great, the total monthly figure was considerable.

Eventually, I managed to track down the person who was almost certainly responsible for the frauds, but I could not obtain sufficient evidence locally to take him before a court-martial. I was so certain, however, that I had found the culprit that I requested military intelligence in Nairobi to initiate inquiries in England to check on his prewar record. I also managed to obtain specimens of his fingerprints without his knowledge and submitted them for checking with Scotland Yard. It did not surprise me when, eventually, a reply came to the effect that the suspect had been convicted for forgery in England before the war.

With this additional evidence to support my theory, I was able to gather together sufficient information against him and to bring him before a court-martial, where he pleaded guilty. This gave me great satisfaction, since I can think of no meaner trick in time of war than to use monies due to the wives and families of military personnel for personal gain.

It was during this year too that I had several interesting cases involving forgeries in the Gujarati script, a language used by many Kenyans of Asian origin. Before carrying out these investigations, I had to learn a great deal about Gujarati symbols: how they are written and in what ways they are linked to each other. If the documents I had to work on had consisted only of forged signatures, I very much doubt that I could have studied them successfully, but in each case they were short letters, with alleged forged signatures appended, addressed to different members of an Asian family in Kenya by a writer in India. When I had them translated, each was found to carry instructions about funds to be sent from Kenya to India. For various reasons, the recipients suspected that the letters were not genuine, and the CID was asked to investigate.

The first thing to do was to obtain indisputable samples of the handwriting of the supposed signatory in the Gujarati script. This proved possible because he had formerly lived in Kenya and worked in a government department; while there, he had written a number of letters to friends and colleagues, several of whom were prepared to swear to his writing. They agreed that the writing on the suspected letters looked like his, in a general way, and suggested that he might have been ill when he wrote them, which would account for the few obvious differences.

As it turned out, the letters handed over to me for comparative study by the official's friends in Kenya proved to be those of a man who had returned to India and died there. It seemed certain from this evidence that a surviving relative was writing the letters in the dead man's name in the hope of obtaining some of his money.

But perhaps the most amazing case I came across during the last few months of my work with the CID in Nairobi was one involving a very clever burglar. For several months there had been a series of burglaries in the suburb of Nairobi usually known as Muthaiga, or the Hill. Finally, one day, the culprit was caught red-handed, carrying his stolen booty, as he came out of one of the premises he had illegally entered. The case came to court, and the man was convicted and sent to prison—but not before a complete record of all ten fingerprints as well as prints of his palms was taken for the CID files.

Then, suddenly, there was a new outbreak of similar burglaries in a different suburb of Nairobi. In each case, they followed the pattern we knew was typical of the man now serving a prison sentence, including the care with which he avoided leaving fingerprints. Then, one day, we found one fingerprint at the scene. To the astonishment of the fingerprint experts, it was identical in every detail to that of the man who was still in jail.

Superintendent Poppy's immediate reaction was that the man must have escaped from prison and that, for some reason or another, he had not been informed. However, a telephone inquiry soon eliminated that explanation. A further spate of burglaries ensued, at which no fingerprints were found, and then another, where one more excellent fingerprint was discovered. This once again was identical to that of the man in prison. As before, Poppy telephoned, only to be told that the prisoner was still under lock and key.

Ever since the day I had first joined the CID, Poppy had stressed again and again that the method of identification by fingerprints was absolutely foolproof, since no two people in the world had identical prints. Yet now we had two prints of a person involved in burglaries in a suburb of Nairobi that were apparently identical to those of a man who had already been convicted for another burglary and was serving a prison sentence. Poppy became really obsessed with this unparalleled state of affairs. He studied and restudied the new prints, but could find no difference at all between them and those of the imprisoned man. In fact, his concern led him to prepare a report for the official organ of Scotland Yard to the effect that the impossible had happened and two people with identical fingerprints had been discovered.

As a scientist, I found it hard to believe this. Yet when Poppy himself showed me two greatly enlarged sets of prints for comparison I had to agree that they seemed identical. Suddenly, a possible explanation occurred to me. I asked Poppy to hold everything for a while and allow me to give some of my Special Branch men the task of solving the problem. I got them to watch the prison. After a few days, during which nothing happened, their patience was rewarded when one dark night they saw a figure emerge from the prison in civilian clothes. They followed him stealthily for some distance and eventually arrived in the suburb where the recent puzzling burglaries had been committed. He was just about to make an unlawful entry into a dwelling there when they arrested him.

It transpired that this resourceful man had found a way of getting out of prison unseen, in civilian clothes that he had somehow managed to secrete, and would then commit a burglary, hide his booty, and return to prison before the warders made their morning check.

My men made one mistake. They ought to have let the suspect enter the house, waited for him to emerge, and then followed to see where he hid his booty. We never did discover his cache, which certainly included money, jewelry, and quite a large number of small objects of value.

When, at last, in May 1945, the war in Europe came to an end, negotiations were speedily put in hand for the release of prisoners-of-war. We were informed that among those to be sent back to Italy first would be the older prisoners, like Count Patrizzi, who had been working at the museum on the insect collection, and Ferucio Menengetti, who had been helping in our technical department. The younger prisoners-of-war, like those at Olorgesailie, would have to wait their turn, since transport problems were a major difficulty at that time. In fact, except for those who had wives and children in Italy whom they were anxious to rejoin, they were happy to continue working for us there. Indeed, della Giustina and his younger brother decided that they would, if possible, remain in Kenya. This they were not allowed to do, but after having returned to Italy, in order to complete their release procedures, they came back to Kenya as legal immigrants. In 1947 the older della Giustina took up a position at Olorgesailie once more—this time on a salary, as warden of the site, which had by that time been opened to the public as a national park.

Mary and I were now faced with several difficult decisions. Naturally, Mary wished to return to England as soon as possible to introduce young Jonathan and Richard to her family, whom she had not seen since 1937. I was not free to go with her, since I had to hand over my duties in connection with Special Branch 6 of the CID. I had also been offered the post of full-time, salaried curator of the Coryndon Memorial Museum, and I had to decide whether to accept the offer or return to England and seek a new grant to continue my research work.

Another idea to which Mary and I had given a great deal of thought was the possibility of inviting colleagues from all over the world to come and see some of our important sites in East Africa—the Miocene of Rusinga and Songhor, the Middle Pleistocene site of Olorgesailie, and, of course, Olduvai Gorge. There were also sites in Uganda that E. J. Wayland was most anxious for colleagues to visit.

It was not at all easy to know what to do. Eventually, we agreed that I should accept the museum trustees' offer and become the full-time curator, with the proviso that, having worked for them voluntarily throughout the war, I be allowed to go to England for a brief visit at their expense before taking up my duties.

Finally, the decision as to whether Mary and the children should go on ahead of me to England or wait until I was free to accompany them was made for us. They were offered berths on a transport ship detailed to take women and children back to England. Accordingly, I sent my family off on what, unfortunately, proved to be an uncomfortable journey on an overcrowded ship, planning to join them at the earliest opportunity.

Meanwhile, I opened negotiations with the Kenya government to find out whether they would favor the idea of holding a special meeting on African prehistory in Nairobi in the near future. For the past twenty years, ever since Raymond Dart's spectacular discovery of the juvenile skull of *Australopithecus* at Taung, South Africa, interest in the prehistory of the African continent had been growing. Now, with the various discoveries made by Mary and me in East Africa and by Wayland in Uganda, and with the additional finds of australopithecine material in the Transvaal by Robert Broom and John Robinson, scientists were at last beginning to believe Charles Darwin's prophecy that the birthplace of both man and the great apes would be discovered in Africa. I felt strongly that the moment was most opportune to inaugurate a Pan-African Congress of Prehistory.

I wrote to colleagues in South Africa, Great Britain, and elsewhere in Europe to gauge their reactions to the proposal. The response was excellent, and I proceeded to the government treasury, with the full support of the museum board of trustees, to seek a grant towards the cost of organizing such a conference. I also got in touch with the governments of Tanganyika and Uganda, both of which promised subsidies for what was to be the first Pan-African Congress of Prehistory and Palaeontology.

Once the war was over, I also approached the trustees with regard to the appointment of John Williams as ornithologist to the museum. Fortunately, the new chairman of the trustees, Sir Charles Belcher, was himself a keen ornithologist, and he pressed the case strongly. The question of a salary for John was successfully taken up with the Kenya government, and we were able to tell him that as soon as he had received his discharge from the Air Force and returned from England (where he was to be married), we should be happy for him to take up the position of museum ornithologist.

In the early postwar years passengers traveling by air from Nairobi to London went by seaplane, which took off from Lake Naivasha, landed on the Nile at Khartoum, again at Cairo and Sicily, and then flew via Marseilles to Southampton. When the time came for me to leave, the museum trustees provided me with a one-way ticket by seaplane to England and sufficient funds to return by ship with my family.

The flight was uneventful until we reached Egypt, where the authorities, to my horror, informed me that my yellow-fever certificate, which was only a fortnight old, was not in order. Their regulations demanded that I should have been inoculated six weeks before arriving in Egypt. They were adamant, and removed me and my luggage from the plane. They then took me to a camp outside Cairo, where I was locked behind barbed wire for twenty-four hours. Fortunately, before their plane left Cairo some of my fellow passengers telephoned the British Embassy to explain my plight. Next morning the British authorities communicated with the Egyptian immigration office, and I was released and brought back to the airport. A new problem then arose.

All flights at that time were, of course, heavily booked, since there were so many people waiting to return to England after the war, and I was unable to get a seat. I was advised, therefore, to go to a hotel and wait until I was informed by the authorities at the airport that there was a plane seat available. This did not suit me at all, and I decided to stay at the airport and hope for the best.

It was a good thing that I did so—in fact, the result was a very good example of what is so often described by my colleagues as "Leakey's luck." Shortly after I began my vigil a plane landed in Cairo on its way to England from India. As one of the passengers came down the airplane steps for the brief stopover, she had the great misfortune to slip and break her ankle, and had to be taken to the hospital. From my point of view, it was most fortuitous, since I was promptly allowed to take her empty seat. Thus I got passage to England in time to have Christmas with my family.

Fifteen

Most of my time in England was spent in making preliminary plans for the Pan-African Congress of Prehistory, to be held in Nairobi sometime in 1947. In particular, it was vital to fix a date that would be acceptable to the greatest number of those concerned. I had long consultations with some of my English colleagues, including Sir Wilfrid Le Gros Clark at Oxford, Kenneth Oakley and Gertrude Caton-Thompson in London, and Miles Birkitt at Cambridge.

I also went over to Paris for discussions with the Abbé Henri Breuil and Professor Camille Arambourg. The Abbé Breuil, the leading world prehistorian of the time, had spent the greater part of the war period in South Africa, at the invitation of General Jan Smuts and Professor C. van Riet Lowe. As a result, he was not on very good terms with the French scientists who stayed behind in Paris when the Germans overran France. I found that others of my colleagues were also being cold-shouldered because it was thought they had collaborated with the enemy. Consequently, Paris at that time as a center of prehistoric study was very tense indeed.

In spite of the strained atmosphere, however, I was determined to persuade at least a few of the French prehistorians to attend the forthcoming congress in Nairobi. It was, in my view, unthinkable that we should hold a congress of prehistory anywhere—let alone in Africa—without the participation of French prehistorians and geologists. It was, after all, to the French that the world owed the origin of the science of prehistory, and they had also done a great deal of pioneer work in Africa, along the northern coast. Besides this, I wanted the Abbé Breuil to be the first president of the congress. In addition, since France's North African possessions ranked as provinces and any decisions affecting them could be made only in the capital, my task was to persuade the French government in Paris to arrange for the North African territories to be represented in Nairobi.

I made it quite clear to those colleagues whom I contacted in both England and France that although the congress would be mainly concerned with prehistory, we would not confine ourselves to the Pleistocene (that is, the chapter of the earth's history immediately preceding the present), but would consider the earlier Pliocene and Miocene periods as well. This was necessary because most of the South African prehistorians believed that the famous *Australopithecus* specimens from Taung and Sterkfontein were of Pliocene age. I, on my part, was determined that our *Proconsul* material from the Miocene deposits in Rusinga should be considered as a possible link in the evolutionary story of man in Africa.

In 1946, the generally accepted view of most anatomists and zoologists was that the South African australopithecines were simply a local variant of an apelike creature similar to the gorillas and chimpanzees, and were in no way directly related to the family of man, the *Hominidae*. But I knew that Raymond Dart, Robert Broom, John Robinson, C. van Riet Lowe, and other likely delegates from South Africa were determined to show that the australopithecines were closely related to man and far removed from the apes, a view with which I concurred.

It was, therefore, with the greatest pleasure that I learned from Sir Wilfrid Le Gros Clark that he was planning to visit Johannesburg and Pretoria before the Nairobi congress to see the original australopithecine material for himself. He ranked, unquestionably, as the leading physical anthropologist of the day, and it was of the utmost importance that he should see the actual specimens and draw his conclusions from them—not, as previously, from casts—before he discussed their affinities at the congress.

One of the problems arising from the early date we chose for the congress—January 1947—was that of raising the necessary funds. The East African governments had promised to provide for local expenditures, but we had to raise additional monies from the European countries to make it possible to invite the overseas delegates. In many cases, the governments concerned gave us direct grants, and General Smuts, Prime Minister of South Africa, even made a military airplane available, to transport not only the South African delegates but also those from Northern and Southern Rhodesia and from the Portuguese territories of Angola and Mozambique.

General Smuts had been interested in botany from an early age and later became a good amateur prehistorian, under the guidance of van Riet Lowe. He also gave vital support to Dart and his colleagues in their search for early hominids in South Africa. He then became interested in human evolution generally, and when he heard of the congress in Nairobi he arranged for the South African delegation to bring with them an invitation for the next, to be held in the Union of South Africa.

I realized, at an early stage in the preparations for the congress, that there would be major difficulties in regard to accommodation and transport during the excursions we planned for the delegates both before and after the meetings in Nairobi. For instance, I wanted to show the visiting scientists some of the important prehistoric sites in Kenya, such as Kariandusi, Gamble's Cave, Hyrax Hill, and the Njoro River Rock Shelter, which would involve their staying two nights in the Nakuru area. This meant finding local residents who would be willing to accept two or three scientists each as overnight guests, since hotel accommodations in Nakuru at that time were wholly inadequate to meet an influx of some eighty to ninety people.

Fortunately, a good many farmers in the Nakuru district had become interested in prehistory when I was working at Gamble's Cave and Bromhead's site—both at Elmenteita—and also when Mary was working at Hyrax Hill. Many of them now rallied to my aid and, among them, they promised to accommodate all the delegates in private homes during the time they were in the district. I also had to arrange for meals for the delegates and their escorts during the excursions.

Another problem that had to be settled well in advance was that of the location for the meetings in Nairobi. We required a large hall for public sessions and a number of smaller rooms for offices and where committees could deliberate without disturbance. Fortunately, the Nairobi Municipal Council agreed to put their main debating chamber at our disposal for the duration of the congress, and they also offered us a number of other rooms to use as we liked. I was grateful indeed for this help, which was largely provided because the mayor of Nairobi at the time was also a member of the museum board of trustees and helped me in the negotiations.

In Nairobi itself, I planned to use the accommodations available at the three biggest hotels, the Norfolk, the New Stanley, and the Avenue, but even so I was unable to book enough rooms in advance and had to call on some of my friends to take in delegates as guests.

The most difficult part of the whole organization was how to get my eighty-one scientists—many of them elderly—to the various sites we planned to visit, particularly Olduvai Gorge and the prehistoric painting areas in the Kondoa Irangi district, both in Tanganyika. So far as Olduvai was concerned, I planned to set up a camp on the rim of the Ngorongoro Crater, adjoining the lodge there (which could then accommodate only about twenty people), and take the group for a day trip to the gorge. I went down to Ngorongoro and booked every room at the lodge for the two days we needed. I told the manager that I would bring tents and bedding for the additional people in our party, but that I would like him to provide food and liquid refreshments for the whole party.

Another important phase of the preliminary work was to ensure that we would be able to hire sufficient tents, beds, bedding, camp chairs, tables, cutlery, and other equipment for the trip to Olduvai and to the rock paintings, as well as enough large, reliable vehicles to transport all the members of the congress and those who were helping to organize it.

The proposed visit to the prehistoric art sites around Kisese was complicated by the fact that there were only footpaths leading from rough tracks to the sites. Especially for the comfort of the elderly scientists, I felt it was essential to have a number of roads made so that such cars as Chevrolet sedans could get as near as possible to those sites we had selected for the visitors to see. I therefore went down on a preliminary safari and was able to arrange with the district commissioner of Kondoa Irangi and with the local chiefs and headmen to have temporary roads cut through the bush a few weeks before we were due to arrive, in time that they would not be overgrown again when we got there.

Mary and I naturally wished to show the congress members

the Olorgesailie site, so we planned to hold one of the sessions there, to discuss the handaxe cultures of East Africa. I also wanted our visitors to see at least part of the handaxe site at Kariandusi, near Gilgil. In this connection, I knew that it would be necessary to open an additional trench, since the 1929 excavations had been filled in.

The Kariandusi site was on land belonging to Lady Eleanor Cole, and she and her son, David, and daughter-in-law, Sonia, were most co-operative. We set up a temporary camp for three weeks and extended the excavation, which we had started in 1929, to expose another part of the living floor. In some ways this site was as rich as any of the living floors at Olorgesailie, but there was only one level. One of the most interesting features of the excavation lay in the fact that the majority of the handaxes and cleavers found were made of shiny black obsidian. This stone was widely used in Stone Age cultures of a much later period, but I know of only two other sites in the world where it was used for making handaxes.

My friend E. J. Wayland wanted some, at least, of the visiting scientists to see the Nsongezi handaxe site he was then in the process of excavating, but it was possible only to arrange for a visit by the few people who could afford the time prior to the congress.

Similarly, a number of those planning to attend the congress wanted to make an excursion to the important Lower Miocene sites of Rusinga and Songhor, but this too could be organized only as a brief post-congress trip, when the main parties had dispersed. Quite apart from the time factor, we knew we could not possibly take more than four or five visitors at a time to Rusinga because of the difficulty of getting to the island.

While all these preliminary arrangements were being made, my staff in Nairobi was busy overhauling some of the museum exhibits, which had had little attention since the outbreak of war. I wanted our museum to look its best for the many visitors who were coming from internationally known museums elsewhere. Accordingly, John Williams reorganized the bird exhibit; Allen Turner hastily arranged a marine biology exhibit, using the casts of fish and the crustacean material he had been preparing during the last two years of the war; Joy Bally undertook to arrange a special exhibit of her flower paintings; and Mary and I, assisted by Donald MacInnes, completely reorganized the prehistoric exhibits and those dealing with palaeontology.

Over the years since 1926, I had been steadily acquiring a relatively complete collection of casts of skulls of prehistoric men from all over the world, and by 1945 I probably had the largest single collection of such material. This had been possible because I had exchanged casts of the various Kenya prehistoric skulls from Nakuru, Elmenteita, and elsewhere for those I needed to build up my collection. I explained all this to the museum trustees, and they managed to persuade the Kenya government to give me a grant so that I could order special cases from England in which to exhibit these casts. I was eventually able to have them all on view in time for the congress.

In December 1946 all our energies were concentrated on completing the final arrangements for this first-ever Pan-African Congress of Prehistory. We had recruited a large staff of voluntary helpers. These included Margaret Tait, Catherine Ellis, Sonia Cole, Eileen Bennett, Kay Attwood, and Jean Harries, who, with our museum staff, made an excellent team to run the congress office and help with the excursions. We also recruited Mr. and Mrs. Howard Williams to help run the safari to Olduvai and to the rock paintings. They were to be responsible for the catering and other camp arrangements. As an afterthought, I also engaged a full-time mechanic and a breakdown vehicle to accompany us everywhere and, lastly, a number of good European drivers for the cars.

The individual members of the congress arrived, one by one, over a period of two or three days. The proceedings were then formally opened by the Governor of Kenya, Sir Gilbert Rennie, in a speech of welcome in the big hall of the Municipal Council's building. Before this official opening we had had a number of preliminary meetings on an *ad hoc* basis and had appointed a management committee for the meetings. We had also chosen the Abbé Breuil of France to be nominated as the first president of the congress, with Professors C. van Riet Lowe and Camille Arambourg as vice-presidents. I was designated the organizing general secretary.

As soon as Sir Gilbert Rennie finished his speech, the Abbé Breuil replied suitably on behalf of all the members of the congress, and the Governor departed. We then had a plenary session, at which we officially appointed the president, vice-presidents, chairman, and secretaries of the various sections of the congress. These sections were devoted to geology, palaeontology, and prehistory.

The task of working out in advance the program and order of papers had been very complex. I had tried to arrange things so that there were never two papers of any importance scheduled at the same time, since most of those present were interested in every subject under discussion. Only a few of our members were specialists in just a single field.

On the first day, a small subcommittee was set up to work out a draft constitution for the congress as an international body that would meet once every four years. A small standing committee to manage the affairs of the congress between sessions was also recommended.

After the opening meeting the congress remained in plenary session for a symposium to discuss the South African australopithecines. Dart and Broom first described their discoveries, starting with Dart's juvenile specimen from Taung found in 1924, and ending with the latest finds of skulls and jaws in the Transvaal limestone caves and fissures at Sterkfontein and Kromdraii, near Johannesburg. A general debate then took place, led by Le Gros Clark, who had come back from South Africa fully converted to the idea of the near-human nature of the australopithecines and their ancestral position in man's family tree. Others who spoke included M. R. Drennan, Oakley, and myself.

A discussion on the relationship of glacial episodes in Europe and North America to pluvial periods in Africa led to a hot debate. Some, like Professor F. E. Zeuner, insisted that glacial periods in the Northern Hemisphere coincided with drier conditions in the equatorial zone, while I and my supporters argued that glacials coincided with pluvials, interglacials with interpluvials.

A preliminary discussion of Pleistocene faunas took place next. Arambourg, Dorothea Bate, Oakley, Zeuner, and myself were the main contributors.

In addition to these symposia, numerous brief individual papers were given.

The session of the congress we had arranged for the Olorgesailie prehistoric site was held in the big new *banda* that had been built with the aid of our Italian prisoners-of-war. The Governor of Kenya also attended this session and formally opened the Olorgesailie site as a museum-on-the-spot. After Sir Gilbert made his speech the Abbé Breuil, as president of the congress, stood up to reply. Just as he rose to his feet, the back part of his braces broke, and he had to keep his trousers in position by holding on to them with one hand while he spoke— much to the silent amusement of the assembled scientists seated behind him!

As soon as these preliminaries were over, I gave a talk on the significance of the Olorgesailie site and explained why we had made it into a museum-on-the-spot for the future benefit of visiting tourists. When my paper was over, but before it was discussed, everyone visited the site. This involved a walk of nearly two miles in the heat of the day. Meanwhile, the *banda* was swiftly transformed into a dining room, where cold drinks and an excellent luncheon were laid out. When the meal was over my paper was discussed.

The idea of making an early Palaeolithic site into a museum-on-the-spot, where part of each of a series of prehistoric living floors was preserved just as it had been found, was a new one. The members of the congress were most impressed. The idea caught on quickly, and soon other countries were following our example.

After the excursion to Olorgesailie the congress resumed its sessions in Nairobi. Prehistoric art in South Africa, Rhodesia, North Africa, and Tanganyika was the subject of a major debate, with van Riet Lowe, A. J. H. Goodwin, and Breuil as the major contributors on South African art, while Mrs. E. Goodall from Bulawayo described recently found sites in Southern Rhodesia and Dr. A. Ruhlmann gave an account of some of the more important North African art styles.

A session was devoted to the Mesolithic and Neolithic of Africa, with the South African contingent maintaining that these European terms ought not to be used and suggesting that the term Middle Stone Age should be adopted to refer to cultures corresponding to those of the Upper Palaeolithic in Europe, Late Stone Age to what would be called Mesolithic and Neolithic elsewhere. Despite this disagreement, the discussion was very valuable, with Anthony Arkell giving us the first information about important new sites in the Sudan and Mary describing her discoveries at Hyrax Hill and the Njoro River Rock Shelter.

Again, many individual papers were read and discussed.

This initial congress was really of an exploratory nature, and one of its most important aspects was the bringing together for the first time of prehistorians, geologists, and palaeontologists whose work was concerned with the African continent. One of the results was the decision I have already mentioned, to hold a similar congress once every four years, and another was the acceptance of General Smuts's invitation for the next one to meet in South Africa. Unfortunately, when the time came this had to be abandoned, because after Smuts's death the new South African government made an unacceptable condition—that nonwhites could not participate. Instead, the second congress was held in Algeria.

The first congress ended with a series of resolutions dealing with the future of prehistory, palaeontology, and Pleistocene geology, together with recommendations to the governments of various African countries that they increase their support of such studies.

As soon as the congress was over, we set off for the first important excursion, to the Nakuru–Naivasha basin, where I had worked from 1926 to 1929 and where Mary had excavated at Hyrax Hill in the late thirties. The sites we visited included Gamble's Cave, Kariandusi, Enderit Drift, Hyrax Hill, and Deighton's Cliff. We also arranged special visits to Lake Nakuru for those who wished to see the bird life there, especially the wonderful spectacle of myriads of flamingos. On the day we visited Gamble's Cave, Mrs. Gamble and her husband most generously provided a magnificent cold buffet at their house for over a hundred people.

After the Nakuru–Naivasha visit the party returned to Nairobi and spent a whole day resting. We knew that the next excursion would be a very tiring one—for some, at least, of the party—since it included visits to the Ngorongoro Crater, Olduvai Gorge, and the prehistoric art sites.

We duly left the next morning and spent the first night at Arusha, where arrangements had been made with the Reverend Hampshire, headmaster of the local school, and his wife for some of the party to be accommodated in the school's dormitories. He also kindly put the school dining room at our disposal for a public lecture that evening by Professor Zeuner.

In the morning we all assembled and set off in convoy for Ngorongoro. Earlier that morning I had sent one vehicle ahead, with instructions to wait for us at the top of the escarpment beyond Mto-wa-Mbu, overlooking Lake Manyara, where there was a wonderful view. Our plan was to have a picnic lunch there before going on to Ngorongoro. When we reached the appointed place, however, there was no sign of the vehicle carrying our lunch. Inquiries from passers-by revealed that it was waiting some seven miles farther on, where there was a similar view of the lake.

After much-needed refreshments we set off again and climbed to the rim of Ngorongoro Crater, reaching it at the point where the interior of the crater is first visible after the ascent. Here we paused so that members of the congress could take photographs of this awe-inspiring view, which has often been called the "Eighth Wonder of the World."

At length we reached the rest camp, and the senior scientists were shown to their sleeping accommodations in charming log cabins, while the rest of us organized ourselves in tents. An impromptu bar was quickly set up in a corner of the lodge dining room. The evening was bitterly cold, and whiskies were very popular!

While our volunteer assistants were helping the scientists get ready for the night, Mary and I joined the Howard Williamses in preparing a picnic lunch to be eaten at Olduvai the next day. I also briefed the drivers of the cars, none of whom had ever been to Olduvai, about the many difficulties they might encounter as they descended from Ngorongoro to the Balbal depression and up along the track on the opposite side. I arranged that one vehicle should precede the convoy; another, driven by Mac-Innes, should be somewhere in the middle; and the breakdown vehicle was to bring up the rear.

Our first stop at Olduvai the following day was by my old Camp 1, where I myself had first seen the gorge, with its magnificent geological sections, at the Second Fault. We then moved on to the Third Fault and stopped again, but did not attempt the descent from there. After having thus shown the party two general views and explained the geological sections, I led the convoy to a point near the junction of the main and side gorges, at FLK, where Mary and I, with Bell, Kent, and White, had made our camp in 1935. From this point it was an easy walk down to the sites at FLK I and VEK II, so that those of us who knew the gorge were able to lead the scientists on foot to see fossils and stone tools *in situ* in the lower levels. One of the sites we visited on this occasion was a bare hundred yards from the spot where, in 1959, Mary was to discover the *Zinjanthropus* skull.

Since it was still early and the day was likely to get much hotter later, I decided to take the whole party down the precipitous track at the Third Fault to see the lava flow and the deeper sections of the deposits in this area. On the way down, we paused briefly to examine the site where Reck had found a human skeleton in 1913. After viewing the sections in the Third Fault area we walked down the dry riverbed, which runs along the bottom of the gorge, to the Second Fault, where I showed the party the Capsian site underlying Bed V deposits. We found that there were still pools of stagnant water nearby, one in a hollow in the lava above the old waterfall and another beneath Black Rock, a few hundred yards farther down. Most of the party decided that they wanted to bathe, in spite of the fact that the water was somewhat odorous. The women retired to the lower pool, and the men bathed in the top one. A long slow climb up the cliffs at the Second Fault in the heat of the day was rewarded by cold drinks and lunch.

Our second night at the crater camp provided great excitement for those who were sleeping in the tents. At about eleven o'clock in the evening a number of buffalo wandered into camp, knocking against the guy ropes and generally spreading fear among the sleepers. Soon after they left two rhinos ambled into view in the moonlight and discovered the sacks of cabbages, carrots, and cauliflowers that were supposed to provide our vegetable courses for the next two days. The rhinos set about eating them, and almost everything was consumed.

Since it was essential to get the lorries off early next morning with all the camp equipment, so that the camp at Kisese could be prepared in advance, the people sleeping in the tents were roused early, and they helped to pack everything up. The senior members of the party, who had spent the night in the log cabins, were allowed a more leisurely rising. The view that morning from the rim of the crater was magnificent, and those with cameras photographed it before breakfast.

To ensure that the lorries reached the camp site before we did, we deliberately traveled slowly. When we arrived at the cliff above Lake Manyara we stopped for more photography, and a few of the cars drove down into what is now Manyara Park to see whether they could catch a glimpse of flamingos, pelicans, and perhaps elephants. From there we traveled on past "the pyramids"—a strange natural phenomenon resembling man-made pyramids when seen from a distance—and so on to Kisese camp.

On arrival I learned that one of the three lorries had not turned up. This meant that about twenty-five of our scientists had neither tents nor bedding nor, indeed, any luggage. John Waechter, Desmond Clark, and some of our African staff set off immediately in search of the missing lorry. They found that it had taken a wrong turning near Babati and by the time the mistake was realized had used up so much petrol that it had to return to Babati and refuel. But by eleven o'clock that evening we finally had everyone safely and soundly fed and asleep, in readiness for a heavy schedule the following day.

As soon as breakfast was over, the convoy set out to visit six of the prehistoric art sites in the cliffs between Kisese and Cheke.

Our first stop was at Kisese 1. We had to leave our vehicles a quarter of a mile from this site. The paintings at Kisese 1 are on the sloping face of an immense granite boulder the size of a large house that forms an overhanging but shallow rock shelter. This site was the place where Mary and I first studied the sequence of art styles, and, with Cheke, it still ranks as one of the most important that she and I have studied. The paintings were viewed with great excitement by the French prehistorians because some of the styles recalled those of the Dordogne; the South African archaeologists were mostly impressed by the differences from what they called "Bushman art" in South

Africa and the resemblances to some of the paintings of Southern Rhodesia.

Nearly all the paintings at this and the other sites we visited were in various shades of red. The earlier styles were mostly line drawings, but the later ones were filled in with color.

We omitted a visit to Kisese 2, because of its inaccessibility, and proceeded to Kisese 3 by car. There the local chief had cut a track for our cars to within a hundred yards of the site.

After seeing these paintings we set off once more, this time for the Chungai rest camp, beyond Cheke, where we had arranged to have a break. We were met there by the chief of the area, who told us that his men had managed to cut a track only to within two miles of the base of the cliff at Cheke. This meant a long walk in the heat of the day before clambering 200 feet up a steep cliff. I therefore suggested to the older members of the party, including Robert Broom and Dorothea Bate, that they not attempt to visit this particular site. In spite of my warnings, they were determined to make the effort. I shall never forget the sight of Robert Broom—then almost eighty years old—wearing, as always, a dark suit, wing collar, and butterfly tie, negotiating the last steep stretch in the heat of the day. It was indeed an amazing feat for a man of his age in such unsuitable clothing. Dorothea Bate, though not as old as Broom, was also wearing completely the wrong clothes and made very heavy weather of the ascent.

After examining the paintings at the Cheke site we went leisurely back to the cars and drove to Kisese, where the African staff had heated plenty of water so that members of the party could have a much-needed wash. We celebrated the end of this excellent, but exhausting, day with sundowner drinks.

The next morning we started back to Arusha, where we occupied the same accommodations as on the outward journey.

We were due to leave early the next day for Nairobi, and since we expected this trip to take only about eight hours, one or two of our delegates had planned to fly home from Nairobi late that evening. I had arranged for us to lunch at the picturesque Namanga River Hotel, about seventy miles from Arusha, a very suitable place to break the journey. But as I have said before, plans in Africa seldom work out the way they are intended.

We had gone only a little way past the village of Longido, on the Kenya–Tanganyika border, when we ran into serious floods. The whole road was under several feet of water, and it was impossible even to wade through, let alone drive the cars across. But the water was subsiding fairly fast, so it was only a question of waiting. Presently, after testing the depth of the water, we decided that it would be possible to drive the vehicles through. Most of the delegates decided they would prefer not to stay in the cars, in case the floodwaters had left potholes that were invisible in the roadway, so they removed their shoes and stockings and waded across. They were led, magnificently, by Robert Broom, who rolled his black trousers up to his knees and strode ahead of everybody. The vehicles crossed safely, and we were able, at length, to drive on again, over wet and muddy roads, to Namanga, where we arrived very late for lunch. Fortunately, the hotel staff had realized that the road was probably flooded and had kept a meal ready for us.

Normally, January is the driest month of the year in Kenya, but the unseasonal floods, not only near Namanga but also right through to Nairobi, made the journey very slow. Around five-thirty, when we were on the outskirts of the town, there was a sudden cloudburst and one of the cars skidded badly, shaking the occupants quite considerably. Our late arrival meant that those who had planned to catch planes to Europe that evening could not make their flights. It had been a distinctly tiring and trying day for all of us.

The next day was a memorable one for the congress. Bernard Fagg, from the museum of Jos in Nigeria, was one of the delegates. His wife, Mary (the Mary Davidson who had worked with us at Hyrax Hill and the Njoro River Rock Shelter), had been staying with her parents in Nairobi for a few months; she was expecting her first baby. Throughout the congress we had all hoped that the baby would arrive in time for it to be christened "the first congress baby." Bernard was a Catholic, and we had planned that if the baby was born in time it should be baptized by the president of the congress, the Abbé Breuil.

When we reached Nairobi that evening we heard that Mary had had her baby. Plans were made immediately for the baptism to take place the next morning. Since the Abbé Breuil had not officiated at any baptism for many years, he requested that another priest help him in the ceremony, which was to take place at Mary's bedside. Accordingly, we arranged for one of the priests from the cathedral to assist, and the few Catholic members of the congress were also present. My Mary, who was brought up as a Catholic, stood in as godfather, since there was a shortage of Catholic males at the congress. It is interesting to note that Angela Fagg, our first Pan-African Congress baby, has since qualified as a prehistorian in her own right.

The congress was now officially over, but a few delegates remained behind.

Mary and I had promised to take Dorothea Bate, Kenneth Oakley, and John Waechter to Rusinga Island when the congress was over. A Mr. Day (who had taken over the fisheries at Kisumu from Mr. Death) had agreed to take us out in his motorboat and stay with us for the three days we planned to be there. In this way we could use his boat to reach various points around the island, and save Dorothea and Kenneth from having to walk too great a distance.

We left Nairobi for Kisumu by car, taking beds, bedding, and food, boarded Day's boat in the harbor, and went over to Rusinga Island, where we settled into the chief's camp before dark. Next morning we took the launch and visited sites along the north side of the island, especially those near Hiwegi Hill, such as R I, R IA, RA I, and R III. We had lunch on the launch, returned to camp past the narrows, and anchored facing the mainland. In the afternoon we walked up the long slopes towards Lunene to visit the Kulu–Waregu fishbeds before returning to camp.

The following day we again went out in the launch, to the far side of the island, to visit the sites at Kathwanga and Kiahera Hill. Late that afternoon, while we were still on Kiahera Hill, Day sent a messenger to find us with a request that we return immediately, since it was getting late and he did not like the idea of circumnavigating the island in darkness. Day did not know the reefs round the island as well as I did, and although I warned him to keep well clear of the headland at Gumba, he went in too close and hit some submerged rocks in the shallow waters. We were completely stuck. The boat began to knock badly, and for a few unhappy moments we thought it would be smashed to smithereens. It was desperately important to get it off the reef as quickly as possible. Those of us who could swim immediately stripped and slipped overboard into the water to see if we could lift the boat off the rocks before it was holed. Our efforts were in vain; we simply did not have enough manpower. A number of fishermen and other local inhabitants spotted our plight and swam out to help us. Soon there were some thirty naked men and a few women milling round in the water, desperately trying to get the boat afloat. Meanwhile, poor Dorothea Bate, who was very Victorian in her outlook, kept her eyes tightly shut to avoid the sight of the naked men, while Mary periodically assured her that all would be well.

After a time Day announced that he could see no hope of floating the boat off the reef until we had many more helpers; therefore, we would have to wait until morning and ask the chief to assemble a hundred men. Since there was very little food and drinking water on board, we decided that Mary and I should escort Dorothea and Kenneth on foot along the seven weary miles to the camp, while John Waechter stayed with Day and the members of the crew. Perhaps the most difficult maneuver was that involved in getting Dorothea off the boat and ashore. The only men available to carry her were stark-naked, and she simply *had* to open her eyes to climb onto their shoulders. Poor Dorothea—she was absolutely covered with confusion and embarrassment! However, we got her ashore in spite of her modesty. The locals very kindly lent us some lanterns, and two of them volunteered to guide us along the tortuous pathways to our camp on the other side of the island. Both Dorothea and Kenneth developed terrible blisters on that walk, but otherwise all was well.

Next morning, with the help of a large number of men recruited by the chief, the boat was finally floated off the rocks, and we were relieved to discover that no serious damage had been done to the hull. John Waechter and Day had spent a sleepless night on board expecting that at any moment the boat would break up.

The First Pan-African Congress of Prehistory was a great success. It resulted in a general feeling that Darwin's prophecy that Africa would prove to be the birthplace of mankind was correct. In particular, Le Gros Clark, as the leading anatomist at the congress, made a major contribution to this end. Since he had just come from South Africa, where he had seen the australopithecine specimens at Pretoria and Johannesburg and discussed them with Dart, Broom, and Robinson, he could speak of them with the authority of firsthand knowledge. At the congress he made it abundantly clear that there was no longer any doubt in his mind that these South African manlike fossils were hominid, not pongid (apelike), and that they were more closely related to man than they were to any ape. The lead thus given by Le Gros Clark was speedily followed all over the world. For the first time since their initial discovery in 1924, the australopithecines were accepted as belonging to the *Hominidae*.

Sixteen

Dr. J. Janmart, who represented Angola at the Pan-African Congress in Nairobi, was at the time chief geologist for a big diamond company based on Dundo, in northern Angola. During the previous few years he had become a keen amateur prehistorian and had found many fine stone tools in deposits varying in age from the Middle Pleistocene to recent times. In fact, many of the gravels exposed in the Angola diamond mines were now known to be implementiferous.

The whole of this very rich and widespread diamond field was blanketed by a variable thickness of red wind-blown sands. The sands made it difficult to locate buried gravel deposits that might be exploited except by digging a network of prospecting pits, sometimes to a considerable depth. The deposits underlying the sands and soils were, inevitably, of many ages. Some dated back to the Miocene period and had not been disturbed subsequently. A few were of early Pleistocene age; the majority were attributable to the Middle Pleistocene; a few younger deposits dated to the late Pleistocene and even post-Pleistocene. The youngest gravels of all were in the present-day stream channels, and most had already been exploited for their diamond content.

The vital question facing the diamond company at the time was to find a way to determine with some degree of certainty the age of gravels in test pits. It was particularly important to decide whether a gravel was of Miocene age or whether it belonged to one of the later periods and, if so, which one. The soils and sands of this region were intensely acid; consequently, fossils, by means of which the various deposits might have been dated, were nonexistent.

A gravel that had been worked and reworked by nature was more likely to produce diamonds in economic concentrations than gravels that had not been frequently water-sorted. Diamonds are relatively heavy; when subjected to flowing water, they tend to concentrate at the base of a deposit. The modern technique of obtaining diamonds from alluvial gravels is an extension of this natural process, and is achieved by first washing the gravels and then passing them through a big centrifuge. The diamonds, because of their weight, settle at the bottom.

Janmart, having failed to find satisfactory geological evidence of faunal associations with which to date the gravels in test pits, wondered whether some other method could be devised for this purpose. He had frequently noted that certain deposits yielded stone tools, or at least a limited number of flakes and broken artifacts.

On his return to Angola after the congress, therefore, he persuaded the diamond company to extend an invitation to Mary and me to visit Angola, to see whether, with our experience of the prehistoric sequences of East Africa and Europe, we could help him to obtain more or less positive indications of the age of a particular gravel.

I should explain that the exploitation of this immense alluvial diamond field, which was blanketed by soil and sands to a depth of as much as 200 feet, was being carried out by running long lines of test pits parallel to each other right across the countryside. A high proportion of the pits reached bedrock without striking any gravel. Every now and again, however, a layer of water-borne stones was reached in the pits, and sometimes it was possible to plot the extent of this gravel over several miles by recording its course from pit to pit. The depth of the gravels was, of course, noted and a close lookout for diamonds made by washing samples. If the gravel samples from the series of test pits marking a single ancient stream could be dated on the basis of the Stone Age artifacts the gravel contained, it would then be possible to decide whether or not the gravel had economic potential. If there were no stone tools at all, the probable age was early Pliocene or even Miocene. If the pits yielded Oldowan-type chopping tools, an early Pleistocene age was suggested. Material representing the Sangoan culture indicated a Middle Pleistocene age, while advanced Sangoan or Tumbian-type tools represented an even later period, with possibly a high diamond potential.

I believe the trip Mary and I made to Angola, to study the prehistoric contents of the gravel beds as a means of deciding the age of the deposits and their economic potential, was the first time that prehistory had ever been used for such a purpose—and possibly also the last.

Soon after Janmart returned to Angola the expected invitation arrived, and we gladly accepted it. So far as I was concerned, it meant taking unpaid leave from the museum, but the opportunity to study the prehistory of a comparatively little-known area was too good a chance to miss.

Our task was not to attempt any detailed study of the tools found in the test pits, but to reach a general understanding of the sequence of Stone Age cultures in the area on the basis of evidence already available in the many mines that had been opened up during previous years. We were also to study the mines that had been partially excavated and abandoned as uneconomic, to find out whether the deposits contained any evidence of Stone Age cultures. In short, we were to endeavor to establish the extent to which it was possible to use prehistory as a basis for mining.

The diamond company offered us first-class air fare to Angola as well as free accommodations and all our other expenses paid. In addition to this, we were to receive a fee for our work. In those days, the only way to reach Angola from Nairobi by air was to fly to Ndola, at the northeast corner of what was then Northern Rhodesia, spend the night there, and go on by train to Elisabethville, in the Congo. After that there was air service to Léopoldville, then the capital of the Congo, and on to Angola.

En route, Mary and I spent a short time in Elisabethville as the guests of Dr. Fr. Cabu, who had been one of the delegates from the Congo at the congress. He had already made a number of important archaeological discoveries in the eastern Congo, and we took this opportunity to look at the large collection of artifacts he had accumulated in his museum. From Elisabethville we flew, via Léopoldville, to a little town on the Angola–Congo border, where we spent the night. This southern area of the Congo was the center of the important diamond field in Katanga, which was then being worked by the Belgians and which extended across the border into Angola.

In the morning we were collected by a representative of the Companhia Diamentes di Angola and driven to our destination at Dundo. Here we were met by Janmart and taken to lunch with the president of the company, after which we were escorted to the bungalow that was to be our home for the duration of our stay. It was a well-furnished little house with a pretty garden; to add to our well-being, we were provided with three servants to attend to all our needs. After unpacking I asked where we might change our travelers' cheques, but was flatly refused permission to do so. Strict instructions had been given that we were to charge all our food, drink, and cigarettes (Mary and I both smoked heavily in those days) to the company. In addition to this, we were provided with a car for our personal use, although, for the most part, we were driven around by Janmart in his car. In fact, so literally was the promise "all expenses paid" meant that when eventually we left Angola to return to Kenya, we had not once handled Angolan currency!

After we were settled in our bungalow, our first task was to examine all the drawings and geological sections that Janmart had already prepared, so that we could get a general picture of the problems facing us. We found that he had done a great deal of valuable preliminary work. It was most interesting to see how the courses of buried river and stream beds, with their gravel deposits, could be plotted on a map on the basis of the evidence revealed by the test pits. We were next taken to the huge mines that were yielding a high proportion of diamonds in relation to the quantity of gravel that was processed in the centrifuges. In some cases, the area covered by one of these mines was as much as a mile long and a quarter of a mile wide. There was no doubt that if we could find some way of deciding the age of a gravel on the basis of the small samples of artifacts from a series of test pits, it would facilitate the decision as to whether it would be worth while to excavate huge areas.

After we visited the mines—both those that were being actively exploited and those that had been abandoned as uneconomic—we began to analyze the collections of artifacts taken from each. We also made a considerable collection ourselves at some of the mines, where tools of a primitive type occurred in gravels but had been overlooked by Janmart.

We found that in some places there was evidence of an ancient and very heavily ferruginized gravel, which contained only crude artifacts of the type known as Oldowan. On the available evidence, we assumed this gravel to be of Lower Pleistocene age. It never contained artifacts of the Sangoan culture, which were numerous in younger gravels. The Sangoan culture had first been recognized and named by Wayland in Uganda many years previously and was present in abundance in certain Angolan deposits.

At some of the mines, where the older ferruginous gravel was exposed and had been mingled with the more ancient Miocene gravels, we were told that it often yielded rather higher concentrations of diamonds than did the true Miocene gravels. All the mines we examined that were of high economic value contained typical Sangoan material or evidence of later cultures.

During our stay in Angola Mary and I frequently found ourselves in the strange position of being referred to not as "Dr. and Mrs. Leakey," but as "Dr. Leakey and Mr. Leakey"! The reason for this was that Mary was a heavy smoker, she quite naturally wore her field clothes—khaki slacks—most of the time, and her hair was relatively short. In Angola, at that time, the wives of the Portuguese in the mines did not smoke—at least, not in public—nor were they ever allowed to wear trousers or drive cars. Consequently, Mary's apparel, plus her smoking and the fact that she drove a car, caused consternation among the many men we met, who were afraid that their wives would be influenced by her behavior. We were, therefore, usually introduced to the workmen as "Dr. and Mr. Leakey," and most of them probably assumed that Mary was my brother.

One evening Mary and I were invited to dine with a very well-known Portuguese social anthropologist, Dr. J. Redinha, who, with his wife and family, had been living in the country for some thirty years. During this time he had published monographs and reports on six or seven of the leading Angola tribes.

During the course of the conversation at the dinner table I asked whether any of the Angola tribes made string figures and remarked that, strangely enough, although string figures were common in East Africa, my own tribe, the Kikuyu, had only a small repertoire of them.

To my astonishment, Redinha replied that in all his thirty years in Angola he had never seen any evidence of string figures or string tricks from any of the tribes. To me, this was almost beyond belief. The biggest ethnic groups north of Angola and in Northern Rhodesia, to the east, all had particularly large repertoires of string figures and tricks. Since there were so many cultural resemblances in other respects between these groups and those of northeast Angola, I found it hard to believe that no Angola tribe practiced this art. However, I did not wish to argue with my host, since he seemed so sure of his facts.

Nevertheless, when we retired to the drawing room after dinner I produced a string from my pocket (I almost always carry a suitable piece everywhere I go in Africa), and, as I sat on the sofa waiting for the coffee and liqueurs to be brought in, I proceeded to demonstrate some of our East African string figures. I was in the middle of a complicated figure known as "the bed," which is very common in Africa, and which is known in the United States as "the tent flap," when a servant came through the door carrying a tray loaded with coffee cups, a silver coffeepot, brandy, and cigars. As he came into the room and saw me his expression turned to one of utter consternation. A white man, *a white man,* doing string figures! He hastily put down the tray and left the room, without serving the coffee.

My host was, naturally, shocked by this display of uncontrolled behavior in one of his highly trained house servants. Redinha was about to rush after the man when I stopped him to explain that I was sure the poor servant had suffered a terrible shock and had better be left alone. He had just seen a foreigner engaged in doing something he probably regarded as sacred and known only to his own people. Something, moreover, there was a strong taboo against performing in front of strangers. I begged Redinha to be patient and to await events, and he agreed. Mary, who is also adept at string figures, and I then proceeded to show our host and hostess and their other guests a large number of figures, from Melanesia, Alaska, Canada, Australia, and Africa.

We explained that sometimes string figures were simply used to illustrate stories, as in the case of an Eskimo example that depicts a man catching a salmon. Sometimes they were illustrations in sequence, like the turtle story from Melanesia. Sometimes they had magic or religious significance, and occasionally, as in parts of the Congo, they were used as passwords for secret societies.

While we were talking I noticed that the door at the far end of the room was opening very slowly, to admit the head of the African servant. Next, at the level of his waist, his wife's face appeared, and then those of three children. A few minutes later the door opened wider, and the cook and his wife and family, as well as a whole bevy of servants and their wives, representing the outdoor staff, stood there. They watched in silence for a while. Then I asked my host if I might invite them to come right into the room. They entered and assembled wide-eyed in front of Mary and me, and we proceeded to show them a number of figures we knew, especially some from the adjoining territories of the Congo and Northern Rhodesia.

Soon I tossed my string to one of the men, and Mary gave hers to one of the women. They hesitated for a few minutes, and then, as one took the lead from the other, we were given a fascinating display of Angola string figures, many of which were wholly new to us. Redinha's face was an absolute mask. Neither surprise nor anger showed—just blank, staring amazement. Finally he relaxed and began to question the members of his staff in their own language. He was completely at a loss to know how he could have lived in the country for so long without ever having seen the people he was studying making such figures.

The news that there were two visiting white "men" who knew how to do string figures spread rapidly through the district. In many places thereafter we were referred to as "white gods." Again and again, as we sat down under a tree to have a quiet smoke or eat our sandwiches, people would appear suddenly from nowhere and stand around staring at us. At first they would be a little apprehensive, but as they gained confidence they would shyly produce strings that had been tucked into their belts and do some string figures for us, to which we in our turn would respond by doing some for them. In this way Mary and I learned many new string figures, and we eventually published a paper entitled "String Figures of Angola," most of which had not previously been recorded.

On our last day in Dundo, the president of the diamond company held a dinner party in our honor. During the course of the conversation, which had turned to social anthropology, I described how the people all over the area had been showing us string figures. After dinner we were asked to demonstrate some of these, and before long we had about sixteen people, including our host, sitting on the carpet with pieces of string learning some of the more elementary African string figures!

I should perhaps explain here that years ago, towards the end of the last century, anthropologists and travelers in Melanesia, Australia, and the Far East had recorded a large number of string figures. One of my professors at Cambridge, Dr. A. C. Haddon, was foremost among the recorders, and he devised a special nomenclature for the task. Studies in the United States followed, and in 1906 Jayne published a monumental book on all the then known string figures of the world. In the preface he wrote for this book, Dr. Haddon noted: "So far no string figures from Africa have been recorded, but recently my friend Cunningham has written to me that he has found some at the south end of Lake Tanganyika."

Today, probably more string figures are known from the African continent than from any other. One of the strange things, however, is that a few tribes, like my own, the Kikuyu, do string tricks rather than figures. Some of these, which I learned as a child, I discovered were being performed on the stage in England in the early 1920s by British conjurers.

Another interesting fact about string figures is that, although there are a few in Great Britain and Ireland that are almost certainly indigenous, the best known, such as "the cat's cradle," originated in China and Korea and were most probably brought to Europe long ago by those who sailed the China seas. From Great Britain they were taken by the Pilgrim Fathers to America; in the United States today, these are commonly referred to as "English string figures," to differentiate them from the native Indian ones.

Dundo, the main center of the diamond industry, was also the cultural center for that area of northern Angola and possessed a very fine museum, which had been built by the diamond company. At the time, the museum was in the process of being reorganized. It had departments dealing with mammalian and reptilian zoology, ornithology, entomology, and also ethnology. As part of the latter, the curators had established the first-ever "folk village," where families from different areas of the country were living in huts and compounds of their own tribal type and leading their normal lives. Here visitors could see the different cultural and behavioral patterns of the tribes represented and were able to examine their varying methods of hut building, basket, mat, and string making, and leatherwork. A band composed of individuals with musical talent drawn from many different tribes and families in the folk village provided entertainment and accompaniment for dancing every Sunday.

In the field of anthropology, one of the most interesting things I saw in Angola was the drawing of what are known in the literature as "dust figures." The Angolan examples were very similar to those that had been recorded from Melanesia by Haddon. In Angola, it was only the women who knew these dust figures, which were competitive. Two women would sit on the ground, face to face, and one would suggest the name of a dust figure. Then each woman would set out in the dust the requisite number of dots for that particular figure. These dots were made in parallel rows with the tips of the three middle fingers of the right hand. There had to be as many rows as there were dots in each row. For example, if a row had twelve dots, there must be twelve rows, making one hundred and forty-four dots in all. Then, starting at one corner, each competitor had to draw, as quickly as possible, the complex figure that had been named. No dot could be omitted from the figure, and no dot could be crossed more than twice. I was informed that, just as in Melanesia, so here in Angola, these patterns had a magico-religious significance. Much later, I learned from some Indian friends of mine that in southern India, as well as in Ceylon, similar dust games were played by children and had become a sort of parlor game no longer linked with any ceremony.

Much to my regret, I saw very little of the wildlife of Angola. We were told that there were plenty of giant sable, numerous lions and leopards, and a large variety of monkeys, but the vegetation of the area was so thick that we seldom managed to catch a glimpse of any of them. We did so only when a road reached one of the many large rivers—which could only be crossed by ferry, since there were still no bridges. From time to time, while waiting for a ferry to arrive, we would be lucky enough to see some animal coming down to the water to drink.

One of the impressions we took away from this part of Angola was that most of the natives lacked the opportunity to obtain an education. A few privileged individuals were educated in the limited number of schools that had been established by the diamond company, and then, if they qualified for a profession, they were ranked as Portuguese citizens and given equality. The majority of the people, however, were not provided with any kind of schooling and were completely illiterate, very badly paid for their work, and treated almost as slaves. In direct contrast, many of the Portuguese working in the mines as technicians or specialists had nice homes and club premises built for them by the diamond company and were, for the most part, accompanied by their wives and families. On the other hand, from what we saw of the numerous half-castes and from what we gathered in conversation, there was a good deal of miscegenation between white men and native women.

Before we finally packed up and left for Kenya we prepared a report on our findings concerning the possibility of utilizing prehistory as an aid to diamond prospecting. At the request of the company president, we also wrote a special account of the prehistory of Angola for publication by the diamond company in the annals of the Dundo Museum. The expedition had been a most interesting one from every point of view, and we were very grateful to the Companhia Diamentes di Angola, Dunda Lunda, for their invitation and for everything they had done for us during our visit.

Once we had returned to Nairobi, I began planning extensions to the Coryndon Memorial Museum exhibit halls and work space. I had been fired with enthusiasm by seeing the wonderful galleries and laboratories in the Dundo Museum and hoped that we might achieve something comparable. Unfortunately, in Kenya we had no diamond company to build, equip, and maintain a large museum, but in spite of this I felt there was much we could accomplish. With the permission of my board of trustees, therefore, I set to work to organize a fund-raising committee. I was lucky to have as chairman of the board of trustees Mr. (later Sir) Ernest Vasey. Since he was also in charge of government finances, he was able to persuade the Kenya government to offer the museum trustees a pound for every pound they collected from the public, up to a total of £30,000. If we were successful in raising our share, this would bring in £60,000 for our building program. It was with this goal in mind that the year 1947 ended in our setting up a committee to launch a major drive to raise museum funds.

Seventeen

The original Coryndon Memorial Museum buildings, even with the addition of the new workroom block, were inadequate for the program of expansion I had in mind. The extensions donated by the Natural History Society had provided excellent space for our study collections of birds, mammals, and insects, but after a time we had also had to accommodate the botanical collection, which was building up under Peter Bally. This situation was somewhat eased after the war by the decision of the government to build a large herbarium to house all the available botanical material in East Africa. There was then a large collection of plant specimens at Amani, in Tanganyika, which had been started just after World War I, at the time when the League of Nations took over the country and vested it in Great Britain as a mandated territory. Other collections had been made by the forestry departments of Kenya and Uganda. In addition to all these, we had a great deal of botanical material housed in the Coryndon Memorial Museum, based on the collections built up first by the Natural History Society and later by Bally.

All this mass of botanical material, mounted on sheets, was packed and moved into the new herbarium building, which was erected after the war just behind the main Coryndon Memorial Museum block. Dr. P. J. Greenway, formerly of Amani, and Peter Bally were jointly in charge. Much-needed storage space was thus made available in the museum's workroom block for the archaeological and palaeontological study collections, which were moved into the old botany room.

In spite of this, space was still our major problem, both in the public hall and in the workrooms. In the past I had deliberately overcrowded the exhibit hall in the hope that this state of affairs might stimulate interest in providing funds for expansion. My plans now included a new hall to house the ornithological exhibits, another devoted entirely to prehistory and palaeontology—including prehistoric art—and a third for botanical specimens, including the large and expanding collection of Joy Bally's beautiful flower paintings and a display of the timbers of East Africa. I also wanted a special gallery for insects and another for reptiles and fresh-water biology. If I could achieve all this, it would mean that the whole of the ground floor of the old building could be devoted to mammal exhibits, mostly in the form of habitat groups, while the upstairs could be used for the important mineral and geological collections.

Dr. Hitching, director of the Geological Survey in Kenya, had presented the museum trustees with his valuable private collection of minerals from all over the world. (In the ordinary course of events, the museum accepted and exhibited only material that was East African in origin, but an exception was made in this case.) All three East African governments were, at that time, carrying out major geological and mineral surveys, and there were many prospectors in the field looking for precious minerals. As curator of the museum, I felt that it was absolutely vital for there to be a really first-class comprehensive exhibit of mineral specimens to which they could refer.

One of our problems in connection with this particular exhibit was, of course, the temptation it offered to thieves. One day, a visitor in rather nondescript clothes chose a moment when there were very few members of the public about to ask the attendant to fetch him a glass of water because he was "feeling faint." While the attendant was out of the gallery the man broke the top of a glass case and escaped with a large and very valuable gold nugget; this was never recovered. After that incident we installed burglar alarms on all the cases containing the more valuable minerals, and for a long time we had no trouble. Then, one day, someone with an expert knowledge of electrical devices found a way of disconnecting the alarm system without setting it off and stole our entire diamond exhibit.

With a view to establishing a display of the local timbers, I had been collecting examples of all the more important types of wood. These were cut in eight-foot-long planks, the upper halves of which were kept in their natural state and the lower halves polished. The whole series, of about a hundred planks, was then used to panel a long wall of the botanical gallery. Each plank was labeled with its correct botanical name as well as its common name, and, where possible, a photograph of the species of tree from which it had been cut was featured. One of the administrative officers in the government whose hobby was cabinetmaking gave additional distinction to the exhibit by making a beautiful round table, about five feet in diameter, composed of segments of fifty-two different hardwood timbers, one for each week of the year. The segments were cut so that they all met in the middle, where a fifty-third specimen of wood, ebony, was carved in the form of a ring. I had this table covered with plate glass, and it proved an excellent way of displaying the more important timbers of Kenya that are used for making furniture.

Once the decision had been taken to build a large new wing onto the museum, a committee drawn from all sections of the community was set up. At its first meeting, the members agreed, in principle, that the cost of building each of the three main new halls should be met by the three wealthiest communities then in Kenya—the British, the Ismailis (followers of the Aga Khan), and the Hindus. The halls were to be dedicated to and named after, respectively, Winston Churchill, the Aga Khan, and Mahatma Gandhi. Since the Aga Khan had always been a regular visitor to the museum and was particularly interested in the history and prehistory of Kenya, it was agreed that the hall to bear his name should be the one devoted to prehistory and palaeontology.

In addition to the money needed for the main halls, there was also to be a central fund to cover the costs of smaller exhibit rooms and galleries. In order to raise the money for this fund, the museum staff decided to hold a fete. This, it was hoped, would bring in £3,000—a sum that would then be doubled by the government's pound-for-pound promise. The fete eventually took place over the 1948–49 New Year weekend, on the grounds that now constitute the playing fields of Nairobi University, just across the Nairobi River from the museum.

Among many other attractions at the fete was a spectacular pageant tracing the history of East Africa, and more particularly of Kenya, from 1870 onwards. It included scenes depicting the activities of the Arab slave raiders, the coming of the white man with his railway, and the opening of the first Christian missions. At the time of the fete the main railway line ran right along the edge of the arena where our pageant was to be staged. The railway authorities most kindly agreed to co-operate in our fund-raising venture by letting us use one of the veteran 1890 engines in the pageant episode depicting the coming of the railway. Twice a day during the fete, this engine, pulling a string of ancient carriages behind it, was "attacked" by an African, in memory of the occasion when a Kikuyu warrior sacrificed his life trying to kill the evil "iron snake" that was invading his country. On their part, the Kikuyu of the time had associated the building of the railway with the terrible successive ravages of smallpox, rinderpest, and famine that swept through East Africa in the late 1800s.

Another great attraction and considerable moneymaker was provided by a Hindu fakir who allowed himself to be "buried alive," six feet underground, for twenty minutes at a time, twice a day—each time emerging in fine fettle.

Still another event, which I myself organized, was a demonstration of the ancient Kikuyu team game of "spearing the hoop," which I had played in my youth with boys my age. This game engendered great interest among the spectators, both African and European—most of whom had not witnessed it before. Now, as I write this chapter in 1972, I feel that a revival of this ancient Kikuyu game in East African schools would be most worth while. Why should our schoolboys play only hockey, cricket, soccer, and rugger when they have a magnificent team game of their own? For that matter, why should boys in England not play an African game that involves speed, planning, skill, and team spirit and is every bit as exciting and beneficial as many Western sports?

The fete was an enormous success. We reached our target of £3,000 and might even have raised more, but for the fact that at the last minute we were not permitted to stage the gambling game known as "crown-and-anchor." We had been given to understand by the police that, providing no objections were made, we would be allowed to run the stall, but, unfortunately, a complaint *was* made and we had to abandon the idea.

Apart from these activities in connection with the expansion of the museum, Mary and I were also anxious to raise funds to support a major excavation of the early Miocene sites on Rusinga Island, where, we were convinced, there was much vital information still to be obtained. At the Pan-African Congress, we had discussed this proposal at some length with Sir Wilfrid Le Gros Clark, Kenneth Oakley, and Dorothea Bate; when the congress was over I had drafted a report for Le Gros Clark, which he submitted to the Royal Society in London.

Towards the end of 1947, we received the welcome news that a grant had been made for work on Rusinga Island during 1948. Subsequently, a letter of mine to the London *Times* setting out the problems we had to face in connection with the transport of our equipment from Nairobi to Kisumu and then on to Lake Victoria aroused the interest of an American-born London businessman, Charles Boise. In due course, he generously offered to give us a lorry, sending us a cheque to buy, equip, license, and insure it. This meant that we could transport our staff and ourselves, as well as all our equipment, by road to Kisumu, thus saving the considerable expense of railway fares and of hiring vehicles. Indeed, the lorry proved to be an invaluable asset. We were also able to use it for our annual trips to Olduvai Gorge.

At this time Mary and I already had a fair idea of the location of the main fossil-bearing beds on Rusinga Island. We planned to concentrate our 1948 season's work on the area around Kathwanga Point and the exposures near the base of Kiahera Hill. Both places were on the far side of the island, some seven miles from the chief's rest camp we had used so frequently in the past. Instead of walking back and forth over the Lunene Pass every day, we decided to set up a tented camp in the Kathwanga area. We chose a site under an enormous fig tree, in which no fewer than three pairs of fish eagles had their nests. This unusual situation was owing to the fact that large and suitable nesting sites were very scarce on Rusinga, so that trees had to be shared, though each pair of birds still had its own fishing territory on the lake. We fetched our water for the camp from the lake in tin cans and went for a swim each evening, when we came back tired and dirty from our day's work. From a camping point of view, the situation was not ideal because of the enormous number of mosquitoes. We had to sleep under nets, but had a large mosquitoproof mess tent in which to eat and write up our notes after dark. Once again, Mr. Day of the Fisheries Department had very kindly brought us to Kathwanga. He had promised to call in three weeks' time to bring us fresh supplies of green vegetables and to find out when we would be ready to make the return journey.

By this time we were well known on the island and had many friends there, including the small group of men who had done fossil hunting for us in the past. Augustino, the camp cook, duly arrived from the far side of the island to take charge of our kitchen again, while Erastus Ndere, Zadok Opuko, and Samson Achieng, together with some of their friends, asked to be taken on as workmen for the duration of our stay. Since we planned to carry out some extensive excavations, especially at Site R.106, near the foot of Kiahera Hill, we were glad to have them. Heselon was, as usual, our headman, and we had with us about five of our own permanent Kikuyu staff, who normally worked at Olduvai or Olorgesailie.

As soon as camp was established, we started two trial trenches at Site R.106, where we had previously found a number of broken primate fossil specimens on the surface. One trench was dug into red beds and the other into stratified gray sandstone. Both of these excavations yielded important material, including upper jaws, lower jaw fragments, and teeth of Miocene primates, as well as quantities of other contemporary fossils, many rodents and antelopes among them.

While these excavations were in progress, Mary and I carried out an intensive search of the cliffs and gullies in the area. For some time we had both had a hunch—if that is the word for it—that something very important was near at hand. The problem was to locate it.

One morning, at about eleven o'clock, I was crawling on my hands and knees over an area on the west side of Site R.106 and had just found traces of a lower jaw of a very large anthracothere (a creature related to the hippopotamus) when I heard

Mary calling me most urgently. I got up and went over the small rise that separated us, to see her standing at the bottom of a little gully and pointing up at some bone fragments on the slope above her head. I swiftly joined her, and she showed me some fragments of skull she had picked up on the scree and also a tooth she had found in the gully below. The pieces of skull appeared to be from a primate, and there was no question at all that the tooth was that of a *Proconsul*. It appeared highly probable that the bone *in situ* on the slope above was part of a *Proconsul* skull—something for which we had been searching for many years.

Mary started, very gently, using a fine camel's-hair brush and a dental pick, to uncover the area around the bone she had sighted on the slope. It was a tense moment. The find was not just a few fragments. As Mary slowly excavated, the greater part of a skull became visible. The facial bones were intact, but badly cracked; the whole lower jaw was present, although warped. The specimen was beautifully fossilized. Slowly each individual piece was picked out and put on a tray in its correct position relative to the pieces already there, so that when the time came to piece together the three-dimensional jigsaw puzzle, the work would not be too difficult.

At last the final piece was extricated, and we carried the tray down to the camp. We knew that we had not recovered a whole skull, but it was already clear that we had much more than half of one. For many, many years we had dreamed of making such a find, and now, at long last, the dream had come true. For the very first time, a large part of a Miocene primate skull had been found—our hunch had been right!

Back in camp, Mary, whose fingers are marvelously dexterous for this kind of delicate work, started to piece together the fragments of the skull. It was merely a preliminary effort, but we wanted to see, straight away, just what was missing before we returned to the site with fine sieves to see if we could recover any further fragments from the rubble. Whatever we pieced together now would obviously have to be taken apart again and assembled more carefully after the specimens were cleaned.

We found that we had the greater part of the face, minus a few fragments and one tooth (the tooth previously recovered in the gully), the whole of the lower jaw, the frontal bone, and a large part of either side of the skull (the parietals). But the back of the skull (the occipital bone) was missing.

We returned to the site for several days, and sieved and searched without much success. We recovered only one or two more small fragments belonging to the skull. Reluctantly, we concluded that the missing pieces must have been swept away by the floodwaters that follow severe storms on Rusinga Island, and were by now at the bottom of Lake Victoria.

We had to endure a period of intense frustration while we waited for Mr. Day, since we could not move or even send a report out until he came. Meanwhile, we were making plans for Mary to go to Nairobi as soon as possible and thence to Oxford, to show Le Gros Clark what we had found.

When at last Mr. Day arrived, he was on his way to Kurungu Bay, farther south, and we had to wait until his return five days later! Then, leaving Heselon and the staff still working on the trial trenches, we set off for Kisumu, where we dispatched a highly excited cable to Le Gros Clark before continuing by car to Nairobi.

It was not possible for both of us to go to England. Since Mary had found the skull, clearly it was for her to go. The general manager of British Overseas Airways in Nairobi at that time, Mr. (now Sir) Malin Sorsbie, kindly agreed to suggest to the airline authorities in London that, in view of the importance of the discovery, they fly Mary and the precious skull free. This they generously agreed to do.

By now the news of our find was out and had been headlined in the world press—"First-ever Miocene Hominid Skull," "The Leakeys Find Important Fossil-Man Ancestor" (which it was not), and so on. The advance publicity was so great that by the time Mary arrived in London the press, the BBC, and many other interested parties were at the airport to welcome her. To satisfy the photographers, she had to go up and down the steps several times carrying her precious parcel, and when she was eventually allowed to disembark she was escorted by two police officers to the VIP lounge at Heathrow Airport, where the press and radio men gathered round once more to take close-up pictures as she opened the box and briefly exhibited the skull. She was then escorted by police all the way to London, where she took a train to Oxford. Le Gros Clark was waiting for her there and drove her to the laboratory.

Some joints in the skull's lower jaw were not quite correctly aligned, so that it was necessary for Mary to dissolve the adhesive with which they had been stuck together and reassemble the pieces in their true position before Sir Wilfrid could make a thorough examination. Once he had done so, he cabled me, sending hearty congratulations on the wonderful results obtained with the Royal Society grant.

Fossil primate skulls are very rare indeed. This was the first to be found. The next one, not so old, was found by Dr. Johannes Hürzeler about fourteen years ago in lignite deposits in northern Italy. A third, the oldest of the three, was found more recently by Elwyn Simons in deposits of Oligocene age in the Fayum of Egypt. Still more recently, parts of one other fossil primate skull have turned up on Rusinga.

Our *Proconsul* skull proved to represent a species named *africanus* and was very interesting indeed. The most important points about it were that the forehead was rounded and smooth, showing no trace of heavy brow ridges over the eyes such as are normally found in apes, both fossil and modern. Second, the lower jaw and its articulation with the skull were of the human type, not like those found in apes. The teeth, however, were more like those of chimpanzees, but the face was short and not as prognathous as expected in primates of this period.

In a great many ways, the new skull suggested a *possible* ancestor for both the later great apes and man. For a good many years now, textbooks have placed *Proconsul* in this position. It was only as recently as 1968-69 that this view was challenged. We now possess several specimens from deposits of the same age on Rusinga that may be more representative of proto-man. These I call *Kenyapithecus africanus*.

It is interesting to note that the first specimen, an upper jaw, representing this new species was also found in 1948 at R.106, not far from where the *Proconsul* skull was discovered, but it was too fragmentary for its importance to be recognized at that time. In our 1951 report on the fossil primates of East Africa, Le Gros Clark and I therefore referred it to *Sivapithecus*, a genus of Asiatic fossil ape, which it somewhat resembled. A fragment of lower jaw was found at the same site and at the same time, but its connection with the upper jaw fragment was not then accepted.

This lower jaw was much longer than that of the medium-sized *Proconsul* species called *nyanzae* and about the size, at least in the depth of the mandible, as *Proconsul major,* the largest of the three species, from Songhor. Le Gros Clark and I had a great argument about this specimen before we published the report on it. It seemed to me that it was much too slender and gracile to be called *Proconsul major.* I wanted to link it with our *Sivapithecus* specimen, but Le Gros Clark objected to this and was quite certain it *should* be assigned to *Proconsul major.* In the end, he won the argument and his interpretation was published. I now believe that both specimens represent what I call *Kenyapithecus africanus,* a very early ancestor of man himself. Both specimens were probably parts of the same individual!

As soon as I received confirmation of Mary's safe arrival in Oxford, I returned to Rusinga to close down the camp and pack up the rest of the material we had found. That season's work, made possible by the Royal Society grant, had given us a wholly new insight into the fossils associated with *Proconsul* in early Miocene times. We had discovered a very large number of fossil genera and species of animals previously unknown to science, in particular, numerous extinct rodents, shrews, and bats, as well as larger animals such as anthracotheres, giant extinct hyracoids, and several new fossil pigs and antelopes. And in the shales exposed in the Kulu-Waregu gully we had found many examples of beautifully preserved fossil fish.

While we were on Rusinga a strange incident occurred—one that caused a great deal of excitement and speculation among the local population. The island was, supposedly, free from all large carnivores. The only carnivorous animals known to exist there were a few wildcats, mongooses, genets, and otters; there were no large felines at all. Then, one morning, a herdboy reported that a leopard had killed one of his flock. A few days later someone else saw the same animal, and it was decided that a trap must be set to catch it. The interesting problem for me was to discover how the leopard had reached Rusinga. The narrows between the mainland and the island are deep, and at certain times a very swift current runs from the Kavirondo Gulf into the lake; at other times the direction is reversed. Leopards are notoriously bad swimmers, and it was inconceivable that one could have swum across the fast-flowing water to the island. Yet a leopard was certainly there.

A wide variety of explanations were offered in an effort to solve the riddle. Most of the old people decided that it was not a real leopard at all, but a wereleopard, like the werewolves of Europe. In other words, it was a human being who had died and been reincarnated as a leopard; it had no physical restrictions, and could come and go as it liked. According to this view, it had come to the island to punish somebody for a past misdeed. The younger generation, most of whom were Christians, did not believe that such a thing was possible, but they propounded an equally unlikely theory. They suggested that some enemy living on the mainland had come over to the island by night with a leopard in his canoe and had released it to harass the islanders.

My own conclusion was based on the fact that papyrus grows in dense masses in the swampy shallows surrounding the Kavirondo Gulf, and from time to time great islands of it break away and drift across the gulf, from north to south or along its length, where they bank up and clog the Kisumu pier. On one occasion I counted over forty such drifting islands visible at the same moment from the boat on which we were travelling to Rusinga.

A variety of mammals, including sitatunga—an animal like a bushbuck, with long specialized hoofs adapted for marshy ground—inhabit the swamps. My explanation of the leopard's arrival on Rusinga was that one night it followed a sitatunga into the papyrus just at the moment when a large floating mass was becoming detached from the mainland. Under such conditions, the leopard would have been marooned until the mass came to rest against another shore, enabling it to get off.

In this context, I suspect that zoologists often do not give sufficient attention to the possibility, or even probability, of animals' reaching islands and continents far removed from their place of origin on floating masses of swamp or other vegetation. I would not even exclude the possibility that sometime during the many millions of years that have elapsed since mammalian faunas came into existence some sort of floating island crossed from West Africa to South America. In his recent study of the Miocene fossil rodents from Rusinga, Professor R. Lavocat has made the suggestion that some of the present-day South American rodents may be related to some of the Miocene fossil ones from Rusinga. I would not dismiss such an explanation as impossible, although I am quite sure that most of my colleagues would disagree.

Eighteen

Early in 1949, I had the unexpected experience of being called in—this time on behalf of the defense—to investigate the evidence in connection with an alleged murder. The case involved a young, well-educated English college graduate who, it was charged, had murdered his wife by shooting her with a twelve-bore shotgun. By the time I was called in the man had already been brought before a magistrate's court for a preliminary hearing and had pleaded not guilty. Nevertheless, he had been committed for trial by the Supreme Court.

The defense counsel was a friend of mine, who was aware that I had been involved in helping with several murder investigations while working with Superintendent Poppy of the CID. Although all the evidence in this case appeared to incriminate the young man, my friend was convinced that there had been a terrible mistake and that he was completely innocent. He therefore asked me to reinvestigate independently and report to him the results of my inquiry. Accordingly, arrangements were made for me to interview the accused in prison, in order to hear his story firsthand.

The young man told me he had been to a public school and then to a university in England, after which he joined the colonial civil service and was posted to Kenya. He was a talented musician, but not a particularly practical man. A few months previously—after coming out to Kenya—he had married a young woman who was also musical, and both had become members of the Nairobi Cathedral choir. The house they acquired was in the Hill district of Nairobi, and since they had heard rumors of a succession of burglaries and housebreakings in this suburb, the young man bought a shotgun and ammunition, which he kept in a cupboard in their bedroom. The gun, he explained, was to frighten away any intruders who might try to enter the house at night. He had no previous experience with firearms, but the shop assistant who sold him the gun showed him the safety catch and trigger, stressed that the gun must be regularly cleaned and oiled, and also told him that the gun was entirely safe, even when loaded, so long as the safety catch was on.

On the evening of the alleged murder the couple adjourned to the sitting room after dinner, where the young man played the piano for a time while his wife sat in an armchair nearby mending a pair of his pajamas. After a time, remembering that he had not cleaned the gun for several weeks, he went upstairs to their bedroom and brought the gun down, together with the necessary cleaning materials. He then sat on the left arm of the chair in which his wife was seated, with the gun held loosely across his lap, the butt end outwards and the barrel towards his right side. He started rubbing an oily cloth over the barrel, presently reaching the area of the trigger and safety catch. He had forgotten that the gun was loaded, and as he cleaned the trigger guard he must have released the safety catch and touched one of the triggers, for the gun went off.

Held only loosely on his lap, the gun gave a tremendous kick and flew off his knees towards the piano. The young man looked round and found that he had shot his wife through the head, making the most terrible mess of her. The shock must have been enormous. As he described it, he did nothing for a long while, unable to think or act. When, finally, he pulled himself together, he picked up the gun and placed it in another part of the room, then walked to a neighbor's house to telephone the police that he had accidentally shot and killed his wife. (At a later stage, the neighbors made a statement to the police that the interval between the time they heard the shot and the man's arrival at their house was between fifteen and twenty minutes.)

The police duly came, made their examination, and questioned the young man. When he could offer no explanation of the long interval between the shot and his phone call to them, other than that he had "just sat still, doing nothing," they became suspicious. Leaving a guard on the house, they took him into custody. The current CID superintendent (Poppy was no longer in Nairobi) took over and began investigating the evidence, and was soon convinced the young man had committed willful murder. To make matters worse for him, a young woman volunteered the information that some weeks earlier she had spent a weekend with the young couple and at breakfast one morning had overheard the man say to his wife, "Oh, I could murder you!" This was taken seriously by the police.

The young man protested over and over again that he had not wished to kill his wife and that it had been a ghastly accident, due to his inexperience with firearms and his forgetting that the gun was loaded.

I asked him to make me a rough drawing, so far as he could remember, of the arrangement of the sitting-room furniture on the night of the accident. When he did this, it became apparent to me that the position of the grand piano in relation to the arm of the chair in which his wife had been sitting was such that if the gun had flown off his knees with a kick, the butt must have dented the piano. Consequently, if his story was true, there should be a distinct mark on its polished surface. When I asked him to give a further description of the room, he said that there was a bookcase in front of the window behind the back of the chair in which his wife had been sitting. On this there was a small rectangular wireless set, which did not touch either the windowsill or the wall, but stood some six inches away from both.

Again provided the young man's story was true, by taking a straight line from the dent (if we found one) on the piano, through the point where his wife's head had been when she was shot, and on towards the window and wall area, one would expect to find blood splashes (1) on the front of the radio and (2) on the wall and the window to its right, but not behind the radio beyond the termination of this line.

Having acquired this information, I asked the man's defense counsel to get me permission to examine the room itself. Permission was readily given by the police, and I was allowed to study the room in detail, in the presence of two officers. I took along a photographer, who had been with me in the CID and was now doing free-lance work in Nairobi. In order that the jury might see it for themselves if they wished, the room where the

234

accident occurred had been kept locked and had been left, as nearly as possible, in exactly the same condition as when the police first saw it on the night of the tragedy. The gun had been taken to the police station, but had not been cleaned.

I first examined the side of the grand piano facing the armchair where the man and his wife had sat. Almost at once I located a dent in the polished woodwork that looked as though it had been made by the metal heel of a shotgun. I had a photograph of it taken and, with the permission of the police, made a cast of the indentation with the material dentists use to make molds of teeth. This positive cast looked exactly like the shape of a gun heel.

I then turned my attention to the blood splashes on the radio, the window, and the wall. There were certainly considerable stains all over the radio and on the whitewashed wall, but those on the wall did not extend beyond a certain clearly defined point about three inches beyond the edge of the radio. By taking a line from the farthest blood splash through the end of the radio and onwards, it was possible to get the exact direction of the shot; this, when continued onwards, went straight to the dent in the piano. All these facts very strongly supported the statement made to me by the accused as to where he had been sitting and how the gun had gone off while lying across his lap.

I then took measurements and made drawings of the room, and also had many more photographs taken, including one from the farthest point of the splash mark through the top of the chair to the dent on the piano. This line passed straight through the place where the woman's head had been.

Next, I had to seek permission to make a negative cast from the butt of the gun itself—which the police were holding. At first they refused to allow me to do this, but in the end they reluctantly agreed. When I had made a mold, it compared very closely with the dent on the woodwork of the piano.

I could find nothing to dispute the statement the accused had made to me and to the police, and everything to support it. The only serious accusation that could be made against him was that he had done nothing for nearly twenty minutes before going to his neighbors' house to telephone the police. This, from my point of view, could be explained by the effects of shock.

While I was engaged in these investigations, the parents of

the dead wife arrived from England, and they were so completely sure their daughter's death had been an accident that they sided entirely with their son-in-law and even helped to pay the cost of his defense.

When the case eventually came to trial before a judge and jury in the Supreme Court, the police built up what seemed to them an absolutely watertight case of willful murder. Then it was the turn of the defense, which introduced the evidence I had gathered strongly supporting the young man's statement, repeated from the witness box and unshaken by cross-examination. The jurors were obviously impressed with the evidence we had produced and by the young man's demeanor. They were probably also influenced by the fact that the parents of the dead girl were solidly behind him and had given evidence about how much the two loved each other.

In his summing up, the judge left little doubt that he was himself greatly impressed by the evidence of the defense, but he gave a fair review of both sides of the story, and the jury then retired. After a very short interval they came back with a verdict of not guilty. It has always appalled me to think how nearly that young man came to being convicted and hanged, had it not been for that tiny dent in the piano and the angle of the splatter of blood on the wall.

Nineteen forty-nine was the year in which Nairobi changed its status from that of municipality to city; the Duke of Gloucester came out from England to represent the king at this ceremony. It was at this time that we had some real indication of the growth of what was eventually to be known as the "Freedom Fighters" movement. A large group of important Kikuyu personalities decided to boycott the celebrations, although they had been invited to attend a garden party given by the governor in honor of the occasion. Instead, they held a ceremony of their own under a sacred fig tree at Kiamba, where they took a solemn oath to do all in their power to free the country from the rule of the white man and to regain control of the land that had been "stolen" from them.

I will not enlarge here upon this whole complex question; on the way in which an extensive part of Kikuyu land was taken over by the British authorities at the turn of the century and made available for white settlement. Nor will I discuss the later settlement schemes after World War I. I have dealt with both these matters in my books *Kenya: Contrasts and Problems*, published in 1936, and *Mau Mau and the Kikuyu*, published in 1952. Suffice it to say that some of the tribes—and the Kikuyu in particular—nursed a very real grievance in connection with land settlement. All efforts to right the wrongs by constitutional means had failed, and these people were suffering from a deep sense of injustice and frustration.

During the time that my father was a nominated member of the government Legislative Council, as the sole representative of native interests, he had frequently attempted to get something done about the Kikuyu land problems and other injustices. I too had written about them on several occasions and had taken part in a committee of inquiry on Kikuyu land tenure. That report had shown clearly how, through British misunderstanding, privately owned Kikuyu land had been taken from its owners. However, all the efforts made by my father and others had been to no avail.

During World War II, many Kenya Africans took part in the war effort against Hitler and his allies and were sent overseas, where they came in contact with people of other nationalities, whose way of life was very different from their own. On returning to their native land at the end of hostilities, they were far more acutely aware of the injustices they had suffered and were no longer content to remain passive in the face of British unwillingness to introduce constitutional changes.

By 1949, a number of Europeans, including my own family, felt strongly that something positive must be done to right earlier wrongs. The question was how to achieve this. Was violence the answer, or was there still a chance of getting saner views to prevail at the Colonial Office? Could British officials change their views before it was too late?

It was at this time that I first began to hear talk of a series of secret oathing ceremonies, somewhat similar to those that had taken place among certain branches of the now banned Kikuyu Central Association before the war. Aware of the grim significance of such activities, I sought a personal interview with the governor, hoping to make him appreciate that it was no longer possible to continue along the lines of the old colonial regime. For example, in the civil service there were three distinct grades—the European, the Asian, and the African—each with its own salary scale, based not on qualifications but on race and skin color. I also tried to warn the governor that Kenya Africans had never regarded the report and recommendations of the Carter Land Commission of 1932 as valid and that it was useless to pretend they would ever accept these findings as a fair appraisal of the situation.

Colonial governors and senior civil servants are not easy people to argue with; and, of course, I was not popular, because of my criticism of the colonial service in *Kenya: Contrasts and Problems*. Had it been possible to make the government open its eyes to the realities of the situation, I believe that the whole miserable episode of what is frequently spoken of as "the Mau Mau rebellion" need never have taken place.

When Mary had been in England with the *Proconsul* skull the previous year, she had taken the opportunity of showing it to Charles Boise, with the result that in 1949 he sent us funds to purchase a much-needed motorboat for our research work on Lake Victoria. No longer would we have to depend upon the help of the Fisheries Department in Kisumu or travel in unreliable dhows. His gift was exceedingly welcome, but the problem was to find a suitable vessel. At the time there were hardly any motorboats on Lake Victoria other than those belonging to the Fisheries Department and to a few private owners, who maintained a passenger service from Kisumu to various places within the Kavirondo Gulf. We failed to find anything suitable in the Kisumu area, but eventually we located a forty-two-foot motorboat for sale in Mombasa. It was a twin-engined vessel, built in South Africa and brought to Mombasa to be used for deep-sea fishing. The fact that it had two engines was important to us, since if one failed a long way out from Kisumu, we would still be able to limp back on the second.

The boat, however, was over twelve feet wide, and the railway had a major problem transporting it from Mombasa to Kisumu. The railway track between the two towns was only a single one, and even at some of the stations where there was a dual track it was not possible for the train carrying the motorboat to pass other trains traveling in the opposite direction. The result was that it took almost three weeks to bring the boat the 500 miles to Kisumu. Also, the lengthy journey caused the timbers to dry out, and no sooner was the boat put into the water at Kisumu pier than it started to sink. We got it into shallow water only just in time to save it. Even so, the engines were flooded and had to be completely overhauled before they could be used.

When the vessel had been made good and some minor modifications carried out, I appointed Hassan Salimu to take charge of it. He had, until that time, been working on launches with the air authority at Kisumu. He was assisted by a crew that varied in number. There was usually at least one extra pair of hands on board, because of the necessity of having someone permanently on the boat during our absences in Nairobi.

We named the vessel *The Miocene Lady*. It served us most faithfully not only as a vessel and as combined sleeping and living quarters, but also as a laboratory, and made it possible for us to explore the island of Mfangano, which we had hitherto been unable to visit. We also used the boat to visit mainland sites around Uyoma, on the northern shore of the gulf, and twice we took it down the east coast of Lake Victoria beyond Rusinga to Karungu, where we studied the Miocene beds that had been discovered in 1913. These were the deposits to which C. W. Hobley, then the commissioner in Nyanza Province, had sent a young assistant called Piggott to make a collection of fossils. Hobley recorded that "most unfortunately, before Piggott was able to make any collection of fossils, he was eaten by a crocodile while crossing a swamp on the way to the site."

About this time our activities in the kennel club were increasing, and we began to exhibit our Dalmatians at dog shows. At that time there was no class for Dalmatians, and the breed had to be entered in the "any other variety – nonsporting" classes. This always intrigued us, because although in the nineteenth century Dalmatians were known as ornamental and carriage dogs, the history of the breed shows clearly that there was a time when they were used for hunting hares.

Our own dogs, which over the years varied in number from three to six, were exceedingly keen hunters. At every conceivable opportunity they would go off to chase such animals as duiker, reedbuck, or Thomson's gazelle, and when Sally, the long-haired throwback, had puppies, she would regularly go hunting and return with a hare or some other small animal with which to feed her young—as though she did not trust us to look after them once they needed solid food! We have often seen Sally and other Dalmatian bitches regurgitate meat for their young, in exactly the same way as jackals, wild dogs, and wolves do. In fact, the Dalmatian breed has many primitive characteristics.

As time went on, we sold many of our puppies, and a flourishing Dalmatian Club became one of the breed clubs in Kenya. The Dalmatians' numbers increased to such an extent that special classes were created for them, and they no longer ranked as "any other variety – nonsporting"! Some of our dogs were sent to Uganda, Tanzania, and Ethiopia, and a few were even exported to the United States. On one occasion Mary's bitch became supreme champion at the big annual open show in Nairobi, judged by a judge from Great Britain.

In addition to running the Dalmatian Club, in time Mary and I became active members of the kennel club, and eventually I was elected the president. I judged many breeds and, on one occasion, the grand challenge classes.

We were living now in a new stone bungalow erected for us by the museum trustees on a corner of the museum land and known as "the curator's house." Unfortunately, it was situated right at a road junction, and, consequently, we were obliged to fence the whole garden to keep our dogs from straying onto the roads. Our own dogs were, therefore, safe from traffic accidents, but one day Mary and I heard the terrible sound of a dog screaming in agony on the road beyond the fence. We rushed to see what had happened and found that a black-and-tan mongrel dog had been hit by a car, which had not stopped. Both of its left legs had been broken, and the poor creature was in terrible pain.

Since our own dogs would have made a fuss if we had brought the mongrel into the house, we took it to a wooden shed at the back of the museum and then telephoned for the vet. When he saw the dog he recommended that it be put to sleep. Mary and I, however, thought differently. We knew, from many years' experience, what extraordinary recuperative powers wounded domestic and wild animals have, provided they are young. We decided that we would nurse the dog at least for a week and see what happened. The vet explained that the fractures were too high up on the legs to allow them to be set satisfactorily. The only thing to do in the circumstances was to keep the animal completely quiet and hope that the fractures would mend by themselves. He accordingly gave the dog a sedative injection, and we laid it on its undamaged side and nursed it night and day. Four times a day we fed it by hand, and every few hours we lifted it so that it could urinate and defecate. At intervals too we moved it slightly, to ease the pain of lying in one position, and administered more painkiller.

During the second week, the injured dog began to stand up on two legs on the same side and balance there. After a bit it learned to take two or three steps at a time on the same two legs of one side—a remarkable achievement. Eventually, it recovered completely, and we found a good home for it on a farm miles away from any traffic. Some years later we saw it again and would never have known that two of its legs had been completely smashed.

The incredible recovery powers of mammals were also demonstrated by one of our own pedigree Dalmatians, Flicker, a year later. While we were on holiday in England, we found homes for our Dalmatians with various friends. Flicker went to a farm near Eldoret, an area that was almost entirely devoted to wheat growing. While there he began to indulge in his old hunting habits, and one day he chased a roedbuck into a neighboring farmer's wheat. This man, seeing a dog and a buck careering through his ripening grain, rushed to fetch a rifle and fired. Flicker was hit high in the shoulder, and his humerus was shattered. Our friends, rightly, in our view, decided not to have the dog put to sleep, but to try to nurse him. They thought that Flicker would never be a show dog again but at least, as a pedigree dog, he might still sire future champions. They cabled us with the news of what had happened, and we agreed that Flicker's life must be saved if possible.

Thanks to magnificent nursing and veterinary care, Flicker not only survived to sire many winners, but he himself, two years later, won in the show ring too! The extraordinary thing was that he never limped at all while he was in the ring, although before and after his events it was obvious that he was lame. On this particular occasion, the judge, who was from England, happened to be dining with us when he suddenly saw the dog to whom he had given the challenge certificate appear with a limp. He inquired what had happened to the dog's shoulder and could hardly believe us when we told him that in spite of having been shot through the shoulder two years previously, Flicker never, under any circumstances, limped when in the show ring.

Another example of the extraordinary recuperative powers of seriously injured animals belongs to a much later date, but I will tell the story here. After we moved into our new house at Langata in 1952, Mary and I encouraged the children to ride and to take part in the activities of the pony club. On this occasion, they and some of their friends had gone off to a drag hunt. During a check, a mare that was stabled at our home panicked and charged through the ring of cars belonging to the hunt followers. She crashed against a car wing, breaking the headlight, and tore from her shoulder a lump of flesh about as big as a leg of mutton. This was hanging by a small strip of skin, and the wound was bleeding hideously. Helped by others, our family caught the mare and halted the flow of blood by using our shirts as bandages. Most of those present urged that the mare be shot immediately to put her out of her pain, but Mary and I were determined to save her life if possible. We sent word to the vet to meet us at home, and meanwhile we coaxed the mare gently to her feet and into a horse box.

When we got home the vet was waiting for us. After examining the wound, he said it was completely hopeless and the mare had better be destroyed. We refused to agree and asked him to give her a general anaesthetic and then stitch up the wound; we would nurse her until she was well again. Most unwillingly, the vet agreed, and once the operation was over and the mare recovered consciousness, we got her into her own stable. Thereafter, night and day, Mary and I and the stableboys took turns staying with her and holding her head so as to prevent her from biting the stitches and otherwise damaging herself. By the end of three weeks she was infinitely better, and the stitches were removed. Two years later, she was once more winning in show jumping.

Let me give one more example, this time of a wild animal. A young male baboon living in the Nairobi National Park lost its right forearm. The wound bled profusely, and the prospects of recovery did not seem at all good. However, after consultation, the warden decided it would be best to leave the animal alone and see how it fared. Since then, I have watched its progress over the years, and now, to my delight, this baboon is one of the "big five" dominating the troop to which it belongs.

Silent but eloquent testimony to the recovery powers of wild animals frequently becomes apparent from the study of skeletons housed in the museums of the world. One quite often finds bones that have received fractures when the animal was young and that have healed, allowing the animal to live to a good age. This applies not only to animals that live on the open plains, like zebra, wildebeest, and hartebeest, but also to monkeys. I believe that a study of the percentage of animals with healed broken bones would be very interesting. Nature helps not only animals with broken limbs to survive; there are also many cases on record where the wounds of animals shot with poisoned arrows or pierced by other weapons have healed and tissue has formed round the offending foreign body, isolating it.

Let me end this chapter by saying that far too often animals are put to sleep when they could be saved through proper care and nursing. The problem is that most people are unwilling, or unable, to devote enough time for this purpose. I am not advocating indiscriminate action in this respect. Clearly, there are occasions when a major injury to some vital organ calls for an act of mercy to end unnecessary pain. To save an animal's life in order that it may suffer indefinitely is something I would never condone. But many people act too precipitously when an animal's limbs are broken or damaged.

Nineteen

In 1950, Mary and I were due for a period of leave in England and had already begun making plans to travel by sea when we received a most unexpected offer from the British Overseas Airways Corporation. We had come in close touch with the company in connection with the flight Mary made to London with the *Proconsul* skull in 1948. Now, when they learned that we were going to England with our three children (our third

243

son, Philip, had been born in 1949), they offered to fly us there free of charge if they could make use of this fact to advertise their East African service. Since our funds were at a low ebb, we readily accepted the offer and eventually took off from Lake Naivasha by seaplane for Southampton. At Southampton we were met by a BOAC driver and taken to a hotel in London. On the following day we were taken on a sightseeing tour and photographed with our children against typical London backgrounds. In this way, the airline obtained publicity material and we had our free flight.

In order to give the children the advantages of English country life during this holiday, we had advertised for a house somewhere in the country, not too far from London. Finally we selected one in the little village of Ewhurst in Surrey. It suited us perfectly, having plenty of room for us as well as for Mary's aunts, whom we had invited to stay with us. From the children's point of view the place was magnificent. Behind the house there were grassy fields and chestnut woods abounding with bird and animal life.

Mary and I had told Charles Boise (the London businessman who had given us the lorry and the motorboat, *The Miocene Lady*) that while we were in Europe we would be happy to go with him to France to visit some of the more important prehistoric art sites. Charles was a connoisseur of art. He had a large collection of paintings by famous artists and was anxious to acquaint himself with art in its more primitive forms. Mary and I were glad to have this chance of revisiting the sites we already knew and of seeing the paintings in the Lascaux cave, which we had not been able to see so far. Mary's aunts declared themselves willing to look after the three children while we were away, so we left with Charles for the Dordogne.

We had an excellent trip and saw many of the famous art sites before we arrived at Lascaux. Here, fortunately, I was acquainted with both the local representative of the Ministry of Fine Arts, who was officially responsible for the prehistoric art sites of the area, and with a French government official. These two men kindly made arrangements for us to visit the caves after normal closing time, which was a great advantage, since then the Abbé Glorie and other prehistorians were able to accompany us and discuss the significance of the discoveries.

We also visited a number of sites in the valley of the Lot that were new to me but had been known to Mary since childhood. Our visit to Pech-Merle, where Mary had worked with the Abbé Lemozie when she was eleven years old, was a particularly memorable occasion for us. This site, or at least a part of it, had been opened to the public. We were very happy to find that the Abbé was still living in the little village. He was, of course, delighted to meet Mary again after so many years and showed us round the site with great pride.

We visited Pech-Merle again a good many years later and were shown very exciting evidence that prehistoric man, towards the end of the Ice Age, had actually made music. In one small part of the cave deep below ground a set of stalactites was discovered showing certain interesting signs of damage. These were left untouched for many years, until the authorities decided to make an experiment. It was then found that when these stalactites were hit with a piece of wood covered with a chamois leather, each produced a different note. The indentations were explained, and the prehistorians found themselves in possession of a prehistoric musical instrument—the earliest known to science!

Our visits to the prehistoric art sites included one to Cap Blanc, to see the wonderful bas-relief of extinct horses. We also looked at a number of the more famous prehistoric sites, such as Le Moustier, La Mouthe, and Niaux, which are of great importance.

Unfortunately, there is tragic evidence to show that the paintings at the French prehistoric art sites are deteriorating, and it has become necessary in recent years to close the Lascaux cave while experiments are being carried out to find the exact cause of the damage. Until this particular site was discovered, it had been entirely cut off from ordinary atmospheric conditions by a fall of rock. After being opened to the public, it was visited by thousands of tourists. A suggestion has been made that the carbon dioxide exhaled from their lungs may have caused the damage to these beautiful paintings, which by any standards must be regarded as some of the finest in the world.

The visit to France not only gave Mary and me a chance to get to know our benefactor, but also fired Charles with an enthusiastic interest in prehistoric art. During the course of the holiday he promised to give us additional funds for our work at Olduvai, and we were delighted when he announced his intention of coming out to East Africa the following year to visit the gorge and see some of the prehistoric art sites in central Tanganyika. Such was his zest, moreover, that he even decided he might accompany us on a trip in the motorboat to see the fossil beds at Rusinga Island.

Soon after our return to Ewhurst we were approached by a neighbor of ours, Mr. (later Sir) Edward Beddington Behrens, who had a manor house a few miles away, at Abinger Common. Behind the house there was a vegetable garden and beyond that a recently ploughed field. After the ploughing and after rain had washed the soil, Edward noticed that in one corner of this field a large number of flint flakes and other signs of prehistoric culture had become visible. He rightly assumed that below the topsoil there must be a land surface that, at one time, had been occupied by a prehistoric camp. He therefore collected a number of specimens and showed them to several experts in Great Britain. Every one of the experts, even those who visited the site, assured him that although the specimens he had picked up belonged to the Tardenoisian culture, similar sites were scattered throughout Surrey and Hampshire and had been used as temporary summer camps of this late Mesolithic hunting people. They had decided, therefore, that this site had no particular significance and had declined to investigate further.

Without telling us any of this, Edward invited Mary and me to come over one day and examine his collection of artifacts. Mary and I found the evidence exciting. There were a great many stone tools washing out from the surface, and we considered that they were far too numerous to indicate only a temporary summer camp.

After our preliminary examination we decided that further investigation would most certainly be worth while. However, since our interests were in African prehistory, we told Edward that we did not really wish to undertake any work in England. We told him, moreover, that in our opinion the investigation should be made by British prehistorians.

Edward then revealed that certain British archaeologists had already examined the place and rejected it as having little scientific value. In the circumstances, he begged us to reconsider our decision. Ultimately, I agreed that if no objections were raised by my British colleagues, Mary and I would undertake a test dig. None were made, and several British prehistorians even went so far as to make it clear that they considered we would be wasting our time if we proceeded with our proposal. Neither Mary nor I shared this view. We told Edward that while we were happy to do what we could in the time available, he must remember that autumn was approaching and such an outdoor excavation in England might be difficult because of the weather. Edward was delighted we were going ahead and promised that as soon as we decided where to make our main trial trench he would have a sixty-foot marquee erected over the area, to protect us from cold winds and rain.

We started by cutting two parallel lines of trial trenches, each trench being five feet long by three feet wide and separated from the next trench by an area of similar dimensions. The trenches were arranged in such a way that those in one line were next to the undisturbed areas of the other line. We plotted the distribution of the artifacts found in these two lines, and it was soon apparent that the number of tools and waste flakes was increasing as we went up a slope. After a time, the edge of what appeared to be an ancient pit dwelling appeared in one of our excavations. Previously, no Mesolithic pit dwellings had ever been found intact in England, although several damaged ones had been revealed by accident during commercial excavations. It seemed likely that we had hit upon the first undamaged example, and this was extremely rewarding.

True to his promise, Edward sent for a sixty-foot marquee and had it erected over the area where the edge of the dwelling was exposed in the trial trench. With the help of additional staff and with the personal assistance of Edward and his wife, we soon uncovered what appeared to be one half of a magnificent pit dwelling. Shortly afterwards the whole dwelling became visible, exposing a hearth, postholes, and a great deal of very exciting material, which we had great difficulty in preserving, since the pit had been dug in greensand and was liable to break down under the pressure of the weather. Our problems were resolved by a Mr. Glossop of the Mowlem Construction Company, who advised us to use a consolidating material. The new technique involved spraying the greensand banks on the sides of the pit and hardening them with silica, which acted as an excellent preservative. In time, the site was roofed over and opened to the public as an example of the earliest known dwelling anywhere in England, and full details were subsequently published. Today this museum-on-the-spot is visited by hundreds of people every year.

While we were concluding the excavations under the marquee we were visited by several of our British colleagues who had earlier tried to discourage our work. They were, of course, delighted by our discovery, but some of them, quite wrongly, as I have demonstrated, attributed the finding of the pit dwelling to yet another instance of "Leakey's luck"!

When we arrived back in Nairobi after our holiday in England, the time had come for us to contact the architect and discuss detailed plans for the new museum extensions. Nearly all the necessary funds had at last been raised, either in cash or in the form of promises from various organizations, and I now felt justified in asking the museum trustees to appoint a building committee to make final plans.

I suppose it is inevitable that conflict should arise over minor details involved in the erection of museum exhibit halls. The architect wishes to create something to enhance his reputation; the curator, on his part, is concerned only with making sure that the galleries have the right amount of wall and floor space and as few windows as possible. (Museum curators never like too many windows, because they take up valuable exhibit space and cause all kinds of disturbing reflections.) The layman, on his part, wants a building that will combine a pleasing exterior with the best possible facilities for viewing inside.

In our case, these differing approaches to our problems came to a head when the building committee—made up of laymen— met to discuss the final plans with the architect and the curator (me). I was adamant as to what I wanted, and the architect was equally determined to stand by his design. Since the committee members appointed by the trustees were not concerned with exhibits as such, the architect's plans were, for the most part, approved. He did, however, make some concessions. For instance, where his original plans showed a high tower at the end of the block, I was able to have this reduced to a much smaller one, in which there was a staircase leading to the upper floor.

My biggest defeat was in connection with the front of the building. The architect's plans included a whole series of large windows on both the ground and the upper floors, and these were duly approved. After the building was completed, I had to block up most of them because of the loss of wall space and because one could see nothing in the cases that faced the windows except one's own reflection. This was a terrible waste of time, glass, work, and money.

In my view, when a museum is planning a new wing or hall the curator and his staff alone should have the decision as to where the windows are to be and how the building is to be laid out. Otherwise, almost inevitably, major alterations have to be undertaken as exhibits are installed.

By this time, we had nearly £50,000 available, which meant that we could start building the five new halls and galleries right away—though we still had the task of raising another £10,000 for electrical and other installations and for interior decoration, furniture, and fittings.

At the end of the year, Mary and I made a brief visit to Olduvai Gorge, taking the children with us. Previously, we had been unable to find a route up onto the plains on the south side of the gorge, and consequently we had been obliged to work from a camp on the north side and explore the side gorge on foot. On this occasion, we decided to try to find a way up the cliffs from the Balbal depression, so as to reach the BK II area with our vehicles. After a day's search, we were successful in reaching a point just above the site. We explored farther and found that it was possible to drive at least part way down the slope and so make a camp that would be sheltered from the howling winds that blow across the open plains at night.

Jonathan had brought a school friend, Nick Pickford, along with him, and the two of them spent most of their time exploring the side gorge, while Mary and I made some preliminary excavations at the BK site and established that it was extraordinarily rich in fossils and artifacts. We also plotted some of the side gorge sites on our map.

We spent that Christmas at the gorge and returned to Nairobi after New Year's, having resolved to spend a great deal of time at the new site as soon as time would permit.

The year 1950 had been an exciting one for the children.

They had flown for the first time and had paid their first visit to England. For Mary and me it had been one of varied and valuable experiences. We had found and excavated an important Mesolithic site in Surrey; we had visited the Lascaux prehistoric cave paintings for the first time; and at last our plans for increasing the exhibit space at the museum were, at least on paper, beginning to take shape. And, finally, we had found a new and shorter way from the Balbal depression to the south side of Olduvai Gorge; since we were still transporting all our water from Ngorongoro, this would mean a considerable saving of time and money in the future. Altogether a memorable year.

Twenty

In early 1951, when Charles Boise arrived in Nairobi, we left the children at home, in the care of a friend, Margaret Lehner, in order to give him our undivided attention during his stay.

We first took him to Olduvai, and although Charles found the heat, wind, and dust exceedingly trying, he nevertheless enjoyed his visit to the gorge. We spent several days showing him the principal geological sections and some of the sites where, with the money he had given us, we planned to carry out our excavations after we completed the current work at BK II. He was particularly impressed by the care with which Heselon and our other trained men were uncovering specimens of the giant extinct bovid *Pelorovis*. Then, leaving most of our staff to continue the work at Olduvai, we set off by car to the rock paintings in the Kondoa Irangi district.

We were a long way from camp and some eighty miles from a service station when one of the springs of the car Mary was driving broke. There was nothing for it but to solve the problem by improvisation. First, I sent one of my men to find, purchase, and slaughter a goat and bring back the skin; meanwhile, I dismantled the spring to assess the damage. The main leaf and three others were broken. We therefore set to work to cut three new leaves from the wood of a tree we felled for the purpose.

This we had done on several occasions in the past and had found that hardwood, when fresh, makes a reasonably good substitute for metal. But the top, or main, leaf of the car spring was broken into three pieces; this, of course, was something we could not replace with wood. We therefore had to fit wooden splints above and below to hold the main leaf together. Next, we cut the goatskin into long narrow strips and tightly wound these round the whole spring. As the skin dried, it shrank and hardened into a tight rawhide sleeve, thus giving us an excellent repair. After a delay of four hours the car was once more roadworthy, and we were able to continue our journey, arriving very late at our camp under the fig tree at Kisese.

During the next few days we showed Charles a large number of the rock paintings that Mary and I had investigated and traced on previous visits, but since Charles did not like walking through thick undergrowth, we were able to show him only those that were not too far from the road. One night, when we camped at Kolo village, the local people told us they had found a site with excellent paintings on a range of hills facing Kolo to the southeast. It was not possible for us to go there with Charles, but Mary and I decided that we would examine this site at some later date.

At Olduvai, for twenty years, ever since 1931, Mary and I had been content to find and record sites and make a general survey of the over-all geology. We had dug occasional trial trenches to determine the exact horizon of artifacts and fossils found on the surface, but we had made no major excavations. Now, in 1951, Mary and I came to the conclusion that the time to stop our general survey of the gorge was rapidly approaching and that we would soon have to begin detailed excavations, with the funds Charles was so generously providing. We decided that the first major excavation in 1952 would be a continuation of our work at BK II, since the site was so rich in artifacts and fossils. Simultaneously, we planned a subsidiary trial excavation half a mile away at Site SHK II. Charles declared himself satisfied with this decision.

I had by now completed writing up detailed notes on the stone tools that had been found at Olduvai since 1931, and my book, *Olduvai Gorge*, was published early in 1951 by the Cambridge University Press. The late Dr. A. T. Hopwood of the

British Museum of Natural History, who had been with us in 1931 and had written a report on the fossils we found that season, contributed a chapter dealing with the fossil fauna of Olduvai Gorge. The late Dr. Hans Reck, who had worked at Olduvai in 1913 and had also accompanied me in 1931, to work on the geology, had promised to provide a detailed report on the geological sections of the gorge from his notes. Unfortunately, he died before he was able to do so, and since his widow was unable to locate either his draft or his field notebooks, I had only a very generalized chapter on the geology of the gorge, which he had written before his death. My main chapters dealt with the sequence of the Stone Age cultures as we knew them at the time. The most important section described the evidence of a wholly new Stone Age culture from Olduvai—the Oldowan—reports of which had been published in *Nature* and other scientific journals.

Previously, claims had been made for a very simple, primitive Stone Age culture from East Anglia in Great Britain and one from Belgium, but these had not been accepted as valid, though I personally had always felt that, in part at least, they must be considered to have a possible human origin. Provisionally, however, in my 1951 edition of *Adam's Ancestors,* I withdrew my support for the validity of the evidence for early Pleistocene Stone Age tools in Europe on the grounds of "not proven." Nevertheless, I kept an open mind on the question of whether or not a hominid had been present in Europe in the early Pleistocene. My view was partly influenced by the fact that early in this century a fossil jaw of *Homo* type had been found in a commercial excavation at Foxhall, in Suffolk, England. The geologists of the time reported that the jaw was contemporary with the extinct animals in the same pit. At that time, the deposits in this pit were dated to the Pliocene, but on modern interpretation they would probably be regarded as early Pleistocene or even the beginning of the Middle Pleistocene.

The "Foxhall jaw" has now been missing for many years. It was reported to have been bought by an American physician and taken to the United States. If it could be found, I feel that a re-examination would be extremely interesting. Modern dating techniques would clearly prove whether or not it was contemporary with the Foxhall gravel bed in which it was discovered.

I have never had any doubt as to the validity of the Kanam mandible we found in 1931—and I have always been interested in the possibility that the Foxhall jaw might correspond with the Kanam specimen, which was certainly of *Homo* type. Thus, I felt that in time simple stone tools would be found in the early Pleistocene in England. Our new discoveries of the Oldowan culture very strongly supported this idea. Although up to 1950 we had not found any hominid remains with the Oldowan culture at the base of the Olduvai series, the fact that primitive artifacts were present in large numbers there enhanced the validity of my claims for the Kanam mandible, as well as the possibility that hominids, represented by the Foxhall jaw, were present at about the same date in England.

During 1951 there were increasing reports of the growth of the political movement then known as Mau Mau and to which I referred in an earlier chapter as the "Freedom Fighters" movement. Though the vast majority of the Kikuyu, including myself, supported the aims of this movement, many of us abhorred the methods being employed to force people to join it—or at least to undertake not to oppose it. We believed that the same objectives could be achieved by less violent methods, and it was for this reason that we tried to establish another basis for negotiations and to form a group to persuade the government to act before the situation exploded. Unfortunately, our representations fell on deaf ears, and there emerged no point of agreement around which discussions could be held.

During the year it became increasingly obvious to Mary and me that we should try to move out of Nairobi into one of the suburbs. Jonathan, Richard, and Philip were growing fast and needed more space in which to play than was available within the limits of the garden at the curator's house. Mary and I therefore started to look for a site outside the city where we could purchase land at a reasonable price and could plan and build our own house.

About the middle of the year, after much searching, we found an ideal five-acre plot on Hardy Estate, in the suburb of Langata, about eleven miles southwest of Nairobi. It had a magnificent view of the Ngong Hills across the plains, and since the land sloped downwards towards the Mbgathi River, our view could never be obscured, even if one day a house was built in front of us. We bought the land and began to design our house. We planned that the rooms would form an open square around a courtyard, in the middle of which there was to be a lily pond. We then recruited an Asian foreman and some African builders who had helped us on previous occasions, and proceeded to buy the necessary bricks, cement, and sand. The house was eventually completed at the end of 1952.

During the second part of 1951 I took unpaid leave from my duties as curator of the museum, and Mary, the children, and I set off to make a base for ourselves in the Chungai rest camp; we wanted to study and make tracings of the prehistoric rock art in the Kondoa Irangi area in much more detail than had hitherto been possible. We went armed with ladders, rolls of cellophane, all kinds of paints, and, of course, full camp equipment. A Mrs. Hollis accompanied us to help look after the children in camp, and we also took with us an African nanny for Philip, who was still quite young and needed a great deal of attention. Jonathan and Richard went along with Mary and me most of the time, either helping with the tracings or hunting for new sites along the cliff faces.

On one occasion, we took little Philip with us when we went to explore a new site we had noticed on the previous day. It proved most exciting, since it had magnificent paintings of animals on the ceiling as well as on the panels at the sides of the rock shelter. On the way back, I was in the lead, carrying Philip on my shoulders through some very high grass in which there were many fallen trees and stumps. I saw what looked like yet another fallen tree in front of me and put my foot on it to cross over. At that moment it reared up in front of me—the biggest python I had ever seen! I beat a hasty retreat, and we made a long detour to get back to our car.

Tracing the paintings was often complicated because of high winds and also by the difficulties of getting within reach of the paintings. It was a task at which Mary excelled, since she had had considerable experience from earlier days, when she worked on cave sites in France. She was the principal worker, therefore, and I acted as her general assistant, holding paints, putting up ladders, building scaffolding (upon which she would sit to trace paintings that were otherwise out of reach), mixing colors for her, and holding the cellophane sheets onto the wall until they could be secured with tape. In fact, I was the "bottle washer" and Mary did the important work. A large part of my time was spent in exploring for new sites, with the assistance of the local men.

The government rest camp at Chungai served us well as a base. The main building had several bedrooms, as well as a big sitting room and a bathroom; it was ideal for our purpose, although in a bad state of repair. It had been built on a small granite outcrop away from the main Chungai cliffs, and on the rocks surrounding this little outcrop there were several small panels of paintings. The main sites we were tracing at that time, however, were much farther away. Most of them involved leaving by car each morning and taking food and water with us for the day.

In some cases the paintings were situated on rocks that were disintegrating severely, and as a result parts of many figures were often missing. In a few cases, water deeply impregnated with silica had seeped downwards onto the face of the rock and then hardened, so that there was an opaque white film all over the surface. We quickly found that if this film was sponged with water, it became temporarily translucent, and we could see through and trace the figures underneath. This was an entirely safe procedure, since the silica was very hard and completely insoluble in water.

In addition to having our main camp at Chungai, we had a lovely tented camp at Kisese Number 3 Rock Shelter. This, a most interesting site, is now open to the public. We also made a camp near the foot of the Kolo cliffs to examine the sites we had heard about during our visit with Charles Boise. These were a long way from the main roads, and everything had to be carried there.

At the Kisese 3 site, one hot afternoon, a huge "dust devil" came whirling through the camp, and hit and carried away the main work tent with all its contents. The heavier things, like chairs and tables, were soon recovered, but some of our important tracings were transported into the bush, and it took a long time to find and recover them. A few were lost irretrievably.

Mary and I, at this time, were making elaborate plans for an exhibition of the prehistoric rock art of Tanganyika in the new Aga Khan Hall then being built for the museum in Nairobi. Our plans involved reproducing the surface texture as well as the general shape of the actual sites, so that when the paintings were transposed onto this new surface in the correct sequence the effect would be almost exactly as if one were looking at the site itself. Mary had the assistance of our talented museum technician, the late Norman Mitton, in preparing the artificial rock surfaces. The final result was extremely realistic. Indeed, today these representations are recognized throughout the world as the most effective technique of recording prehistoric art ever used. Many museums have copied the idea.

It will be recalled that at the time of the first Pan-African Congress of Prehistory, held in Nairobi in 1947, General Smuts had sent an official invitation for the second Pan-African Congress to be held in Johannesburg. The invitation had been gladly accepted, because South Africa had a long record of studies in prehistory, going back to the end of the last century, and there were many sites there that congress members were anxious to visit.

Accordingly, we had nominated Dr. Berry Malan of the University of Witwatersrand in Johannesburg as the organizing secretary and Professor C. van Riet Lowe—who was vice-president of the congress in Nairobi—as president-elect.

Unhappily, these well-laid plans were nullified by a change of government in Pretoria. The new government refused to endorse General Smuts's earlier invitation, and van Riet Lowe wrote informing me that the next congress could not, after all, be held in South Africa. This news was received so late that there was no time to find another host country and make all the necessary preparations in time for a meeting in 1951. It was, therefore, decided that the second congress would have to be postponed.

As a result of this change of plan, the Abbé Breuil and I were involved in a great deal of correspondence. Eventually, the government of Algeria invited us to hold the second congress in Algiers, with Professor L. Balout as organizing secretary. This was agreed to by the interim committee, and the second congress was held there in 1952, five years after the first.

As the retiring organizing secretary, as well as the founder, of the first Pan-African Congress of Prehistory, I went to Algeria well before the start of the second meeting to hand over the minute books of the Nairobi congress to my successor and to assist him with the general plans.

So the year 1951 ended, and with it the twenty years I have allocated to this, the second volume of my memoirs. I think I might be allowed to indicate here that the promises of the twenty years just described were to be more than fulfilled in the next twenty. The Mau Mau movement developed into a major confrontation with the British government; in the end, Kenya achieved self-government and at the time of writing is a happy and prosperous republic, under Jomo Kenyatta. Our discoveries at Olduvai Gorge of a very primitive Oldowan culture were followed by the finding of numerous fossil hominid remains, both of true man and near-men, or australopithecines.

Our sons, who were well grounded in field work in their youth, have all, in one way or another, assisted us in our work. Jonathan found some important remains near Baringo, although he is mainly concerned now with a study of the snakes of Africa. Richard has taken over from me as director of the Nairobi National (formerly the Coryndon Memorial) Museum and is making fantastic discoveries on his own account in the area around the northeast corner of Lake Rudolf. I have never, as I said earlier in this chapter, had the slightest doubt as to the validity of my Kanam jaw of 1931. Now, forty-one years later, Richard's finds include clear confirmation of the existence of men similar to those represented by the Kanam jaw in the earliest Pleistocene.

Philip, while mainly concerned with safari tours, has helped me to locate a potentially important site dating back to about 7 million years ago, on which I plan to start work before this book is in print. All these things and much else I shall hope to write in the third volume of these memoirs.

London
September 30, 1972

Publisher's Epilogue

Louis Leakey did not live to carry out the plans he speaks of here. On October 1, 1972, the day after he completed this book, he died, in London, of a heart attack.

It is a pity he could not finish the story himself. His last twenty years were at once the most wrenching and the most rewarding of his life. The Mau Mau revolt affected him deeply; it was a nightmare come true, a bloody, desperate attempt to revenge wrongs he himself had warned of in vain. Even before Leakey was born, soldier-diarist Richard Meinertzhagen had predicted that the Kikuyu, the most intelligent of the African tribes he had met, would be one of the first to demand freedom from European influence and would "cause a lot of trouble."

That prophecy was an understatement. For four years, from 1952 to 1956, Mau Mau terrorists kept Kenya in a virtual state of siege. Kikuyu who refused to take the Mau Mau oath were the main victims; 2,000 of them were murdered. Among the thirty-two white civilians killed was Louis Leakey's cousin Gray Leakey, who was buried alive near a Mau Mau hideout. Earlier Gray had been forced to watch as his wife was strangled.

A price was also put on Louis Leakey's head by Mau Mau

leaders. (Ironically, many of them were his "blood brothers," members of the *Mukanda* age group with whom he had been initiated.) His crimes were his anti-Mau Mau radio broadcasts to the Kikuyu and his participation in counter-oathing campaigns. There was also his role as official interpreter at the trial of Jomo Kenyatta on conspiracy charges. That took place in 1953, in Kapenguria, an isolated district of western Kenya, and Leakey spent three months wrangling with the defense attorneys before blowing up at their repeated charges of bias and refusing to serve further. In this same period he wrote two books, *Mau Mau and the Kikuyu* (1952) and *Defeating Mau Mau* (1954), in an attempt to explain the background of the revolt and, as he put it, "heal the mental wounds that have been inflicted on all races in Kenya."

At Olduvai Gorge, Louis and Mary Leakey spent the period from 1952 to 1958 in locating and uncovering a series of camp sites at which early men had butchered and eaten the game they killed. (Until the Leakeys discovered their existence, it had been thought that any such living floors had long ago been destroyed by natural agencies.) But human fossils, save for two huge milk teeth of uncertain origin, remained as scarce as ever.

Then, in 1959, came the breathtaking discovery of *Zinjanthropus*. As it happened, Louis was in camp with a fever that day; it was Mary who first saw the small fragment of bone and two teeth, black-brown and shining, eroding out of the slope. She rushed back to get her husband, and together the two knelt to examine the treasure.

Zinjanthropus was the first early hominid find capable of being dated absolutely—in this case, by the newly discovered potassium-argon method of radiometric dating. The determination that it was 1,750,000 years old radically changed the prevailing views about the time scale of human evolution, then wholly based on admittedly fallible geological estimates of the age of rock formations.

The patience Louis and Mary Leakey brought to the uncovering of Olduvai sites is almost beyond belief. At FLK, where *Zinjanthropus* was found, there were 2,275 stone tools and flakes. Each one was carefully studied and identified, and its position mapped, to provide a vivid picture of early human activity.

In the last decade of his life, his greatest hopes were centered on the work being carried out by another Leakey—his son Richard—in Ethiopia and northeastern Kenya. In 1967, Richard, though only twenty-three at the time, led the Kenya team on an international expedition to the Omo River basin of southwestern Ethiopia. The French and American teams found australopithecine teeth and jaws ranging in age from 2 million to almost 4 million years, thus extending the fossil record of this genus back into the Pliocene.

Though his activities were impeded, in the final years, by an arthritic hip and a failing heart, Louis Leakey never let up in his lifelong battle to extend man's understanding of his own origins. He lectured widely, attended scientific meetings all over the world, and wrote and edited books designed for students. At his death, as this book attests, he was planning to open up yet another fossil site. Like Isaac Newton, he was obsessed by the thought of what was yet to be done, of "the great ocean of truth that lay all undiscovered" before him.

It was Isaac Newton too who said that if he saw far, it was because he stood on the shoulders of giants. Louis Leakey was a giant of our time, and our horizons are immeasurably widened because of him.

Index

Index